The Biblical Seminar
69

READING AND WRITING IN THE TIME OF JESUS

READING
AND
WRITING
IN THE TIME
OF JESUS

Alan Millard

Sheffield Academic Press

Copyright © 2000, 2001 Sheffield Academic Press
Reprinted 2001

Published by
Sheffield Academic Press Ltd
Mansion House
19 Kingfield Road
Sheffield S11 9AS
England
www.SheffieldAcademicPress.com

Typeset by Sheffield Academic Press
and
Printed on acid-free paper in Great Britain
by Antony Rowe Ltd
Chippenham, Wiltshire

British Library Cataloguing in Publication Data

A catalogue record for this book is available
from the British Library

ISBN 1-84127-070-9

CONTENTS

LIST OF ILLUSTRATIONS

Chapter 1

Chapter 2

Chapter 3

Chapter 4

Chapter 5

Chapter 6

Chapter 7

Chapter 8

Thousands of papers flowed across the desks of officials in ancient Rome every year. They were stored in a great archive building, the Tabularium. To-day the papers have perished and the Tabularium is the basis of an apartment block. To know about the administration of ancient Rome we have to depend upon the remarks of Latin writers, formal inscriptions on stone and graffiti scribbled on walls; the ordinary written documents of daily life have disappeared. That makes it difficult, too, to measure the extent of literacy in the imperial city. The same situation is true for most parts of the Roman empire. Only in Egypt are there quantities of the paper-work Roman bureaucracy generated and of the letters, notes and deeds private citizens produced or kept. The extent of literacy in ancient Greece and Rome has been studied repeatedly, with the Greek papyri from Egypt playing an important part. In recent decades the unexpected discoveries of written records in ancient Palestine have opened new areas for investigation with the additional richness and complication of several languages current side by side. Not only the questions of who wrote and why need to be answered, but also of which languages were used for which purposes and whether there were differences between the religious, the literary and the legal and between the written and the spoken. Yet as in Rome and even in Egypt, only a small fraction of the information survives, whether in actual ancient documents or in the reports of ancient authors.

Palestine deserves special attention in the study of ancient literacy because Jesus of Nazareth lived and taught there. Jesus never wrote a book and it is common opinion that the major sources about him, the Four Gospels, were not written until some 40 years or more after his death. In their nature the Gospels appear unique, they cannot be fitted neatly into any category of literature current in the first century; they contain biography and instruction together, yet tell very little directly about their hero, his appearance, his youth, his habits. The fact that there are four Gospels and that they do not present identical portraits has turned Gospel criticism into a major industry over the past two centuries, stimulating various approaches and techniques of analysis all centred upon the question of what is credible, how far the Evangelists did report what was said and done and how far they altered and expanded traditions or invented episodes or sayings to support a view or doctrine of the early Church. With most scholars assuming the Gospels were not written until after the Fall of Jerusalem in AD 70, there would be ample time for the stories of Jesus to grow and diversify, especially if information about him was only preserved by word of mouth. For trying to retrieve sayings which can be attributed to Jesus himself, emphasis has been put on the study of oral tradition and its sources almost exclusively; the possibility of written reports circulating from the start has rarely been allowed. By re-examining long-held arguments in the light of the contemporary documents now available and the practices seen elsewhere in the Roman Empire, this study aims to redress the balance by showing that written reports about Jesus could have been made during his lifetime. Wherever the Gospels were finally composed, Palestine, especially Galilee and Jerusalem, was the scene of Jesus' work and the home of memories about him. The recent documentary discoveries demand a new survey of the uses of writing there and a reassessment of the possibility that some people who heard Jesus speaking may have recorded his words.

That any books have survived for two thousand years is remarkable, given the fragile nature of papyrus, the ancient paper, and the enormous history of destruction inflicted by man and nature upon the countries around the Mediterranean where the Gospels first circulated. Religious devotion kept the Gospels from annihilation, appreciation of literature and science ensured others were not lost, but very many books disappeared, like almost all the administrative papers of the whole of the Roman empire. The survival and recovery of ancient books and documents of the Graeco-Roman world in general is, therefore, the topic of the first chapter. Before exploring the first-century situation with regard to Palestine, the importance of writing for Christians when theirs was an illicit religion deserves notice, so a survey of examples of their books surviving from second and third centuries occupies the second chapter. Those Christian books are important witnesses to the shift from the roll form to books with pages (the *codex*), a change still poorly understood, the subject of Chapter 3. Between the earliest Christian manuscript and the composition of the Gospels is a gap of several decades and there was another interval between the Crucifixion and the writing of the first Gospel. Accordingly, in the fourth chapter examples of writing from Palestine of the first century BC and AD are surveyed, to begin to discover how writing was used. The variety of texts leads to a consideration of the languages current in the polyglot society of Herodian Palestine and, in particular, of the language(s) Jesus would have spoken (Chapter 5). The surviving examples of writing also stimulate the question explored in the sixth chapter, Who Read and Who Wrote ? Emphasis on writing brings us face to face with current opinion which gives the role of oral tradition a major place in all discussions of the origins of the Gospels. Again, this is a matter that has to be assessed in the light of ancient practices and the place of the word of mouth balanced against evidence for writing in different activities of daily life. Chapter 7 investigates this question. The final chapter adduces books from the Dead Sea Scrolls and other ancient writings to support the argument that some among the audiences and followers of Jesus did keep notes and reports of his activities, first-hand documents which the Evangelists could weave into their narratives.

The intention of this study is to display the wide range of written sources available from the first century which relate to the question of literacy and the uses of writing in first-century Palestine. Inevitably, there are major realms of scholarship which are relevant but which can only be alluded to or summarized, in particular in the study of the Gospels. The footnotes and bibliography indicate where more information may be found. They also indicate the sources used, for it should be apparent that a study such as this cannot be the result of first hand knowledge of, or inquiry into, every area it touches.

One of the seeds for this study was planted in May 1984, while I held a Fellowship at the Institute of Advanced Studies in the Hebrew University at Jerusalem. During a visit to the University of the Negev at Beer-sheba, Elisha Qimron entertained me in his home and generously read through the Dead Sea Scroll known as *MMT*, which he and John Strugnell had just described to colleagues. The ideas stimulated at that time could not be developed until the formal publication had appeared in 1994 and the leisure of a year's study leave, made possible by a Leverhulme Fellowship in 1996, allowed me to gather other material and prosecute this research. During that period H.Y. Gamble's volume *Books and Readers in the Early Church* was published, covering, in more detail, some of the same ground as I have done, and I have bene-fitted from that.

Among many friends and colleagues who have helped my work Professor Philip Alexander, Dr Alan Bowman, Dr Walter Cockle and Professor Graham Stanton deserve especial thanks for reading a draft of this text and generously commenting on matters relating to early Judaism, papyrology and Gospel Criticism, offering additional refer-ences and correcting some errors. Discussion with colleagues led by Professor Edwin Judge and Dr Alana Nobbs, during a short visit to Macquarie University, Sydney, proved especially stimulating and I am grateful for their interest and advice. In addition to the resources of the University of Liverpool's Library, the use of Tyndale Library for Bibli-cal Research at Cambridge has been an immense benefit and I am indebted to the Librarian, Dr David Instone-Brewer for his help in many ways and to the Warden, Dr Bruce Winter and Mrs Winter for their ready hospitality. My wife's loving support has sustained me throughout.

Alan Millard
Whitsun 1999

ABBREVIATIONS

AB	Anchor Bible
ABD	David Noel Freedman (ed.), *The Anchor Bible Dictionary* (New York: Doubleday, 1992)
AJA	*American Journal of Archaeology*
ANET	James. B. Pritchard (ed.), *Ancient Near Eastern Texts Relating to the Old Testament* (Princeton: University Press, 3rd edn, 1969)
ANRW	Hildegard Temporini and Wolfgang Haase (eds.), *Aufstieg und Niedergang der römischen Welt: Geschichte und Kultur Roms in Spiegel der neueren Forschung* (Berlin: W. de Gruyter, 1972–)
BA	*Biblical Archaeologist*
BARev	*Biblical Archaeology Review*
BASOR	*Bulletin of the American Schools of Oriental Research*
BR	*Bible Review*
BSOAS	*Bulletin of the School of Oriental and African Studies*
CBQ	*Catholic Biblical Quarterly*
CII	*Corpus Inscriptionum iudaicarum*
CIL	*Corpus Inscriptionum latinarum*
ConNT	*Coniectanea neotestamentica*
CR	*Critical Review of Books in Religion*
CRAIBL	*Comptes rendus de l'Académie des inscriptions et belles lettres*
DJD	Discoveries in the Judaean Desert
EncJud	*Encyclopaedia Judaica*
ExpTim	*Expository Times*
GRBS	*Greek, Roman and Byzantine Studies*
HDB	James Hastings (ed.), *A Dictionary of the Bible* (5 vols.; Edinburgh: T. & T. Clark; New York: Charles Scribner's Sons, 1898–1904)
HTR	*Harvard Theological Review*
HUCA	*Hebrew Union College Annual*
IEJ	*Israel Exploration Journal*
JAC	*Jahrbuch für Antike und Christentum*
JBL	*Journal of Biblical Literature*
JewEnc	*The Jewish Encyclopaedia*

JEA	*Journal of Egyptian Archaeology*
JEH	*Journal of Ecclesiastical History*
JHS	*Journal of Hellenic Studies*
JRAS	*Journal of the Royal Asiatic Society*
JRS	*Journal of Roman Studies*
JSJ	*Journal for the Study of Judaism in the Persian, Hellenistic and Roman Period*
JSNTSup	*Journal for the Study of the New Testament*, Supplement Series
JSOTSup	*Journal for the Study of the Old Testament*, Supplement Series
JSS	*Journal of Semitic Studies*
LSJ	H.G. Liddell, Robert Scott and H. Stuart Jones, *Greek–English Lexicon* (Oxford: Clarendon Press, 9th edn, 1968)
MUSJ	*Mélanges de l'Université Saint-Joseph*
NovT	*Novum Testamentum*
NovTSup	*Novum Testamentum*, Supplements
NTS	*New Testament Studies*
RB	*Revue biblique*
RevQ	*Revue de Qumran*
SNTSMS	Society for New Testament Studies Monograph Series
TynBul	*Tyndale Bulletin*
VC	*Vigiliae Christianae*
VTSup	*Vetus Testamentum*, Supplements
ZPE	*Zeitschrift für Papyrologie und Epigraphik*

Chapter 1

ANCIENT BOOKS AND THEIR SURVIVAL

Recently a friend handed me a supermarket bag, 'There's something here for you', she said. In the bag was a tattered piece of papyrus inscribed in Greek; it is part of a fourth century account book written in an early Christian community. Someone had found it while sorting through the house of an elderly lady whose husband had been a pastor, but she had no knowledge of its history. No doubt the papyrus originally came from Egypt, brought to Britain as a souvenir, mounted between sheets of glass and displayed as a sample of early writing, then put away and forgotten after its owner's death until its rescue, so one torn sheet has reached a caring home! How many others may have been thrown away by Egyptian peasants who found them, or by the ignorant descendants of early tourists who had bought them, no one can tell. This inquiry into writing in first-century Palestine begins by describing the ways books from Greece and Rome have survived, first those preserved in libraries, then those uncovered at ancient sites, like that papyrus.

The Fates of Books

'If it agrees with the Qur'an, there's no need for it; if it disagrees, it should not exist.' With that opinion, the story goes, the Caliph Omar sealed the fate of the greatest collection of books made in the ancient world, the Library of Alexandria. His general, Amr ibn al-As, had captured the city in 641 and asked his master to tell him what to do with the books. On hearing the Caliph's reply, Amr sent them off as fuel to heat the city's baths. Whether or not there is any truth in the story is questionable. The history of the Library is not well recorded. The first Greek king of Egypt, successor of Alexander the Great, Ptolemy I, Soter (305–282 BC), had planned the Library and his son Ptolemy II,

Philadelphus (282–46 BC) had had it created to embrace 'the books of all the peoples of the world'. It grew rapidly to contain, ancient writers asserted, 500,000 rolls, including the Greek translation of the books of the Hebrew Bible, the Septuagint. The Library became a centre for study and research where scholars edited and commented upon the standard classics, its holdings continually increasing until another library was created in the temple of Serapis. Unhappily, Alexandria, as Egypt's capital city, was a goal for military adventurers and so open to the risks of attack and capture, pillage and fire. Several times before the Muslim conquest it fell into enemy hands and the Library suffered. The fire started by Julius Caesar to destroy the Egyptian fleet when he was besieged in the city in 48 BC spread to storehouses near the harbour where it destroyed, reportedly, 40,000 rolls. Mark Antony brought 200,000 more from the library at Pergamum as a gift for Cleopatra. The city suffered through war on later occasions, although there is no clear record of the fate of either of the Libraries. The main one may have perished when the palace quarter of the city was destroyed soon after 270, and when the Christians destroyed the Temple of Serapis in 391 they may have destroyed its library, too.[1] Copyists who replaced the roll by the codex (see Chapter 3) may well have reduced the size of the collection, exercising some selectivity as they transferred works to the new format, so bringing about the eventual extinction of the books they rejected. Changes in taste caused by the spread and acceptance of Christianity also contributed to the disappearance of numerous Greek and Latin books, although it was appreciation by educated or interested Christian scribes that caused the copying of most of the classical texts read today.

Alexandria held the greatest library, but there were many others in major cities of the Roman world, each holding hundreds, if not thousands of books. Pliny the Elder, in the Preface to his encyclopaedia, *Natural History*, mentions that he had read two thousand volumes in the

1.   See A.J. Butler, *The Arab Conquest of Egypt* (revd P.M. Fraser; Oxford: Clarendon Press, 2nd edn, 1978), pp. lxxv-vi, 401-26; P.M. Fraser, *Ptolemaic Alexandria* (Oxford: Clarendon Press, 1972), pp. 320-35; E.A. Parsons, *The Alexandrian Library: Glory of the Hellenic World* (London: Cleaver-Hume, 1952); L. Canfora, *The Vanished Library: A Wonder of the Ancient World* (trans. M. Ryle; Berkeley: University of California Press, 1989); A.K. Bowman, *Egypt after the Pharaohs: 332 BC–AD 642* (London: British Museum, 1986), p. 225.

Figure 1. *View of the reconstructed facade of the Library of Celsus at Ephesus. Built early in the second century AD, niches in the inside walls
could hold up to twelve thousand book rolls. (Photograph by Colin
Hemer, by courtesy of Tyndale House, Cambridge.)*

course of his research.[2] Beside those centres of learning, there were
civic archives where official documents and legal deeds were deposited,
often running into tens of thousands (see Chapter 6). All of those libraries and archives have vanished, there is no book that can be identified as a relic from the shelves of Alexandria, no document from the
archive cupboards of imperial Rome. The major Greek and Latin texts
we possess today are copies of copies, almost all from the Middle Ages,
and the extant archival texts are only those that have accidentally survived burial and been found in the last two hundred years. The quantity
of literary works that have been lost is worth noting, followed by the
changes archaeological discoveries have made to the picture. While
deliberate destruction or neglect have been responsible for the loss of

---

2.   Pliny, *Natural History*, Preface §17.

enormous numbers of old books, it is well to recognize that past ages had a different attitude to ours, they did not share the present-day concern for 'heritage' and so what was old or worn was usually replaced and discarded; the monk whom Constantine von Tischendorf found feeding pages of old books to the fire to warm St Catherine's Monastery in May 1844 was not doing anything unusual or disgraceful in the eyes of his colleagues. It was Tischendorf's concern to rescue what is now called the Codex Sinaiticus that would have seemed eccentric to them. That manuscript is precious because of its age and the type of biblical text it carries (see below, Chapter 2, pp. 43, 44), but the Bible continued to be copied throughout the Dark Ages. Other Roman books were not so popular; few have descended to us in such early forms and some basic to modern knowledge of ancient history and culture narrowly escaped extinction.

The first century or so of the Roman Empire was an epoch-making time, a fact some authors alive then recognized and so they wrote about it. Of greatest merit is the Roman historian, Tacitus, who composed his *Annals of Imperial Rome* to cover the years from Tiberius's accession in AD 14 to Nero's death in 68. He divided his work into 18 books. Today books 1-6 are available in several mediaeval copies, the oldest of which was copied in Germany about 850; Books 11-15 are known from a single copy, made about 1050 at Montecassino in Italy, but Books 7-10 and 17 and 18 are not preserved at all, robbing us of vital historical information. A senator named Velleius Paterculus, who fought as an officer in the army under Tiberius before he became emperor, wrote an account of Tiberius's reign. One copy of his work, which was made about 800, was available in the sixteenth century and its text was printed, but later the manuscript itself was lost, so scholars have to rely on that early printed version of it alone. The Roman encyclopaedist, Pliny the Elder, who was killed while observing the eruption of Mt Vesuvius in AD 79, wrote over six books made up of over 60 volumes (rolls) beside his *Natural History*, a treasury of Roman knowledge about the world, but only the 37 volumes of that last book survive, some in copies made as early as the fifth century. The story is the same for many other outstanding Roman authors.[3]

3. See L.D. Reynolds (ed.), *Texts and Transmission: A Survey of the Latin Classics* (Oxford: Clarendon Press, 1983).

The climate in Italy and the western provinces of the Empire did not normally allow books to survive if they were buried in ruined buildings, but accident has preserved one Roman library, although it is severely damaged. Between one and two thousand rolls were found in the Villa of the Papyri at Herculaneum, overwhelmed by the eruption of Vesuvius in AD 79. The hot liquid mud that overwhelmed the villa carbonized the rolls but did not annihilate them. Some remained as brittle rolls, some broke into lumps and many were badly damaged in the eighteenth-century excavation before scholars realized what they were (at first they were thought to be lumps of coal). With great patience, some have been unrolled or separated to reveal the writing. So far as the books can be read, they contain principally philosophical treatises, mainly the works of Philodemus from Gadara in Transjordan. He flourished in the first century BC and was a follower of Epicurus. There are some books on different topics in Greek and in Latin, including the famous Latin poem, *On the Nature of Things* written by the Epicurean Lucretius.[4]

Some pieces of Latin books have been retrieved from the dry sands of Egypt, but they are very much in the minority, little more than 100 pieces of Latin works to over 3000 of Greek, the majority of the Latin texts being writings to do with law. Beside those are a few parts of books by the historians Livy and Sallust, a fragment of one of Cicero's orations, several of Vergil's *Aeneid* and other poems and unidentified compositions.[5]

Greek literature was preserved by copyists in the eastern end of the Mediterranean, but it suffered in much the same way as Latin. Plato's most outstanding book, *The Republic*, survives in many mediaeval copies, of which the oldest was made in the ninth century. A few papyrus fragments show it was being read in the second and third centuries, but add nothing of value to the text.[6] The famous Athenian playwright Euripides wrote 66 tragedies in the fifth century BC. Sixteen of them survive complete; the oldest mediaeval manuscript was made in the

4. M. Capasso, *Manuale di papirologia ercolanese* (Lecce: Galatina,1991); M. Gigante, *Philodemus in Italy: The Books from Herculaneum* (trans. D. Obbink; Ann Arbor, MI: University of Michigan Press, 1995).

5. R.A. Pack, *The Greek and Latin Texts from Graeco-Roman Egypt* (Ann Arbor, MI: University of Michigan Press, 2nd rev. and enlarged edn, 1965).

6. See G. Boter, *The Textual Tradition of Plato's Republic* (Leiden: E.J. Brill, 1989).

tenth or eleventh century. Papyrus rolls offer many fragments of those 16 and of some of the otherwise lost plays, but most remain unknown.[7]

However, the losses to Greek literature through neglect and deliberate destruction have been partly made up by the recovery of the papyri. While often there are only tantalising tatters of rolls, occasional happy exceptions allow whole books to be restored to knowledge. In 1889 some complete Greek rolls were acquired for the British Museum by Ernest Wallis Budge, among them a lost book by Aristotle or his disciples, *The Constitution of Athens*, a copy made at the end of the first century on the back of a set of accounts for AD 78–79.[8] The Greek playwright Menander, who lived in Athens late in the fourth century BC, wrote 108 plays, according to ancient sources, yet not one survived complete in mediaeval manuscripts. The papyri have presented one play in full and large parts of six others, enabling the high reputation he enjoyed in his lifetime to be appreciated to-day. An older contemporary of Menander was the orator Hyperides, who spoke against the Macedonians. Ancient scholars wrote about 52 of his speeches known to them. Some were preserved in a mediaeval manuscript kept in the royal library at Buda, but that was destroyed when the Turks captured the city in 1526, before any scholar had printed its text, so his work was lost. From 1847 onwards the recovery of several papyrus copies restored speeches by Hyperides to knowledge.[9] Books, whether classical or Christian, survive from the Graeco-Roman world, therefore, by chance rather than by design and every attempt to understand that world needs to take this phenomenon into account. Despite the existence of much of that literature in our libraries, including probably all the outstanding works, even more has perished.

Writing Materials

The earliest written documents known today are clay tablets from Babylonia created during the fourth millennium BC for the emerging

---

7. See C. Collard, *Euripides* (Oxford: Clarendon Press for the Classical Association, 1981); S.G. Daitz, *The Jerusalem Palimpsest of Euripides* (Berlin: W. de Gruyter, 1970); C. Collard, M.J. Cropp and K.H. Lee, *Euripides: Selected Fragments. Plays* (Warminster: Aris and Phillips, 1995).

8. See Sir E.A. Wallis Budge, *By Nile and Tigris* (2 vols.; London: John Murray, 1920), II, pp. 137, 147-48.

9. See G. Colin, *Hypérides: Discours* (Paris: Les Belles Lettres, 1946).

cuneiform script. Although a few scribes were still writing in cuneiform on clay in Babylonian towns in the first century AD and a little later, their techniques were not current further west then, so clay tablets are not relevant to this study.

Stone was recognized as a permanent material from an early time for memorials honouring the dead or the living, royal or official decrees, dedications and standard measures. Even so, later generations might re-cycle such blocks for new buildings, slighting the once-significant words, cutting through or abrading them (cf. the Pilate Inscription from Caesarea, Chapter 4, p. 127). Except in the case of gems or engraved seals, writing on stone was not part of daily life and so the quantity of inscribed stones is limited and their use as vehicles for literature very rare indeed.[10] Writing on metal was also unusual and restricted to official decrees and records like the diplomas issued to Roman veterans upon their retirement. Scores of examples of the latter exist, often dam-aged, yet they are only a minute number out of all that were issued and the official lists of the veterans that were displayed on bronze plaques in Rome have entirely disappeared.[11] Few of the many formal Roman inscriptions on bronze plates, the normal way of making a permanent record of the senate's decisions, have survived at all, although thous-ands were once visible in Rome—Tacitus reports that the emperor Ves-pasian ordered the restoration of 3000 which had been destroyed in the fire of AD 69.[12] When the Jewish historian Josephus quoted decrees in favour of the Jews which the Roman Senate issued during the Macca-baean period, he declared they were 'still to be found engraved on

10. Two examples exist in Anatolia: the Deeds of Augustus carved on the walls of his temple in Ankara and at other sites and the philosophical treatise of Diogenes at Oenoanda, some 25,000 words engraved on slabs lining a public building in the second century; see E.G. Hardy, *The Monumentum Ancyranum* (Oxford: Clarendon Press, 1923) and M.F. Smith, *Diogenes of Oinoanda: The Epicurean Inscription* (Naples: Bibliopolis, 1993) and *idem, The Philosophical Inscription of Diogenes of Oinoanda* (Vienna: Austrian Academy, 1996).

11. See M.M. Roxan, *Roman Military Diplomas 1954–1977* and *Roman Military Diplomas 1978–1984* (Occasional Papers 2, 9; London: Institute of Archaeology, 1978, 1985).

12. *Histories* 4.40.1; see C. Williamson, 'Monuments of Bronze: Roman Legal Documents on Bronze Tablets', *Classical Antiquity* 6 (1987), pp. 160-83 and *idem*, 'The Display of Law and Archival Practice in Rome', in H. Solin, O. Salomies and U.-M. Liertz (eds.), *Acta Colloquii Epigraphici Latini* (Helsinki: Societas Scienti-arum Fennica, 1995), pp. 239-51.

bronze tablets in the Capitol' (*Ant.* 14.14.188), although whether he had himself seen the originals or Vespasian's replacements, or was drawing upon another authority is unclear. The most impressive survivor is the incomplete piece from Lyons, 192 × 137 cm (6 ft 4 in × 4 ft 6 in) bearing a speech of the emperor Claudius issued in AD 48.[13] The metal was used for public display in the hope of giving authority and permanence to the texts.

Papyrus

The usual writing material of the Graeco-Roman world was papyrus, the ancient paper, made from strips of pith taken from the papyrus reed growing in the marshes of the Nile delta.[14] One row of the fibres was laid horizontally then a second row placed across them at right angles and the two hammered together, the natural sap being a sufficient adhesive. When dried and polished with a smooth stone or bone, papyrus sheets were almost white and quite flexible, so the scribe could write on either face, but most commonly the writing was done along the horizontal fibres (the *recto*). The papyrus was made into sheets, the average sheet being about 30 cm high and 20 cm wide (about 11 × 8 in), although there were variations. Sheets could be glued side by side to make rolls, the usual form of ancient book. A roll could reach any length, but more than 20 sheets, three to three and a half metres (about 9 to 12 ft), was unusual. The rolls were often bisected horizontally to give lesser depth, sometimes down to 10 cm (4 in). The papyrus strip could be rolled quite tightly, to look like a thick piece of stick, 2-6 cm (0.75-2.5 in) in diameter. Often a blank sheet was left at the outer end to protect the text and, in Roman times, a tag of papyrus or parchment sewn to it to bear the title of the work.

The oldest papyrus roll yet discovered lay in a cylindrical wooden box among the equipment of an Egyptian tomb of the First Dynasty, about 3000 BC—to the archaeologists' disappointment, it was blank, as it had been left ready for the dead man's use.[15] The earliest written

13. G. Walser, *Römische Inschrift-Kunst* (Stuttgart: F. Steiner, 1988), pp. 18-25; for illustrations see A. Degrassi, *CIL Auctarium Inscriptiones Latinae Liberae Rei Publicae, Imagines* (Berlin: W. de Gruyter, 1965), pp. 383-99.

14. See N. Lewis, *Papyrus in Classical Antiquity* (Oxford: Clarendon Press, 1974).

15. W.B. Emery, *Archaic Egypt* (Harmondsworth: Penguin Books, 1961), p. 235.

papyri are accounts for a mortuary temple of pharaoh Neferirkare, pre-pared c. 2350 BC.[16] Papyrus continued to be imported into Europe until supplanted by paper in the Middle Ages. Papyrus could be re-used by washing and scraping the old ink, although the fibres made it difficult to clean.[17]

Egypt exported papyrus to countries bordering the Mediterranean, probably from very early times. The *Story of Wenamun* tells of an Egyptian envoy presenting many 'gifts' to the prince of Byblos about 1100 BC in exchange for cedar wood; among the gifts were 500 rolls of papyrus, to be used, there is little doubt, as writing material.[18] The trade flourished over the centuries, for, although the papyrus reed grew in other places, there is no sign that the writing material was manufactured outside Egypt. Being a vegetable material, papyrus decays rapidly in damp environments and when buried, so books and documents only survive in arid situations or if carbonized, as at Herculaneum (see above, p. 21) and as found in the ruins of a church in Petra probably destroyed in the earthquake of AD 551.[19]

Leather and Parchment
Whereas papyrus was restricted to Egypt, leather could be obtained in most places, but its preparation was more complicated, requiring careful treatment in tanning, stretching and smoothing.[20] The best quality was obtained from the skins of spring lambs, two months old. As such a skin would give a sheet only 30.5 × 60.1 cm (12 × 24 in), a first class roll of any size would demand the slaughter of many animals. More mature animals could provide sheets up to 124 × 104 cm (4ft × 3ft 5 in), according to an early fifteenth-century European manuscript.[21]

16. P. Posener-Krieger, J.-L. de Cenival, *Hieratic Papyri in the British Museum, Fifth Series* (London: The British Museum, 1968).

17. R.A. Caminos, 'Some Comments on the Reuse of Papyrus', in M. Bierbrier (ed.), *Papyrus: Structure and Usage* (British Museum Occasional Paper, 60; London: Department of Egyptian Antiquities, British Museum, 1986), pp. 43-61.

18. J.A. Wilson, 'The Journey of Wen-Amon to Phoenicia', *ANET*, pp. 25-29.

19. G.L. Peterman, 'Discovery of Papyri in Petra', *BA* 57 (1994), pp. 55-57, 152 papyri.

20. R. Reed, *Ancient Skins, Parchments and Leathers* (London: Seminar Press, 1972); *idem, The Nature and Making of Parchment* (Leeds: Elmete Press, 1975).

21. *Western Manuscripts and Miniatures* (Auction sale catalogue; 17 June 1997; London: Sotheby), p. 68.

Leather rolls appear at a date only slightly later than papyrus ones, the earliest examples coming, again, from Egypt, c. 2200 BC.[22] The 'Louvre Leather Roll' from the reign of Ramesses II is a good example. Dated c . 1274 BC, the present text gives details of brick-making, but it had been used for an earlier record, the first writing having been washed off, demonstrating an advantage the smooth, more durable surface of the leather held over papyrus.[23] Ink could be washed off the leather sheets several times, whereas papyrus could not stand repeated re-use. Single sheets of leather bearing messages sent by a Persian governor of Egypt from Babylonia to his local staff in the fifth century BC were recovered in Egypt, still in their post-bag.[24] Circumstances have not allowed any to survive in Babylonia, but cuneiform tablets of the same period mention leather rolls. The Akkadian word used, *magillatu*, is probably a loan-word from West Semitic, cf. Hebrew m^e*gillâ*. The cuneiform determinative sign (*mašku*) standing before the word indicates the roll was made of leather. The most famous examples of ancient leather rolls are the Dead Sea Scrolls written in the last two centuries BC and the earlier part of the first century AD. They represent about 800 rolls containing religious literature, the best preserved being a copy of the book of Isaiah made of sheets of goatskin sewn together to create a roll 26 cm high and 7.34m long (10 in × 24 ft). See Chapter 4, pp. 119, 120.

Wooden Tablets and Waxed Tablets

The prehistory of the book with pages can also be traced to an early date in the Near East. Egyptian scribes wrote in ink on wooden boards, sometimes painted with white gesso, while from early in the second millennium BC, if not before, Babylonian scribes impressed cuneiform signs on wax-covered wooden boards. In the second half of the millennium such boards were widely used in the Near East. The Hittites in

22. Reference in A. Lucas, *Ancient Egyptian Materials and Industries* (revd edn J.R. Harris; London: Edwin Arnold, 4th edn, 1962), p. 364.

23. See K.A. Kitchen, 'From the Brickfields of Egypt', *TynBul* 27 (1976), pp. 137-47 (141-43).

24. G.R. Driver, *Aramaic Documents of the Fifth Century B.C.* (Oxford: Clarendon Press, 1954; reduced and revised edition, 1965); re-edited by B. Porten and A. Yardeni, *Textbook of Aramaic Documents from Ancient Egypt* I (Winona Lake: Eisenbrauns, 1986), pp. 102-29.

Anatolia apparently wrote their hieroglyphic script on waxed tablets and the Minoans and Mycenaeans in Crete and the Aegean probably used them for their Linear A and B scripts. They might be single, like a clay tablet, or they might be hinged together with the inner faces recessed so that each could hold the wax without one face damaging the other.[25] An example of two hinged boards which can be dated about 1300 BC was retrieved from a shipwreck off the coast of Turkey. To our frustration, the sea water and silt which had preserved the two wooden boards and their ivory hinges had dissolved the wax, so any message incised on it has disappeared.[26] Writing boards maintained their place as convenient materials for ephemeral records, notes, lists and school exercises in the first millennium BC, both in Egypt and elsewhere, the soft wax surface being suitable to receive any script. They are shown on sculptures in Assyria and northern Syria and examples of wooden ones have been found at Nimrud, preserved in the sludge of a well, having seen hard use and been repaired. A single ivory panel, once hinged to another, was excavated at Assur and a *de luxe* set of 12 ivory writing boards, hinged at alternate edges, was found at Nimrud, in the same well as the wooden ones. It was inscribed for Sargon of Assyria (721–705 BC), according to a notice on the outside, with thousands of lines of an omen collection in minute cuneiform writing, a few of them legible on small pieces of wax still adhering to the ivory.[27]

25. See E. Lalou (ed.), *Les tablettes à écrire de l'antiquité à l'époque moderne* (Turnhout: Brepols, 1992); for Egypt see also P. Vernus, 'Schreibtafel', *Lexikon der Ägyptologie* 5 (1984), pp. 703-708; at Ugarit note the references to *lḥt* (= Heb. *luaḥ*); J.-L. Cunchillos, 'Correspondence', in A. Caquot, J.-M. de Tarragon and J.-L. Cunchillos, *Textes Ougaritiques*, II (2 vols.; Paris: Cerf, 1989), index; see also D. Symington, 'Late Bronze Age Writing-Boards and their Uses: Textual Evidence from Anatolia and Syria', *Anatolian Studies* 41 (1991), pp. 111-23; for Middle Assyrian texts see J.N. Postgate, 'Middle Assyrian Tablets: The Instruments of Bureaucracy', *Altorientalische Forschungen* 13 (1986), pp. 10-39 (22-25).

26. G.F. Bass *et al.*, 'The Bronze Age Shipwreck at Ulu Burun: 1986 Campaign', *AJA* 93 (1989), pp. 1-29 (10, 11); R. Payton, 'The Ulu-Burun Writing-Board Set', *Anatolian Studies* 41 (1991), pp. 99-110.

27. D.J. Wiseman, 'Assyrian Writing Boards', *Iraq* 17 (1955), pp. 3-13; M. Howard, 'Technical Description of the Ivory Writing-Boards from Nimrud', *Iraq* 17 (1955), pp. 14-20; M.E.L. Mallowan, *Nimrud and its Remains* (2 vols.; London: Collins, 1966), I, pp. 152-60; for the ivory board from Assur see E. Klengel-Brandt, 'Eine Schreibtafel aus Assur', *Altorientalische Forschungen* 3 (1975), pp. 169-71.

Figure 2. *Set of five ivory writing tablets small enough to hold in the palm of the hand, Roman period. (Römische-Germanisches Museum, Cologne D 3788. Photograph by courtesy of the Museum.)*

When the Greeks borrowed the alphabetic script from the Phoenicians a little after 900 BC, they are likely to have received writing tablets as well, something they had forgotten, together with the scribal skills, during the Dark Age. The hinged wax tablets, Greek *pinax*, plural *pinakes*, continued in use throughout the Classical period to become the everyday writing material for tax collectors, administrators, businessmen and scholars in Hellenistic and Roman times. Official and legal texts were inscribed on them as well as business records. However, works of literature were excluded; except in the schoolroom, those belonged on rolls. Their function as note-books is well-attested. According to one ancient report, Philip of Opus, Plato's secretary, copied his master's work *The Laws* on to papyrus from unfinished drafts the philosopher had left on wax tablets, a work that occupies 418 pages in a standard modern edition.[28] In Latin the words for tablets

28. Diogenes Laertius, *Lives of Ancient Philosophers*, III §37.

were *tabula* and *caudex* or *codex*. Paintings from Pompeii, sculptures from various parts of the Roman Empire and actual examples dug up at many sites scattered from Egypt to Hadrian's Wall display the wide-spread use of the tablets and their shape. They could be a pair hinged together, or any number up to ten, with leather thongs threaded through holes in one edge to keep them in order. Pieces of two internal leaves from a multiple-leaved set were recovered from caves used by Jewish refugees in the Second Revolt (AD 132–135), with the wax still attached, but no sign of writing.[29] The normal tablets were convenient to hold in one hand, 22-25 × 13-15 cm (8.5-10 × 5-6 in), others were 'pocket sized' (*pugillares*), one example being 7.2 × 4.5 cm (2.8 × 1.8 in), and others were much larger, tall and narrow survivors measuring up to 33 cm high and 10 wide (13 × 4 in).[30] The writers scratched the letters on the wax with the point of a stylus which was flattened at the other end for erasing unwanted messages. Bronze and iron styli survive in large numbers all over the Roman Empire, attesting the widespread use of the wax tablets.

In recent years a different form of wooden writing material has become better known. Several hundred wooden leaves have been found at the fort of Vindolanda on Hadrian's Wall in Britain, surviving be-cause they lay in waterlogged rubbish. These leaves were carefully cut to be wafer thin and in some cases were folded in the centre, like a pair of pages; in other cases they were held vertically and hinged bottom to top. The Latin messages were written in on them in ink. Dating from the end of the first century, they deal with affairs of the garrison's daily life.[31] Rare examples of the same type are known from other sites, including one with a letter in Aramaic from a cave near the Dead Sea (see Chapter 3, p. 67). It is now suspected that such wooden leaves or

29. P. Benoit, J.T. Milik and R. de Vaux, *Les grottes de Murabba'ât* (DJD, 2; Oxford: Clarendon Press, 1962), p. 44.

30. R. Marichal, 'Les tablettes à écrire dans le monde romain', P. Cuaderlier, 'Les tablettes grecques d'Egypte: Inventaire', and J.L. Sharpe III, 'The Dakhleh Tablets and Some Codicological Considerations', in Lalou (ed.), *Les tablettes à écrire de l'antiquité à l'époque moderne*, pp. 165-85, 63-94, 127-48. A.K. Bowman and J.D. Thomas, *The Vindolanda Writing-tablets: Tabulae Vindolandenses* II (London: British Museum, 1994), p. 46 n. 33, add examples to Marichal's list.

31. Bowman and Thomas, *The Vindolanda Writing-tablets*; A.K. Bowman, *Life and Letters on the Roman Frontier: Vindolanda and its People* (London: British Museum, 1994).

slats were a more common writing material throughout the Roman empire than either waxed tablets or papyrus.

Whitewashed wooden boards carried public notices in Rome, set where they could be conveniently read. They had content of less permanent value than the information engraved on bronze, consisting of draft statutes, lists of jurors and so forth.[32]

Figure 3. *Wooden writing tablet from Vindolanda; a letter from two officers to the prefect Cerialis wishing him success when he met the governor. A.K. Bowman, J.D. Thomas,* Vindolanda: The Latin Writing Tablets *(Britannia Monograph Series, 4; Gloucester: Alan Sutton, 1983), pp. 102-105, no. 21. (Photograph by Alison Rutherford, reproduced by permission of the Vindolanda Trust, by courtesy of A.K. Bowman.)*

Potsherds, ostraca

All the writing materials described so far had to be specially manufactured and so cost something. For ephemeral notes and jottings and school exercises, free writing materials lay ready to hand in every town and village in the form of broken pottery. Ancient pottery was mostly earthenware, terra-cotta, which breaks easily, so that ancient sites were strewn with pottery fragments and are still, as every archaeologist working in Egypt and the Near East knows. Wherever writing was done

32. C. Williamson, 'Monuments of Bronze: Roman Legal Documents on Bronze Tablets', *Classical Antiquity* 6 (1987), pp. 160-83 (163-64).

with ink, potsherds were the ancient form of scrap-paper and thousands of these ostraca have been found in Egypt, smaller quantities in other countries. If there was no ink to hand, messages could be scratched on the sherds.

Figure 4. *Greek ostracon from Egypt, receipt for poll-tax of 16 drachmas, paid by Pekysis, issued by the overseers of the Sacred Gate at Aswan on 12 July 144. (Private collection; Photograph A.R. Millard.)*

Ink

Scribes made their black ink by mixing soot or lamp-black with gum to make a small hard cake which they moistened with water when they wanted to write. The dry conditions in Egypt allow us to examine ancient scribes' equipment, their pen-cases, pens and cakes of ink. From Roman times there are pottery and metal ink-wells, with traces of ink; a few have been found at Khirbet Qumran where some of the Dead Sea Scrolls were almost certainly written.[33] When documents are first

33. For examples from Palestine see N.I. Khairy, 'Inkwells of the Roman Period from Jordan', *Levant* 12 (1980), pp. 155-62; S. Goranson, 'Qumran: A Hub of Scribal Activity', *BARev* 20.5 (1994), pp. 36-39; note also Y. Nir-El and M. Broshi, 'The Black Ink of the Qumran Scrolls', *Dead Sea Discoveries* 3 (1996), pp. 157-67.

Figure 5. *Pottery ink-pot from the excavations at Khirbet Qumran by the Dead Sea, first century* AD. *Height approx. 5 cm. (Israel Antiquities Authority; photograph by David Harris, Jerusalem.)*

uncovered, the ink is often surprisingly black and that made from soot and gum does not fade. Ink made with iron compounds from the second century AD onwards does fade. Ink writing on potsherds is quite easily rubbed or washed off, a risk excavators have to be alert to. Egyptian scribes also made red ink from powdered ochre for writing headings and they painted coloured pictures in some texts. A few passages in red ink are found in manuscripts among the Dead Sea Scrolls, notably in a copy of the book of Numbers. They may have indicated the beginnings of sections in a lectionary system.[34] Classical and Jewish sources tell of books decorated in various colours, with miniature paintings or with words written in gold and silver on parchment dyed purple. Specimens of such splendid manuscripts written in the sixth century still survive

See further the discussion on 'Pens and Writing in Antiquity' in P.M. Head and M. Warren, 'Re-Inking the Pen: Evidence from P. Oxy 657 ($\mathfrak{P}^{13}$) Concerning Unintentional Scribal Errors', *NTS* 43 (1997), pp. 466-73 (467-69).

34. N. Jastram, '4QNum[b]', in E. Ulrich and F.M. Cross, *Qumran Cave 4: VII* (DJD, 12; Oxford: Clarendon Press, 1994), pp. 205-67, Pl. xlix (210-11).

(e.g. Codex Sinopensis of Matthew, now in Paris, Codex Petropolitanus Purpureus of the Gospels, in St Petersburg with stray leaves in other places, and the Cotton Genesis in the British Library).[35]

Survivors

Originally supple and nearly white, the papyri in modern collections are brittle and brown because they have been buried in Egypt where they have become dehydrated over the centuries. The majority lay in rubbish tips of towns which had stood around the Fayyum depression, the remains of an ancient lake, now largely dry, some 50 miles up the Nile from Cairo, or at Oxyrhynchus (now Behnesa), 120 miles south of Cairo. Most of them were books that were worn out, or unwanted or dangerous to own and so thrown away, maybe torn up or crumpled, to be covered by other refuse or earth. In the dumps insects might attack them and a degree of decay occur from contact with harmful waste. Consequently, literary texts uncovered in these heaps are usually a few columns or single pages, often damaged and incomplete. Far outnumbering the pieces of books are the papyri from daily life, from government offices and personal files; over 40,000 have been published in modern times and as many more await publication. Occasionally documents were thrown out by the basketful—baskets were the ancient files—so related texts remain side by side. The dehydration that has allowed papyri to remain for treasure-hunters and scholars to recover in their myriads from the ruins and rubbish heaps of certain Graeco-Roman towns and villages in Egypt is a rare circumstance and does not apply in Palestine and most other countries where almost every settlement lies in an area of some rainfall, bringing damp and decay. Rubbish was thrown outside the towns in the same way as in Egypt and the dumps often set on fire. Writings on leather, papyrus or wood that escaped the flames would decay and perish. (Compare the description of Jerusalem's refuse tip, the valley of Hinnom, in Aramaic Gehenna, where the worm is always active and the fire always burns, Mk 9.48.)

Old papyrus rolls could be recycled by turning them inside out. Several rolls of accounts were reused in this way by people who wanted to make copies of literary works, as with Aristotle's *Constitution of Athens*, already noted, and a copy of the Gospel of Thomas which was

---

35. For a summary of these see B.M. Metzger, *Manuscripts of the Greek Bible* (New York: Oxford University Press, 1981), pp. 17, 45.

written on the back of a land survey (see Chapter 2, p. 50). Old codices did not provide any clean surfaces, but bookbinders would stick unwanted pages together to make boards which they then covered with leather. Significant scraps of a late second-century Gospel manuscript (Chapter 2, p. 50, no. 2) were preserved in this way in the binding of the book which, as described below, was bricked up in a house wall.

Rubbish tips are not the only sources of ancient texts. Some books have been found in the ruins of houses and others carefully buried in tombs, perhaps imitating the Egyptian custom of placing a copy of the Book of the Dead by the deceased for guidance in the next world. Books of special value might be hidden from enemies or carefully buried when worn or damaged. A good example of the first is a book which was allegedly found in a house at Coptos in Upper Egypt, bricked up in a niche in the wall, apparently to evade a search. Although this is a copy of two essays by the first-century Jewish philosopher Philo of Alexandria, it was probably copied by or for a Christian in the latter part of the third century.[36] An attitude of respect for an old religious volume is shown by a copy of the Gospel of John in the Sahidic dialect of Coptic which was discovered in a jar in the ruins of a small church in Upper Egypt in 1923 (at Qau el-Kebir, south of Luxor). Copied in the fourth century, it saw hard use in the church and so needed to be replaced. Its pages were worn, the first three and the last three of the original 50 leaves had disappeared and another one had worked loose, but rather than being thrown on to the rubbish tip, the Gospel had been neatly wrapped in cloth and tied with thread before its reverent burial.[37] Consequently, books hidden in such ways are in relatively good condition in contrast to most papyri, with dozens of intact

36. See C.H. Roberts, *Buried Books in Antiquity* (London: The Library Association, 1963), pp. 11-14; *idem*, *Manuscript, Society and Belief in Early Christian Egypt* (The Schweich Lectures, 1977; London: Oxford University Press for the British Academy, 1979), p. 8; E. Schürer, G. Vermes, F. Millar and M. Black (eds.), *The History of the Jewish People in the Age of Jesus Christ* (rev. edn, 3 vols.; Edinburgh: T. & T. Clark, 1973–87), III.2, p. 823 n. 37.

37. Sir Herbert Thompson, *The Gospel of St John According to the Earliest Coptic Manuscript* (London: British School of Archaeology in Egypt, 1924); note Sir Flinders Petrie's account of the discovery, pp. ix-x. See also R. Kilgour, *Four Ancient Manuscripts in the Bible House Library* (London: British and Foreign Bible Society, 1928), pp. 15-38 and B.M. Metzger, *The Early Versions of the New Testament* (Oxford: Clarendon Press, 1977), pp. 116-17.

Figure 6. *A page from the copy of St John's Gospel in Coptic found in a jar in Egypt. The page shown contains Jn 8.37-43. Sir Herbert Thompson,* The Gospel of St. John According to the Earliest Coptic Manuscript *(London: British School of Archaeology in Egypt, 1924), pl. 41. (Photograph by courtesy of the British and Foreign Bible Society.)*

pages, giving valuable information about the physical production of the books, such as the numbering of pages, their arrangement in quires, their binding and the way unrelated books could be copied in the same volume. For example, one volume in the Bodmer Collection (see Chapter 3, p. 79) contains part of the Greek historian Thucydides' work, the apocryphal Story of Susanna, a section of Daniel and a collection of good advice, all copied in the fourth century.

Some of the Dead Sea Scrolls were deliberately placed in jars and secreted in caves where they could lie undisturbed and, happily, the dryness of the region preserved them. Others of the Scrolls, which are mostly of leather, a few of papyrus, lay torn and damaged on the cave floors, covered with bat droppings, again preserved by the aridity. In a similar way, papyrus and parchment texts have survived in caves lining valleys west of the Dead Sea near En-gedi where they were hidden during the Second Jewish Revolt, led by Simon Bar Kochba in AD 132–35. Where those arid conditions do not exist, the only writings we may expect to find are ostraca, graffiti and occasionally inscriptions on metal or stone. That is the situation for most places in the Near East, including Palestine.

The thousands of papyrus documents and books from Egypt and the very much smaller numbers from other places are astonishing survivors of life about two thousand years ago and they are rightly highly valued. Yet whereas some proportion of ancient literature has perished, these papers are only a tiny proportion of the written material that was produced by central and local administrative offices, by scribes and by individual citizens for legal and private purposes. Egypt, again, provides the most telling figures. The local administration created reams of paperwork annually. Accounts from the archive of Zenon (see below, Chapter 4, p. 106) record that in the winter of 258–57 BC there were two secretariats and three offices at work on the business of Apollonius, the finance minister. In one month the three offices used 434 rolls of papyrus, some of them of 50 sheets, that is to say, up to 12 metres long (40 feet). One purchase of 1800 rolls is noted. The length of the rolls varied, but these amounts remind us of the vast quantities of written paperwork produced in Hellenistic Egypt, almost all of which is lost.[38]

38. P.W. Pestman, *A Guide to the Zenon Archive* (Leiden: E.J. Brill, 1981); C. Orrieux, *Les papyrus de Zenon: L'horizon d'un grec en Egypte au IIIe siècle avant J.C.* (Paris: Editions MACULA, 1983); W. Clarysse and K. Vandorpe,

The writing office of another place listed 247 documents deposited there in a four-month period in the mid-first century AD, including deeds of sale, leases and loans, contracts of all sorts, while a Roman prefect received 1804 petitions in three days in AD 210, which were to be publicly displayed in Alexandria.[39] Imperial rule created further demands. For example, every 14 years from AD 19 to 257 a census was taken of every household in Egypt. One scholar has calculated, 'If the average household size was 5 persons and the population is deliberately estimated low at 3.5 million, and we have less than 1000 surviving census returns, the survival rate is *c*.1: 12,000. Of course, this is only a rough estimate' and based on Egypt where, alone, census returns have been found.[40] Returns of some sort were surely made in every province of the Empire where a census was carried out, including Judaea (for Luke's report [2. 1] should not be rejected as fiction, whatever the problems it raises), so the quantity of census documents empire-wide would be many times greater. There is no reason to suppose the amount of paperwork generated in Egyptian towns was notably larger than that created by the bureaucracies in Rome, Antioch, Caesarea, Jerusalem or any other major centre. The dampness of the climate in those cities, as in Alexandria, capital of Roman Egypt, and most others, has robbed us of that parallel material.

Outside Egypt and Palestine, manuscripts of any sort from the Roman period are rare. A recent find of papyrus and leather documents from the mid-Euphrates joins the larger quantity of pieces unearthed by the excavators at Dura-Europos there (over 150),[41] but no others are known from the whole of Mesopotamia. Further east, in the Avroman district of the Zagros Mountains, someone found parchment leaves in a tightly sealed jar in a cave about 1909. Three of them were brought to

Zenon, un homme d'affaires grecs à l'ombre des pyramides (Louvain: Presses Universitaires, 1995).

39. E.G. Turner, *Greek Papyri* (Oxford: Clarendon Press, 1968), pp. 134, 142.

40. K. Hopkins, 'Conquest by Book', in J.H. Humphrey (ed.), *Literacy in the Roman World* (Journal of Roman Archaeology Supplement Series, 3; Ann Arbor, MI: Journal of Roman Archaeology, 1991), p. 133 n. 2.

41. For the texts from Dura see below, p. 46, and the survey by G.D. Kilpatrick, 'Dura-Europos: The Parchments and Papyri', *GRBS* 5 (1964), pp. 215-25. For the newly found texts, see D. Feisel and J. Gascou, 'Documents d'archives romains inédits du Moyen-Euphrate (IIIe siècle après J.-C.)', *CRAIBL* (1989), pp. 535-61; J. Teixidor, 'Deux documents syriaques du IIIe siècle provenant du moyen Euphrate', *CRAIBL* (1990), pp. 144-66.

London where they were read and shown to concern ownership of a vineyard. Two of them are in Greek, dated 88/7 and 22/1 BC and one, dated AD 53, is in Pehlevi, the Persian language of the Parthian kingdom written in a descendant of the Aramaic script.[42] A single Greek document on leather has come through the antiquities market from somewhere in Afghanistan.[43] Archaeologists working at Aï-Khanoum, where the Oxus River flows out of the Pamir Mountains, also in Afghanistan, recovered some of the text of a papyrus and of a parchment roll of the second century BC. Although the materials had perished, a negative print of the ink-written characters was transferred by dampness to the mud on which the rolls fell, the mud dried out and pieces were rescued during the excavation. Parts of four columns of a philosophical dialogue can be read from the papyrus, while the parchment had apparently carried a poetic work, perhaps a play.[44] A comparable discovery was made in Cave 7 by the Dead Sea: three small pieces of mud bear imprints of papyrus fibres and Greek text.[45]

Calculations based upon knowledge of the Roman army express the amount of documentation lost in one aspect of military life alone where physical survivors are minimal. Each legionary was paid three times a year, each legion had five thousand men, making 15,000 payments, many, if not all of them noted on pay vouchers. Throughout the Empire there were at least 25 legions, producing 375,000 vouchers annually, so

42. E.H. Minns, 'Parchments of the Parthian Period from Avroman in Kurdistan', *JHS* 35 (1915), pp. 22-65; D.N. MacKenzie, 'Avroman Documents', in E. Yarshater (ed.), *Encyclopaedia Iranica*, III (3 vols. so far; London: Routledge & Kegan Paul, 1989), p. 111.

43. J.R. Rea, R.C. Senior and A.S. Hollis, 'A Tax Receipt from Hellenistic Bactria', *ZPE* 104 (1994), pp. 261-80; P. Bernard and C. Rapin, 'Un parchemin gréco-bactrien d'une collection privée', *CRAIBL* (1994), pp. 261-94. Several dozen letters and legal deeds on leather, written in the Bactrian language in the fifth to eighth centuries AD have also been brought out of Afghanistan in recent years, see N. Sims-Williams, 'Nouveaux documents sur l'histoire et la langue de la Bactriane', *CRAIBL* 1996, pp. 633-54.

44. C. Rapin, 'Les textes littéraires grecs de la trésorie d'Aï Khanoum', *Bulletin de Correspondance hellénique* 111 (1986), pp. 225-66.

45. 7Q19: M. Baillet, J.T. Milik, R. de Vaux, *Les 'Petites Grottes' de Qumran* (DJD, 3; Oxford: Clarendon Press, 1962), pp. 145-46, pl. xxx. C.P. Thiede has argued that this may be part of a Christian writing, 'Das unbeachtete Qumran-Fragment 7Q19 und die Herkunft der Höhle 7', *Aegyptus* 74 (1994), pp. 123-28; the evidence is insufficient for so small a piece.

in the three centuries of the Roman Empire from Augustus to Diocletian there would have been 225,000,000 individual pay records. Hardly any have been identified from the whole of that period![46]

Discoveries of a different sort of object also point to the amount of documentation that once existed. Lumps of clay (bullae) bearing the imprints of seal-stones on one face carry the impression of papyrus fibres on their backs, the fingerprints, as it were, of the vanished documents which the clay bullae once sealed. Examples are found from the later centuries of the second millennium BC in Canaan as well as in Egypt and in greater numbers from the first millennium when papyrus was used by Israel and her neighbours.[47] In the Greek and Roman periods the quantities of bullae found testify to the former presence of papyrus documents, at some places in enormous numbers. At Mampsis in the Negev (modern Kurnub) archaeologists excavating a burial of the second century AD cleared the remains of a burnt wooden box and in it lay 27 clay sealings. Marks of papyrus fibres on the backs are proof that there had been documents there in the box which, for some reason, the mourners burned.[48] Very much larger collections of sealings found in other countries are a telling reminder of the extent of archives now lost. A room at Delos, burnt in 69 BC, contained over 5000 sealings from documents which had apparently belonged to two generations of one family.[49] In the ruins of a temple at Carthage, burnt by the Romans in 146 BC, lay another hoard of over 5000 bullae, representing 2500 documents, if there were two seals on each document, as has been supposed.[50] An archive spanning a century at Nea Paphos in Cyprus is

46. See R.D. Fink, *Roman Military Records on Papyrus* (Cleveland: Case Western Reserve University Press, 1971), pp. 241-42.

47. See J.N. Tubb, 'Preliminary Report on the Fourth Season of Excavations at Tell es-Sa'idiyeh in the Jordan Valley', *Levant* 22 (1990), pp. 21-42 (28 Fig. 11), for examples from the thirteenth century BC, and N. Avigad, *Hebrew Bullae from the Time of Jeremiah: Remnants of a Burnt Archive* (Jerusalem: Israel Exploration Society, 1988) for a large group from the seventh century BC.

48. A. Negev, 'Seal-Impressions from Tomb 107 at Kurnub (Mampsis)', *IEJ* 19 (1969), pp. 89-106.

49. See M.-F. Boussac, 'Sceaux déliens', *Revue archéologique* (1988), pp. 307-38.

50. D. Berges, 'Die Tonsiegel aus dem Karthagischen Tempelarchiv', *Mitteilungen des deutschen archäologischen Instituts, Römische Abteilung* 100 (1993), pp. 249- 68.

Figure 7. *Clay bullae which once sealed papyrus rolls, bearing impressions of Roman signets, second or third centuries* AD. *(Private collection; photograph D.J. Restall.)*

Figure 8. *The backs of two clay bullae showing imprints left by the fibres of long-perished papyrus documents. (Private collection; photograph D.J. Restall.)*

represented by over 14,000 sealings.[51] At Seleucia on the Tigris, south of Baghdad, more than 24,000 clay sealings were recovered from public archives of the town sacked shortly after Carthage, in 141 BC, the majority of them bearing seals of municipal officers. Even if there were as many as six seals to a single deed, the number of documents held there in the city's last year was high.[52] Smaller numbers have been recovered from Roman cities in Syria.[53] An enormous amount of writing was done throughout the Near East in Hellenistic and Roman times, most of it for administrative and legal purposes.

51. See K. Nikolaou, 'Oriental Divinities Represented on the Clay Sealings of Paphos, Cyprus', in M.B. de Boer and T.A. Edridge (eds.), *Hommages à Maarten J. Vermaseren* (Etudes préliminaires aux religions orientales dans l'Empire romain, 68.2; Leiden: E.J. Brill, 1978), pp. 849-53.

52. A. Invernizzi, 'Ten Years' Research in the Al-Mada'in Area, Seleucia and Ctesiphon', *Sumer* 32 (1976), pp. 167-75 (169-71) and 'Seleucia sul Tigri: Gli archivi', in *idem, La terra tra i due fiumi* (Turin: Il Quadrante, 1985), pp. 92-93, 124-26, 175-78 (colour ill.); for other Hellenistic bullae from Babylonia see R.H. McDowell, *Stamped and Inscribed Objects from Seleucia on the Tigris* (Ann Arbor, MI: University of Michigan Press, 1935) and J. Oelsner, *Materialien zur babylonischen Gesellschaft und Kultur in hellenistischer Zeit* (Budapest: Eötvös University, 1986), pp. 257-58; see also essays in M.-F. Boussac and A. Invernizzi (eds.), *Archives et sceaux du monde hellénistique: Archivi e sigilli nel mondo ellenistico, Torino, Villa Gualino, 13–16 gennaio 1993* (Bulletin de Correspondance Hellénique, Sup 29; Athens: Ecole française d'Athenes, 1996).

53. See H. Seyrig, 'Cachets d'archives publiques du quelques villes de la Syrie romaine', *MUSJ* 23 (1940), pp. 85-107.

Chapter 2

EARLY CHRISTIAN MANUSCRIPTS

The most remarkable of all the survivors are the Christian books. Like
other Greek texts, many biblical manuscripts made in the early centuries of our era perished in the Dark Ages, the few exceptions preserved in libraries justly attracting great attention (see p. 43). To them
the past hundred years of discovery in Egypt have added some dozens
of copies on papyrus, often small pieces, many of them made in the
period before AD 312, in the time when Christianity was an illegal and
occasionally fiercely persecuted religion whose books might be
officially destroyed.

The New Testament is the foundation document of the Christian
faith. Not surprisingly, therefore, it was copied and recopied endlessly
before the invention of printing for public reading in church and for
private study. At present over three thousand manuscripts of the New
Testament, or parts of it, written in Greek on parchment are known.
They date from the third century AD to the fifteenth. The majority of
them belong relatively late in that period and present forms of the
traditional Greek text, the Byzantine *Textus receptus.*

The First Complete Bibles

Since the fourth century the history of the Christian Scriptures is clear:
the Gospels were revered as the official accounts of the life and teaching of Christianity's founder, the other books as the authoritative statements of his closest followers. From the moment when Constantine the
Great made Christianity a permitted religion in the Roman Empire
(312), anyone could lawfully own those books and reproduce them.
Two years after Constantine refounded Byzantium as his new capital
city, naming it Constantinople, in 330, he wrote to his friend Eusebius,
who was bishop of Caesarea in Palestine, ordering Bibles for the
churches of his city. The order was for 50 copies of the Greek Bible to

be carefully written on parchment, 'easy to read and conveniently portable'. When completed they were to be despatched in two state-owned carriages across Syria and Anatolia to Constantinople.[1] Caesarea was the home of the leading Christian book-producing workshop at the time and the Emperor wanted the best for his new foundations.

Like the majority of books made in antiquity, Constantine's copies have all disappeared. They were either read until worn out and then thrown away, or left rotting in old buildings, or burnt in wars and raids. The two famous manuscripts in Rome and London, Codex Vaticanus and Codex Sinaiticus, belong to only a slightly later date, and may be the products of similar commissions by wealthy patrons following the Emperor's example. Scholars have found reasons for suspecting they were made in Egypt, at Alexandria, and so did not form part of Constantine's own order, although his Bibles and these two were probably very much alike. They are the oldest examples of more or less complete Bibles to survive, and they are massive parchment books, formal copies of the Scriptures for public reading rather than private study books. Codex Sinaiticus is the larger. Originally it contained the Old Testament, including the Apocryphal books, and the New Testament with some early Christian writings, but only two of the last are left, the *Letter of Barnabas* and part of *The Shepherd* of Hermas. To-day it has 390 leaves out of an original total of at least 730. Had Constantine Tischendorf not arrived at the Monastery of Saint Catherine in May 1844 and recognized the great age of the parchment sheets waiting in a basket to be fed as fuel to the monks' fire, doubtless all would have been consumed. He counted 129 leaves and obtained 43 which he presented to the king of Saxony. They have remained ever since in Leipzig. Not until 1859, on his third visit, was Tischendorf able to gain more of the precious book, the 347 leaves he presented to the Tsar and which the Soviet government sold to the British Museum in 1933. (Thirteen more pages, from Genesis, were found at Saint Catherine's Monastery in Sinai in 1975.[2]) The pages are large, now 38.1×34.5 cm (15×13.5–14

1.   Eusebius, *Life of Constantine* 3. 1; 4.36, 37.

2.   See L. Politis, 'Nouveaux manuscrits grecs découverts au Mont Sinaï, rapport préliminaire', *Scriptorium* 34 (1980), pp. 5-17; J.H. Charlesworth, 'The Manuscripts of St Catherine's Monastery', *BA* 43 (1980), pp. 26-34. A colour photograph of a page from the book of Judges (6.1-25, agreeing with Codex Vaticanus) is presented in M.S. El-Din *et al.*, *Sinai: The Site and the History* (New York: New York University Press, 1998), opposite p. 110.

in), having been trimmed from about 45 × 37.8 cm (16.85 × 14.85 in). Codex Sinaiticus is unique in having four columns on each page, except in the poetical books of the Old Testament where there are two. Codex Vaticanus is a little smaller and when complete had about 800 leaves. The present 759 leaves measure 27.5 × 27.5 cm (10.9 × 10.9 in), each with three columns of writing. It covers both Testaments and the Apocrypha, having lost a few leaves from the Old Testament and everything after Heb. 9.14. No other complete or nearly complete Greek Bibles have lasted from the fourth century, the standard handbooks list pages or parts of pages from twelve other New Testaments in Greek on parchment of that date.[3] Whether any of them belong to Constantine's order of 50, or not, is impossible to say, although all except one are smaller than Codex Vaticanus, which makes it less likely. (A fragment of Paul's Ephesian letter now in Florence, does come from a large copy, with a page size 34 × 27 cm [13.4 × 10.6 in].[4]) Such pieces are undoubtedly survivors from a very much greater number of biblical books in Greek copied on parchment in the east Mediterranean lands during the fourth century. Wherever they may have been written, all of these have been discovered in Egypt. Even with a script of reduced size, a whole Bible would make a very bulky book, as the measurements given show, so it is likely that the copies Constantine and his contemporaries ordered were among the first examples of all the books of the Bible collected in one cover.

Earlier Parchment Copies

Obviously, large, expensive volumes of the Scriptures could not be made when the Church was suffering harsh persecution, as it did frequently from its birth until Constantine's conversion in 312. During Diocletian's 'Great Persecution', beginning in 303, for example, all Christian Scriptures and liturgical books were ordered to be burnt. The

---

3.   See K. and B. Aland, *The Text of the New Testament* (trans. E.F. Rhodes; Grand Rapids: Eerdmans, 1987), for standard lists of manuscripts and papyri of the Greek New Testament. The texts dated before about AD 300 are given in P.W. Comfort and D.P. Barrett, *The Complete Text of the Earliest New Testament Manuscripts* (Grand Rapids: Baker Book House, 1999), with dates for some rather earlier than those followed here.

4.   Uncial MS 0230 in the standard list.

careful preparation of the skin of over 350 sheep or goats needed to make Codex Sinaiticus was not a task that could be done secretly or without cost. In dangerous times, owning and carrying big books would be awkward, and hiding them difficult, so to have a whole Bible in a single volume would be impracticable. Rather, groups of books, like the Gospels, or Paul's Letters, could be collected under one cover, or kept separately. They were written on smaller leaves, with only one column on each page, so they could more easily fit in the fold of a robe or be slipped into a hiding place. Examples of these more manageable books written on parchment before AD 300 are rare; only five New Testament manuscripts are currently given that early date. They are:

(1) parts of 2 pages from Matthew (10.17-32) and Luke (22.41-64), originally about 15 × 12 cm (5.9 × 4.7 in), with 23 or 24 lines of writing on each side and two columns on each page, dated c. AD 300;[5]

(2) a piece from a page of John's Gospel (2.11-22), 16 × 15 cm (6.2 × 5.9 in), with 19 lines, from the third or fourth centuries;[6]

(3) a page from Acts (5.3-21), 18 × 11.5 cm (7 × 4.5 in), with 32 lines, variously dated second/third or third/fourth century;[7]

(4) a piece of a page from Romans (3.8-13; 4.23-25), originally about 15 × 13 cm (5.9 × 5.1 in), with 24 lines, from the third or perhaps the fourth century;[8]

5. In Florence and Berlin; uncial 0171; J. van Haelst, *Catalogue des papyrus littéraires juifs et chrétiens* (Paris: Publications de la Sorbonne, 1976), no. 356; Aland, *Text*, p. 105, Pl. 17; E.G. Turner, *The Typology of the Early Codex* (Philadelphia: University of Pennsylvania Press, 1977), NTParch 51+15a (third/fourth century); T.C. Skeat gives a date 'c. 300' in 'The Oldest Manuscript of the Four Gospels', *NTS* 43 (1997), pp. 1-34 (32 n. 20).

6. In New York; uncial 0162; van Haelst, *Catalogue*, no. 436; Aland, *Text*, p. 105; Turner, *Typology*, NT Parch 56 (4th cent).

7. In Berlin; uncial 0189; van Haelst, *Catalogue*, no.479; Aland,*Text*, p. 104, Pl. 27; Turner, *Typology*, NT Parch 76 (4th cent.).

8. 'Wyman fragment'; uncial 0220; van Haelst, *Catalogue*, no. 495; Aland *Text*, p. 60, Pl. 14; Turner, *Typology*, NTParch 82 (third century?); sold at Sotheby's, London, on 21 June 1988, for £104,500 (Western Manuscripts, lot 47), M. Schøyen and E.G. Sørenssen, *The Schøyen Collection: Checklist of Manuscripts 1—2393* (Oslo: In Principio Press, 1997), p. 13, MS 113.

(5)   a page from John's Second Epistle (1-5; 6-9), 9.9 × 8.8 cm (3.9 × 3.5 in) originally with 20 lines of writing, copied in the third or fourth century.[9]

In addition to these, there is a page of one of the so-called Apocryphal books of the New Testament, the *Acts of Peter*, assigned to the third century, (9.8 × 9 cm, 3.9 × 3.5 in),[10] parts of a copy of Genesis on parchment, with two columns per page (X × 16.2 cm, X × 6.4 in) and of Tobit (8.5 × 8.5 cm, 3.4 × 3.4 in) of the same date,[11] and of Exodus (measurements uncertain) and the Psalms (31.1 × 10.5 cm, 12.2 × 4.1 in) from the third/fourth century.[12] As these last four leaves from the Old Testament are from books with pages, not from rolls, they are likely to be the work of Christian, not Jewish, copyists (see Chapter 3, pp. 79-80). One other obviously Christian parchment fragment has to be noted, a part of a harmony of the Four Gospels, the *Diatessaron* which Tatian composed in the second century. This part of a sheet, 10.5 × 9.5 cm (4.1 × 3.7 in) which has 14 lines on one side only and so probably came from a roll, was not found in Egypt, like the other pieces, but at Dura-Europos on the Euphrates in Syria. The sacking and desertion of the site in AD 256 gives the latest date for the copying of this book.[13]

9.   C.H. Roberts, *The Antinoopolis Papyri* (London: Egypt Exploration Society, 1950), pp. 24-26, no. 12; uncial 0232; van Haelst, *Catalogue*, no. 555; Aland, *Text*, p. 124, there assigned to the fifth/sixth centuries; Turner, *Typology*, NTParch 107.

10.   B.P. Grenfell and A.S. Hunt, *The Oxyrhynchus Papyri*, VI (London: Egypt Exploration Fund, 1908), pp. 6-12, no. 849; Turner, *Typology*, NTApocrypha 13.

11.   Genesis: A.S. Hunt, *The Oxyrhynchus Papyri*, VII (London: Egypt Exploration Fund, 1910), pp. 1-3, no. 1007; van Haelst, *Catalogue*, no. 5; Turner, *Typology*, OT 2; Tobit: B.P. Grenfell and A.S. Hunt, *The Oxyrhynchus Papyri*, XIII (London: Egypt Exploration Fund, 1919), pp. 1-6, no. 1594; van Haelst, *Catalogue*, no. 82; Turner, *Typology*, OT 186.

12.   Exodus: Turner, *Typology*, OT 29B; Psalms: B.P. Grenfell and A.S. Hunt, *The Oxyrhynchus Papyri*, XI (London: Egypt Exploration Society, 1915), pp. 2-4, no. 1352; Turner, *Typology*, OT 121.

13.   C.B. Welles, R.O. Fink and J.F. Gilliam, *The Excavations at Dura-Europos, Final report V, Part I, The Parchments and Papyri* (New Haven: Yale University Press, 1959), pp.73, 74, no. 10 ; now numbered uncial 0212; van Haelst, *Catalogue*, no. 699; Turner, *Typology*, NT Parch. 2. For photographs see B.M. Metzger, *Manuscripts of the Greek Bible* (New York: Oxford University Press, 1981) Pl. 8; Aland, *Text* , p. 58, Pl. 13.

Dating the Books

In the descriptions of the parchment texts the dates have all been given vaguely. That is because ancient Greek copyists did not commonly date the books they made in the way printers have usually done since the fifteenth century. The oldest Greek manuscript dated by its scribe was written in the sixth century.[14] Without such a date, the only ways to discover when a manuscript was written are by references within it, by its provenance, or by comparative study of the handwriting. Obviously, if a book refers to an historical person, then it cannot come from a time before that person's birth. Thus the copy on papyrus of a Christian martyr's self-defence cannot date much before his death about 307, although the style of handwriting might suggest it should be placed earlier.[15] Discovering a manuscript in an archaeological context may help to assign a date to it. The stock example is the books found at Herculaneum, all buried in the eruption of Vesuvius in AD 79; all are older than that, although how much older may be open to debate—some books in the library there apparently belonged to a philosopher who died about 40 BC (see above, Chapter 1, p. 21). The fragment of the *Diatessaron* from Dura-Europos is a comparable case, for we know when the town was destroyed.

Many ancient documents bear dates for legal or administrative reasons, so the styles of handwriting they display may be compared with the script of undated texts, but the handwriting in books was usually more careful and formal than the products of the government offices or commercial secretaries. Consequently, the dates palaeographers assign to the ancient books and documents are very approximate, with a margin of 50 years and possibly more being understood, a point important to remember. In the context of biblical manuscripts this is significant, especially as experts can differ widely, sometimes by more than a century. For example, the first editor of a page from a copy of Genesis placed it about AD 90, another scholar (C.H. Roberts) set it in the second century and another (E.G. Turner) in the second or third.[16]

14. See Metzger, *Manuscripts*, p. 50.

15. E.A. Judge and S.R. Pickering, 'Papyrus Documentation of Church and Community in Egypt to the Mid-Fourth Century', *JAC* 20 (1977), pp. 47-71 (60).

16. P. Yale 1: C.B. Welles, 'The Yale Genesis Fragment', *Yale University Gazette* 39 (1964), pp. 1-8; C.H. Roberts, 'P Yale 1 and the Early Christian Book', in A.E. Samuel (ed.), *American Studies in Papyrology*. I. *Essays in Honor of*

Presuppositions can also play a part. When the first examples of pages from biblical books were recovered at the end of the nineteenth century, scholars placed them in the fourth century because they did not believe that type of book (the codex) existed in previous centuries, despite the style of script which clearly pointed to an earlier date for some of them. Once it became certain that the codex was current before that time, a number of texts were placed in earlier centuries and the form of book is no longer used as a dating criterion.[17] In this chapter the dates used are taken wherever possible from the work of the papyrologist Sir Eric Turner, who was conservative, that is, he tended to prefer later rather than earlier dates, and so fewer manuscripts will be found to be assigned to the third and second centuries than in standard handbooks of New Testament textual criticism and in the important works of C.H. Roberts and T.C. Skeat.[18] The occasional attempts to give dates in the first century to various papyrus books have not won support and are disregarded (for the most recent, see pp. 53-57). It seems wiser to err on the side of caution in discussing the evidence these texts give about early Christianity, than to make greater claims for their age which could later be proved wrong.

Christian Books before Constantine

Early Christian Writers and Readers

Several aspects of the books the papyrus leaves represent are worth exploring. The first is their witness to the spread of Christianity. By AD 150 people were reading the Gospels in middle Egypt, far from the metropolis of Alexandria. It is not a case of a solitary individual whose souvenir of a visit to Jerusalem has happened to survive, as the 'Ethiopian' eunuch's scroll of Isaiah (Acts 8.27-39) might have done in the

C. Bradford Welles (New Haven: American Papyrological Society, 1956), pp. 25-28; van Haelst, *Catalogue*, no. 12; Turner, *Typology*, 164, OT 7; see S. Emmel, 'Greek Biblical Papyri in the Beinecke Library', *ZPE* 112 (1996), pp. 289-94, with a fresh edition on pp. 289-91. The papyrus is illustrated in Metzger, *Manuscripts*, Pl. 5. For other examples of varying dates assigned to manuscripts, see Turner, *Typology*, p. 3 and C.H. Roberts and T.C. Skeat, *The Birth of the Codex* (London: Oxford University Press for the British Academy, 1983), pp. 40-41.

17. Turner, *Typology*, p. 3 (documentation p. 11 n. 8).

18. See the discussion by S.R. Pickering, *Recently Published New Testament Papyri: P89-P95* (Sydney: Ancient History Documentary Resource Centre, Macquarie University, 1991), pp. 12-14.

ruins of the Nubian capital Meröe, in the Sudan, but of readers in different places who bought and used books, or even copied them for themselves, those readers being, in all probability, it is worth repeating, only a small proportion of those who studied the Gospels. Had the great city of Alexandria, yielded dessicated rubbish heaps, the number of second century Gospel manuscripts to be expected would surely be far higher than those from Middle Egypt.

1. *The Third Century*

Various manuscripts attest the growth of the church and an increase in Christian readers in Egypt throughout the century before Constantine's conversion. The Christian codices currently known comprise parts of 29 copies of New Testament books or groups of books, parts of 30 or so Old Testament books or groups of books, four of the New Testament apocrypha (the *Gospel of Mary*, the *Acts of Peter* and two copies of the *Acts of Paul*), three copies of *The Shepherd* of Hermas, five copies of writings of the great early Christian scholar Origen (who lived c. 185–254) and one volume in Coptic containing 1 Peter and other writings.[19] The majority of these are single pages or fragments of pages, preserving only a few verses on either side. Notable among these books, or fragments of books, are two from the Bodmer Collection (see Chapter 3, p. 79), a copy of John's Gospel made in the first half of the century, perhaps as early as 200 ($\mathfrak{P}^{66}$), and one of Luke and John made in the middle of the century ($\mathfrak{P}^{75}$). The other major collection is the Chester Beatty Papyri, 11 codices bought in 1931 by an American collector who settled in Dublin where these manuscripts are kept in the Chester Beatty Library, with many others. The papyri are principally biblical, copies of books of the Old Testament in Greek made in the second, third and fourth centuries, with other books early Christians read (*Enoch*, *Apocalypse of Ezekiel* and the *Easter Homily* of Melito, who was bishop of Sardis late in the second century). There are three papyri of New Testament books. Papyrus Chester Beatty I once contained the four Gospels and the Acts of the Apostles ($\mathfrak{P}^{45}$), Papyrus II held many of Paul's Epistles and Hebrews ($\mathfrak{P}^{46}$) and Papyrus III Revelation ($\mathfrak{P}^{47}$). As they belong to the third century and are quite extensive, despite damage,

---

19. Texts published before 1975 are listed in Turner, *Typology*, pp. 143-85; details of papyri published more recently are given annually in the periodical *Aegyptus*.

they have high value for the study of the New Testament text, for they exemplify an apparently established tradition of copying and collecting books of similar content under one cover.

2. *The Second Century*

Codices of every sort dated across the boundary of the second and third centuries number between 20 and 30, 15 or so pagan, one probably Jewish and seven Christian. Five of the last are Old Testament Greek texts: the Yale Genesis (see above, p. 47), another Genesis fragment, a copy of Numbers and Deuteronomy and two fragments of copies of the Psalms. The sixth is the 'Sayings of Jesus' fragment, one of the first Christian papyri identified among the thousands of fragments harvested from Oxyrhynchus (Oxyrhynchus Papyrus no. 1), actually found on the second day of the excavations in 1897, which is now known to be part of the Gospel of Thomas.[20] The other is a fragment of Matthew's Gospel from the same site, recently published.[21]

Not surprisingly, the number of Christian manuscripts allotted dates within the second century is small. The New Testament manuscripts are:

(1)   fragments of one page of Matthew, Oxyrhynchus Papyrus 2683 + 4405, $\mathfrak{P}^{77}$, late second or early third century;

(2)   fragments of Matthew in Magdalen College, Oxford and in Barcelona, and larger parts of Luke in Paris, $\mathfrak{P}^{4+64+67}$ (whether the two books belong together or not has been disputed for some time, but re-examination by the veteran papyrologist T.C Skeat satisfied him that they do[22]), carefully written, with two columns per page, late second century;

20.   See R. Cameron, 'Thomas, Gospel of', *ABD* ,VI, pp. 535-40 (535).

21.   J.D. Thomas, 'New Testament', in E.W. Handley and U. Wartenberg, *The Oxyrhynchus Papyri*, LXIV (London: Egypt Exploration Society, 1997), pp. 5-7, no. 4403 ($\mathfrak{P}^{103}$).

22.   These are the pieces from the binding of a codex of Philo, mentioned earlier (Ch. 1, p. 34), described by J. Merell, 'Nouveaux fragments du Papyrus 4', *RB* 47 (1938), pp. 5-22. See P.W. Comfort, 'Exploring the Common Identification of Three New Testament Manuscripts: $\mathfrak{P}^4$, $\mathfrak{P}^{64}$ and $\mathfrak{P}^{67}$', *TynBul* 46 (1995), pp. 43-54; C.P. Thiede, 'Notes on $\mathfrak{P}^4$ = Bibliothèque Nationale Paris, Supplementum Graece 1120/5', *TynBul* 46 (1995), pp. 55-58; Skeat,'The Oldest Manuscript of the Four Gospels', pp. 1-34.

(3)   a fragment from a page of Matthew, Oxyrhynchus Papyrus 4404, $\mathfrak{P}^{104}$ late second century,[23]

(4)   a fragment of John, Oxyrhynchus Papyrus 3523, $\mathfrak{P}^{90}$ perhaps late second century;[24]

(5)   the Rylands fragment of John, $\mathfrak{P}^{52}$, perhaps a little before 150.

Figure 9.   *Fragment from a leaf of a codex of John's Gospel ($\mathfrak{P}^{52}$), usually dated a little before* AD *150, but perhaps to be set slightly later. The fragment covers Jn 18.31-34 and 37-38. C.H. Roberts,* An Unpublished Fragment of the Fourth Gospel, in the John Rylands Library *(Manchester: University Press, 1935). (Photograph by courtesy of the Director and University Librarian, the Rylands University Library, Manchester.)*

To these can be added the British Museum's 'Fragments of an Unknown Gospel', Papyrus Egerton 2, perhaps to be identified as part

23.   Thomas, 'New Testament', pp. 7-9.
24.   T.C. Skeat, 'Theological Texts', in A.K. Bowman *et al.*, *The Oxyrhynchus Papyri*, L (London: Egypt Exploration Society, 1983), pp. 3-8; see Pickering, *Recently Published New Testament Papyri*, pp. 11-17.

of the apocryphal *Gospel of Peter*,[25] and another fragment of the *Gospel of Peter*, Oxyrhynchus Papyrus 4009, placed in the second rather than third century by its editors,[26] and one fragment of the Greek Old Testament, now in Baden, which is identified as Christian rather than Jewish, containing a verse from Exodus and part of Deuteronomy.[27]

Eight items, all very fragmentary, seem at first sight to be meagre in comparison with the third century figure, which is ten times greater, and so may imply a much smaller Christian presence in Egypt (see Chapter 3, pp. 77-79), nevertheless, they are witnesses to Christian reading and copying in Oxyrhynchus and possibly other parts of the country (the provenances of some pieces are unknown). The books of the New Testament, it is generally agreed, were completed before AD 100. Why do no copies from the first century exist? The disappearance of the authors' autographs puzzles some people, yet it would be extraordinary if they had survived. William Shakespeare wrote his poems and plays only 400 years ago and none of his originals are extant, nor are there any original manuscripts of the famous Latin writers such as Julius Caesar, Vergil or Cicero. If they had been treasured in the authors' families or as collectors' rarities in Rome or any other city of private villa in the Mediterranean region, the centuries of turmoil, war, destruction and neglect, not to mention physical processes of decay, would have reduced their chances of survival to the minimum. Two of the most prized books in the Vatican Library are copies of Vergil's works in Latin. Like the Codex Vaticanus and a few other biblical manuscripts, they have endured the Dark Ages and later troubles, whether kept throughout in Rome or elsewhere is unknown. If older copies of Rome's 'national epic' were not saved, not even the author's text, the likelihood of an illegal, persecuted sect being able to preserve the autographs of books they prized, in Rome or in any other place, is negligible. Chapter 1 has demonstrated how the random element dominates

25. H.I. Bell and T.C. Skeat, *Fragments of an Unknown Gospel and other Early Christian Papyri* (London: The British Museum, 1935); van Haelst, *Catalogue*, no. 586; Turner, *Typology*, NT Apocrypha 7; see D.F. Wright, 'Papyrus Egerton 2 (the *Unknown Gospel*)—Part of the Gospel of Peter?', *The Second Century* 5 (1985–86), pp. 129-50; K. Erlemann, 'Papyrus Egerton 2: "Missing Link" zwischen synoptischer und johanneischer Tradition', *NTS* 42 (1996), pp. 12-34.

26. P.J. Parsons and D. Lührmann, *The Oxyrhynchus Papyri*, LX (London: Egypt Exploration Society, 1994), pp. 1-5.

27. van Haelst, *Catalogue*, no. 33; Turner, *Typology*, OT 24.

our recovery of ancient manuscripts and documents and that applies to Christian as much as to pagan literature. In addition, we can be sure St Paul's letters or the first copies of the Gospels were read regularly and repeatedly, until they were literally read to pieces. Unless the authors' sheets had reached an ancient rubbish heap which was very dry, or been secreted in a well-sealed container, none would last for almost two millennia, as already explained. Furthermore, ancient people, like many modern ones, generally preferred fresh, new copies to old, well-used ones, so worn and damaged books were discarded, sometimes as rubbish, sometimes reverently buried (see Chapter 1, pp. 33-36). While educated Greeks might have an interest in the manuscripts of Aristotle (see Chapter 7, pp. 201-202), there is no hint of early Christians prizing manuscripts by Paul or other writers of the apostolic period.

First Century Fragments?

The will-o'-the-wisp lure of first century New Testament manuscripts has led various people to make claims they have discovered some. Apart from the satisfaction of finding copies from so close to the authors' lifetimes, an element of apologetic enters the scene, for if a text of a Gospel can be dated within a few years of the time of Jesus, that would challenge the consensus of scholarly opinion on the date of the Gospels (about AD 70 and after) and allow a shorter period for reports of his activities and teachings to be exaggerated or altered to suit new situations. In fact, even reports made at the time of an event, or immediately afterwards, need not be more accurate than one set out later and memories of someone's words can vary widely within a few hours of their delivery, or be recalled accurately long afterwards.

In 1860 a Greek, Constantine Simonides, visited Joseph Mayer of Liverpool, a prosperous silversmith and collector, to inspect Egyptian antiquities he had acquired. Simonides claimed to be able to read Egyptian and, after unrolling and mounting some Egyptian papyri in Mayer's museum, was presently permitted to take away some for study at his lodgings. After a short time, he announced that he had found among them three parts of a Greek text of Matthew's Gospel, written at the evangelist's dictation by 'Nicolaus the deacon' in the fifteenth year after the Ascension. With them were pieces of the letters of James and Jude, Genesis and several other non-biblical works. Drawings of the texts were soon published, leading scholars to condemn them as undoubted forgeries, concocted by Simonides and introduced by him into Mayer's collection, which formed the basis of Liverpool Museum where those forgeries are preserved.[28] Simonides, who sold genuine manuscripts to the British Museum and other libraries, but who had created other forgeries, had not sought financial gain but reputation. He further tried to attain that in 1862 when he claimed that he himself had made the Codex Sinaiticus in 1840, while resident at the monasteries on Mt Athos in Greece. Although he was well informed about ancient manuscripts and Greek texts, there is no room for doubt about the falsity of these claims. Simonides died in Alexandria in 1867.

In 1955 archaeologists exploring caves near the Dead Sea hoping to find more "Dead Sea Scrolls" entered one (Cave 7) and extracted 18 pieces of Greek papyrus rolls from the floor, with three small lumps of mud which carried in reverse the writings of other fragments transferred by dampness from papyrus which had later perished (see Chapter 1, p. 38). Intensive scrutiny enabled M. Baillet, who edited the fragments for the official publication, to recognize one piece as Exod. 28.4-6 and another as part of a copy of the apocryphal book of Baruch, containing 6.43-44.[29] The others were left unidentified until 1972 when a Spanish papyrological scholar, J. O'Callaghan, published his identifications of some of them as remnants of books of the New Testament.[30] As it is usually supposed the owners deposited the papyri in the caves at the same time as the Dead Sea Scrolls, that is about AD 67 or 68, his work won wide publicity, for none of the Gospels had usually been dated so early. Were these fragments from New Testament books made before that date? The cave could have served as a hiding place later than the main collections of Hebrew scrolls, but the style of the Greek script set these pieces in the early part of the first century AD, or earlier, so their age is not really in doubt. As soon as O'Callaghan's study was circulated, responses flowed from New Testament scholars and palaeographers, all agreeing that the pieces are too small to support the

---

28. C. Simonides, *Fac-similes of Certain Portions of the Gospel of St. Matthew, and of the Epistles of St. James and St. Jude, Written on Papyrus in the First Century* (London: Trübner, 1861); see the review in *The Athenaeum* 1780 (7 December 1861), pp. 755-56; J.A. Farrer, *Literary Forgeries* (London: Longmans, Green & Co, 1907), pp. 39-66.

29. Baillet, Milik and de Vaux, *Les 'Petites Grottes' de Qumran*, pp. 142-46.

30. J. O'Callaghan, 'Papiros neotestamentarios en a cueva 7 de Qumran', *Biblica* 53 (1972), pp. 91-100; trans. W.L. Holladay, *JBL* 91.2 (1972), Supplement, pp. 1-14.

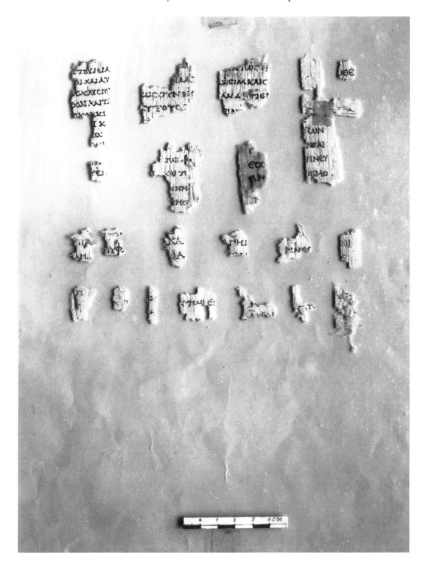

Figure 10. *Fragments of papyrus rolls from Qumran Cave 7. Some have claimed the second piece in the second row to be from the Gospel of Mark 6.52-53. M. Baillet, J.T. Milik, R. de Vaux, Les 'Petites Grottes' de Qumran, Pl.xxx.5. (Photograph by courtesy of the Israel Antiquities Authority.)*

identifications proposed, some arguing that others could be made from non-Christian Greek books. Interest waned as those most competent to judge showed that basis for the identification was weak. The fact that these fragments could not be identified is not unusual in the study of Greek papyri where many pieces, some much larger, suffer the same fate. It is equally true for some of the tatters among the Dead Sea Scrolls. Without an ancient copyright library holding an example of every published book, it is impossible to expect to place each piece in a known book, and, in any case, a fragment may come from a unique work that only ever existed in a single copy which modern students could have no hope of identifying unless a considerable amount of text or some key words survived. However, further study has shown that three of the pieces fit together and they have been identified as parts of a Greek version of the book of Enoch.[31]

A renewed attempt to maintain the identity of 7Q5 as part of Mark's Gospel was mounted in 1984 and has been continued. C.P. Thiede drew on papyrology, statistics and forensic microscopy to try to prove O'Callaghan's case, yet without convincing the majority of leading specialists. The surviving letters are too few—nine are clear, nine are debatable—and the words or parts of words they spell too uncertain to permit the identification without making certain assumptions and barring alternatives.[32] Where other scraps of papyrus have been identified with known works, they have shown sufficient letters to correspond with the existing text (as with the line of Vergil at Masada, see Chapter 4, pp. 130-31). In this case variations from the existing text have to be accepted in order to obtain the correspondence and there is too great an area of uncertainty for the identification to be allowed as more than the smallest percentage of possibility. Since others of the small pieces have been identified as parts of Enoch (see above), the possibility increases that 7Q5 belongs to that or a similar work.

31.   E.A. Muro, 'The Greek Fragments of Enoch from Qumran Cave 7', *RevQ* 18.2=70 (1997), pp. 307-12; E. Puech, 'Sept fragments de la Lettre d'Hénoch (Hén 100, 103 et 105) dans la grotte 7 de Qumrân (=7QHén gr)', *RevQ* 18.2=70, pp. 313-23.

32.   C.P. Thiede, *The Earliest Gospel Manuscript* (Exeter: Paternoster Press, 1992). For critiques see S.R. Pickering, 'Looking for Mark's Gospel among the Dead Sea Scrolls: The Continuing Problem of Qumran Fragment 7Q5', *New Testament Textual Research Update* 2 (1994), pp. 94-98; S. Enste, 'Qumran-Fragment 7Q5 is nicht Markus 6, 52-53', *ZPE* 126 (1999), pp.189-93.

Thiede followed his efforts on the Qumran fragment by claiming to have dated three tiny pieces of a papyrus page from a copy of Matthew's Gospel to the middle of the first century AD. The pieces, in the library of Magdalen College, Oxford, come from the same book as one in Barcelona and, perhaps, parts of Luke in Paris (see above, p. 50, no. 2), but Thiede directed his attention to the Oxford examples alone. By comparing the handwriting with that in a few other Greek manuscripts of the first century BC or AD among the Dead Sea Scrolls, from another cave in Nahal Hever, near the Dead Sea, from Herculaneum and one written in AD 66 in Egypt, he suggested similarities of script 'could point towards a first century date for' the Magdalen papyrus.[33] Again, he spoke against the consensus dating of the fragments at about AD 200, proposed by the papyrologist who edited them and accepted by those best qualified to judge. As said earlier, dating by the style of handwriting is a matter of judgment and can only give an approximate answer, yet the assessment has to be made in the light of wide knowledge and constant acquaintance with the styles of the centuries in question. By singling out certain letters for comparison and basing his conclusions on them, Thiede only undertook part of the exercise, for it is the whole range and style of the script that has to be compared with others, including the flow of the lines and the spacing as well as the shapes of individual letters and the ways they were formed. Some of the points Thiede noted are evident to the layman, such as the apparent serifs on the letters *g*, *n*, *t*, while some are far from compelling. For example, the horizontal and vertical strokes of the letters, he asserted, are equally thick, whereas in the photographs he published the horizontal strokes are clearly thinner than the vertical! When his comparisons with other manuscripts are investigated in detail, they fail.[34]

33. C.P. Thiede, 'Papyrus Magdalen Greek 17 (Gregory-Aland $\mathfrak{P}^{64}$): A Reappraisal', *ZPE* 105 (1995), pp. 13-20; C.P. Thiede and M. d'Ancona, *The Jesus Papyrus* (London: Weidenfeld & Nicholson, 1996).

34. See P.M. Head, 'The Date of the Magdalen Papyrus of Matthew (*P.Magd. Gr.17* = $\mathfrak{P}^{64}$): A Response to C.P. Thiede', *TynBul* 46 (1995), pp. 251-85, with photographs of three of the papyri used for comparison by Thiede and of others. Reviewers have made these and other points, e.g. D.C. Parker, 'Was Matthew Written before 50 CE? The Magdalen Papyrus of Matthew', *ExpTim* 107 (1995), pp. 40-43; E. Puech, 'Des fragments grecs de la grotte 7 et le Nouveau Testament? 7Q4 et 7Q5, et le papyrus Magdalen grec 17 = $\mathfrak{P}^{64}$', *RB* 102 (1995), pp. 570-84; M.-E. Boismard, 'A propos de 7Q5 et Mc 6,52-53', *RB* 102 (1995), pp. 585-88; P. Grelot, 'Note sur les propositions du Pr Carsten Peter Thiede', *RB* 102 (1995), pp. 589-91;

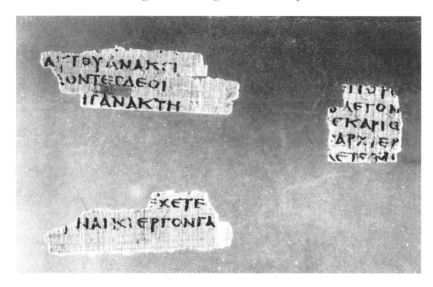

Figure 11. *Fragments of Matthew from a codex of the Four Gospels ($\mathfrak{P}^{64}$), late second century* AD. *The passages shown are from Mt. 26.7-8, 10 and, in the second column, 14-15. C.H. Roberts, 'An Early Papyrus of the First Gospel', HTR 46 (1953), pp. 233-37 (Photograph by courtesy of the President and Fellows of Magdalen College, Oxford.)*

No first century copies of any Christian books have yet been found, although there can be no doubt they existed. Strangely, the oldest example of Christian writing may be in Latin. Scratched on the plaster of a pillar in a public exercise yard at Pompeii and on the wall of a private house remained the word square

K. Wachtel, '$\mathfrak{P}^{64/67}$ Fragmente des Mattäusevangeliums aus dem 1. Jahrhundert ?', *ZPE* 107 (1995), pp. 73-80; J.K. Elliott, review of *The Jesus Papyrus* (London: Weidenfeld & Nicholson, 1996), by C.P. Thiede and M. d'Ancona, in *NovT* 38 (1996), pp. 393-99; P.A.L. Hill, 'Review Article', *Buried History* 32 (1996), pp. 82-95; B.M. Metzger, 'The Emperor's New Clothes', *BR* 12.4 (1996), pp. 12, 14; J. Chapa, review of *Rekindling the Word: In Search of Gospel Truth* (Leominster: Gracewing, 1995), by C.P. Thiede, in *JTS* 48 (1997), pp. 221-27. Skeat supported a date late in the second century in his examination of the Magdalen, Barcelona and Paris pieces 'The Oldest Manuscript of the Four Gospels', as did Thomas, 'New Testament', p. 1.

```
ROTAS
OPERA
TENET
AREPO
SATOR
```

in which the repeated word TENET makes a cross. The Latin words make little sense. However, the letters can be rearranged, with N at the centre of a cross, to read

```
              P
              A
              T
              E
              R
PATERNOSTER
              O
              S
              T
              E
              R
```

the opening words of the Lord's Prayer, with the surplus AS and OS serving for Alpha and Omega at each end of the cross.[35] This interpretation is not universally accepted. A complicated argument has been made for the square's Mithraic origin, using more abstruse patterns and numerical values of letters, and other possibilities have been canvassed.[36] According to the two scholars who have been editing inscriptions from Roman Britain, 'the arguments for a non-Christian origin are even more strained than the Christian explanation and are not conclusive',[37] suggesting that 'Our Father' had become a secret sign among Latin-speaking Christians in Italy before AD 79. Only the recovery of

35. See D. Atkinson, 'The Origin and Date of the "Sator" Word-Square', *JEH* 2 (1951), pp. 1-18; K. Aland, 'Noch einmal: der ROTAS/SATOR-Rebus', in T. Baarda *et al.* (eds.), *Text and Testimony: Essays on New Testament and Apocryphal Literature in Honour of A. F. J. Klijn* (Kampen: Kok, 1988), pp. 9-23.

36. W.O. Moeller, *The Mithraic Origins and Meanings of the Rotas-Sator Square* (Leiden: E.J. Brill, 1973); M. Guarducci, 'Dal gioco letterale alla critografio mistice', *ANRW* II 16.2 (Berlin: W. de Gruyter, 1978), pp. 1763-73 (1743-45).

37. S.S. Frere and R.S.O. Tomlin, *The Roman Inscriptions of Britain*. II, fasc. 6. *Painting and Graffiti* (Stroud: Alan Sutton, 1994), p. 51, no. 2494.98, cf. Vol. II, fasc. 4, *Tools, Decor, Ornaments etc.* (Stroud: Alan Sutton, 1992), p. 72, no. 2447.20, for comment.

an example definitely dated earlier than the second quarter of the first
century AD could exclude that possibility. The square continued in use
all over the Roman empire, evidently spreading rapidly—four examples
were found at Dura Europos, one has come to light in a late second-
century context in Manchester and others at places in between, and it
was still known in the Middle Ages.

Chapter 3

THE FORM OF THE BOOK: PAGE VERSUS ROLL

The Christian manuscripts described in Chapter 2 are almost all books with pages, codices, making a strong contrast with the other Greek books of the same centuries which are predominantly rolls. The statistics for non-Christian books of the second century presented by C.H. Roberts and T.C. Skeat in 1983 show 857 rolls to 14 codices,[1] yet the number of Christian codices adds half as many again. The same scholars counted something over one hundred Greek literary texts in codex form assigned to the third or third/fourth centuries and over 60 Christian ones against 460 rolls and about 150 codices. The growing use of the codex as an acceptable type of book for Greek literature is apparent, for now there is about one codex for every four rolls, but the favour the codex had with the Christians is astonishing, the proportion of their texts on rolls is small and in most of those cases the roll is an old one, reused.

The Roll

The roll was a straightforward form of book and could be very capacious. The longest roll is an ancient Egyptian one, the Great Harris Papyrus recording the achievements of Ramesses III, which was written in the reign of his son, Ramesses IV, about 1150 BC.[2] It is 43 cm (17 in) high and 40.5 m (133 ft) long. Not so large, yet still quite big is a Greek papyrus roll of the second century AD containing Books 23 and 24 of Homer's *Iliad*. It is 24.75 cm (9.75 in) high and 6 m (20 ft)

1. *The Birth of the Codex*, p. 37.
2. P. Grandet, *Le Papyrus Harris I (BM 9999)* (Cairo: Institut francais d'Archéologie orientale, 1994).

long.[3] It has been estimated that a slightly smaller papyrus roll 18 cm high and 6 m long (7 in × 19.5 ft) could easily contain one of the Gospels.[4] Leather rolls could also be large. The Temple Scroll, the largest of the Dead Sea Scrolls, is 8.2 m long (27 ft). Standard book rolls in Egypt were not so large and heavy (see Chapter 1, p. 24) and were therefore easier to carry and read.

Figure 12. *Man with papyrus roll, woman with tablets and stylus, wall painting from Pompeii. (Photograph Scala, Florence.)*

3.   British Museum Pap. 128; F.G. Kenyon, *Books and Readers in Ancient Greece and Rome* (Oxford: Clarendon Press, 2nd edn, 1951), pp. 50, 54.
    4.   Roberts and Skeat, *The Birth of the Codex*, p. 47.

Despite its use for over 3000 years, the roll held some major disadvantages. It was uneconomical in space, for the writing was done on one side only, so very long rolls became cumbersome and their weight added to the danger of tearing. A 'scroll written on both sides' (Rev. 5.1) was very unusual, although the back of an old roll might be used for another text if someone was short of papyrus or was writing something of lesser importance, making a personal copy of a literary text, for example. The roll was easy for readers on one hand because the eye could move swiftly from the foot of one column to the head of the next, unrolled ready, yet, on the other hand, it was clumsy for consultation and reference, even if the columns were numbered (see below, p. 68). While the habitual reader no doubt became adept at handling rolls, comparing one passage with another would still involve rolling and unrolling repeatedly, an awkward process which may have stimulated the memorization of standard or sacred texts (see below, Chapter 7). However, papyrus or leather rolls had one advantage, they could be extended to an indefinite length, suiting them for cumulative records in administrative offices, hence their continued use through the Middle Ages.[5]

The Codex

The origin of this familiar shape of book and the reason for its adoption by early Christian scribes are topics of continuing debates which can only be summarized here.

During the first century AD, while wooden tablets were common writing materials for everyday purposes, it appears a type of note-book was introduced, made up of sheets of parchment fastened together, although no examples have been found. Just as writing could easily be erased by smoothing a wax surface, so ink could be washed off parchment, providing a convenient vehicle for temporary records, and one a little less bulky than the wooden tablets. These note-books were termed *membranae*. The Roman orator Quintilian, writing in the latter part of the first century mentions them as an alternative to wax tablets[6] and they were what St Paul was especially concerned that Timothy should bring to him in Rome (2 Tim. 4.13).

---

5. See Roberts and Skeat, *The Birth of the Codex*, p. 51.
6. *Institutio Oratoria* 10.3.31, cf. 30, 32.

Figure 13. *Woman writing in a codex, wall painting from the 'tomb of Lucian'*
(Q1) third century AD, at Abila, Quweilbeh, Jordan. (Photograph
by courtesy of C. Vibert-Guigne.)

At the same time, the Roman poet Martial made reference to literary
works written on *membranae*, even hand-size ones, as economical in
space and convenient for the traveller. No one else in the first century
has left any mention of these books, so the verdict has been passed 'that
Martial's experiment was still-born'.[7] While that could be the case, the
evidence of fragments of books found far away in Egypt deserves to be
considered before Martial's testimony is dismissed.

7.   Roberts and Skeat, *The Birth of the Codex*, p. 29.

If Martial failed to persuade his contemporary authors of the advantages the book with pages offered over the roll—he does not mention the matter in his later poems, nor does any other Roman writer of the first century—the invention was not ignored for long, if, indeed, it was at all. Among the hundreds of Greek literary manuscripts dated to the second century found in Egypt, two, possibly three, are written on parchment in page form, one a text of Demosthenes, one a play of Euripides and one a copy of Hesiod's *Catalogue* (which could be from early in the third century). Beside them is a comparative rarity in Egypt, a scrap of a Latin text, part of a vellum page (8.6 × 5 cm; 3.4 × 2 in) from a book about wars in Macedonia, copied early in the century.[8] Pages of the same date made of papyrus are few. At present parts of perhaps 15 books have been identified; all are formal books rather than notebooks. (Notebooks on papyrus and parchment are known from the third century onwards in Egypt.[9]) Several of these books contain standard works of Greek literature, such as Plato's *Republic*, Pindar's *Paeans* and Xenophon's *Cyropaedia*. Others have medical and lexical compositions. Seven of them are Christian books, a surprisingly high proportion, a matter to be discussed shortly. Although 17 is a minute fraction of the total number of Greek books copied in the second century and found in Egypt (over 870, see above), the fact that there were scribes putting traditional classical texts into codices proves that that book form was known and acceptable in some circles, both pagan and Christian. The unanswered question is, How did this different fashion arise ?

All the physical evidence comes from Egypt. The literary references, that is Quintilian, Martial (and Paul), come from Rome. Was Martial trying to propagate a fashion which his publisher had recently begun in the capital, a fashion which, while not taking the literary world by storm, did gain some followers ? The presence of the three manuscripts on parchment among those pages found in Egypt may point to a source outside that country. Certainly, it is rare to find parchment rolls there. In contrast, despite the relatively laborious method of preparation, parchment or leather was common throughout the Near East, as we have seen

---

8.   See Turner, *Typology*, pp. 37-39, nos. 47, 80, 94a; the Latin text is no. 497, published by B.P. Grenfell and A.S. Hunt, *The Oxyrhynchus Papyri*, I (London: Egypt Exploration Fund, 1898), no. 30.
   9.   Roberts and Skeat, *The Birth of the Codex*, p. 21 n. 2.

(Chapter 1, pp. 25-26, 37, and further below), because papyrus had to be imported from Egypt. In Palestine, where aridity has preserved writings hidden in the first and second centuries AD, leather rolls far outnumber papyrus ones for copies of books, both canonical and noncanonical, whereas letters and legal deeds are mostly on papyrus (see the examples from Qumran, Masada and Wadi Murabba'at described in Chapter 4). Yet no major distinction is apparent, for biblical and other important works were copied on papyrus rolls as well as on leather (examples are Aramaic Tobit and Greek Leviticus fragments;[10] the 'letter' known as *MMT*, see Chapter 8). Not enough manuscripts survive from the second century for meaningful comparisons to be made. It is worth noting that papyrus was used for legal documents and letters involving men of high rank in Syria during the third century. A collection of 12 papyrus and nine leather documents from the region of Dura-Europos on the mid-Euphrates includes 17 legal deeds written in Greek and two in Syriac.[11] At Dura-Europos itself excavators found 144 legal and other documents and 11 or 12 literary texts, and noted a shift in the writing materials: 'In general, before the Roman occupation the standard writing material in Dura was parchment... With the third century parchment was relegated to a secondary rôle, and for a handsome text military or civilian scribes used the papyrus sheet.' Rome's control of Egypt and her extensive network of communications perhaps made papyrus more readily available. However, Aramaic and Iranian texts found at Dura were written on leather only.[12] Further east, there were deeds on leather, drawn up in the first century BC and the first century AD in western Persia and in the second century BC in Afghanistan.[13]

Quinitilian's comment, Martial's remarks, Paul's reference, and perhaps the parchment leaves from Egypt, may indicate Rome was the

10.   J.A. Fitzmyer, '4Qpap Tobit[a]ar', in J. VanderKam (ed.), *Qumran Cave 4: VIII Parabiblical Texts, Part 2* (DJD, 14; Oxford: Clarendon Press, 1995), pp. 7-39, 4Q196; E. Ulrich in P.W. Skehan, E. Ulrich and J. Sanderson, *Qumran Cave 4.IV: Palaeo-Hebrew and Greek Biblical Manuscripts* (DJD, 9; Oxford: Clarendon Press, 1992), pp. 168-86, 4Q120=pap4QLeviticus[b].

11.   See p. 37 n. 41.

12.   See C. Bradford Welles in Welles, Fink and Gilliam, *The Excavations at Dura-Europos*, p. 4.

13.   See p. 38 nn. 42, 43.

place where the transition from the parchment note-book to the parchment book, the codex, was made. The fact that the Greek language had no word for this new invention and borrowed the Latin term, *membranae*, is another pointer to a Roman home. Innovations of this sort can take time to be accepted, especially when facing long-established practices, so for Roman legal writers, likely to be conservative in their opinions, to recognize this new form as a book early in the third century, as two did, may imply it was taking root there for a considerable period before that.[14] Commenting on the fragment of a page of a book in Latin from Egypt, dated early in the second century, E.G. Turner concluded, it 'does not seem to be an experimental type of book, and its mere existence is evidence that this book form had a prehistory'.[15] Additional evidence flows from a second-century private letter in which a man tells his father of an encounter with someone the same papyrologist described as 'a touring bookseller' who offered six *membranae* for sale. They were unacceptable, but the writer mentioned that he had collated eight others at a cost of 100 drachmae.[16]

Tracing that prehistory led Roberts and Skeat to the waxed writing-tablets familiar in the Graeco-Roman world from primary education and from business (see Chapter 1, pp. 26-29). Physically the wooden tablets could not be folded in quires and sewn as the papyrus sheets which made codices came to be, and signs of hinging by alternate edges may make them a slightly less obvious prototype, although some were tied together at one edge. The wooden leaves or slats, exemplified at Vindolanda and in the Bar Kochba caves, offer a closer model, for some of them were folded in concertina fashion.[17] The flexible papyrus

14. Roberts and Skeat, *The Birth of the Codex*, pp. 30-34.

15. Turner, *Typology*, p. 38.

16. U. Hagedorn, D. Hagedorn, L.C. Youtie and H. Youtie, *Das Archiv des Petaus* (*Pap. Colon.* IV) (Cologne: Westdeutscher Verlag, 1969) no. 30; Turner, *Greek Papyri*, p. 204; see J. van Haelst, 'Les origines du Codex', in A. Blanchard (ed.), *Les débuts du codex* (Bibliologia, 9; Brepols: Turnhout, 1989), pp. 13-35, especially 21-23.

17. M. Haran, 'Codex, *Pinax* and Writing Slat', *Studies in Memory of Abraham Wasserstein*, I, *Scripta Classica Israelica* 15 (1996), pp. 212-22. A length of papyrus folded in this way came from the Pachomian Monastery library; see J.M. Robinson, *The Pachomian Monastic Library at the Chester Beatty Library and the Bibliothèque Bodmer* (Occasional Paper, 19; Claremont, CA: Institute for Antiquity and Christianity, Claremont Graduate School, 1990), photo.13.

sheets could be turned back on themselves at each alternate fold to create a more manageable packet in a way the wooden leaves could not. After cutting the folds at the edges of the pile, the writer could inscribe each page on both sides in sequence, rather than using all on one side before turning the whole over to write on the back.

The reason for the form of book still needs to be supplied. Convenience and economy cannot be dismissed, although they are easily exaggerated.[18] On economy, we may note the comment of the younger Pliny that his uncle, Pliny the Elder, bequeathed to him 160 notebooks of selected passages which were rolls written on both sides 'so that their number is really doubled'.[19] At the initial stage, the production of a codex was more complicated than making a roll. Early codices were made by taking rolls and folding them as described above to produce sheets of equal size—in some examples the joins between the sheets of the rolls appear in the middle of a page. The sheets were then folded in the centre and sewn. The outer edges had to be trimmed to form even pages, with the result that the innermost pages of each quire were slightly narrower than the outer ones.[20] The whole process demanded extra time and skill, so the cost of a blank codex may have been higher than the cost of a blank roll. There is evidence that some books were copied after the pages had been fastened together, although it seems to have been more usual to write on the loose pages before they were sewn. That meant the pages had to be carefully kept in order and there is a possibility that sometimes they were numbered in the way sheets making rolls were sometimes numbered.[21] While the page numbers in many codices were added later, in a few cases they may be the work of the copyists who followed the practice of numbering columns found in some rolls and used in administrative documents.[22]

---

18. T.C. Skeat, 'The Length of the Standard Papyrus Roll and the Cost-advantage of the Codex', *ZPE* 45 (1982), pp. 169-75; 'Roll *versus* Codex: A New Approach?', *ZPE* 84 (1990), pp. 297-98; Roberts and Skeat, *The Birth of the Codex*, pp. 45-51.

19. *Letters*, 3.5.

20. See A. Wouters, 'From Papyrus Roll to Papyrus Codex: Some Technical Aspects of the Ancient Book Fabrication', *Manuscripts of the Middle East* 5 (1990–91 [1993]), pp. 9-19.

21. E. Tov, 'Scribal Markings in the Texts from the Judaean Desert', in D.W. Parry and S.D. Ricks (eds.), *Current Research and Technological Developments in the Dead Sea Scrolls* (Leiden: E.J. Brill, 1996), pp. 41-77 (68, 69).

22. Turner, *Typology*, pp.73-79; see also Josephus's reference, Ch. 6, p. 175.

If the codex was a first-century invention, in Rome or somewhere else, the absence of first-century examples from Egypt may result from its slow adoption. Whether inscribed with manuals for craftsmen, or notes for speakers or literary compositions, the codex did not take the scribal world by storm, unless accidents of survival and discovery have skewed the witness of the papyri, a factor which should not be overlooked.[23] All in all, an origin for this new form of book in Rome in the first century seems likely, given the meagre information available at present.[24]

Distinctive Features of Christian Books

New Testament manuscripts are set apart from other Greek literary copies, including those in codex form, by certain features peculiar to them. It is the presence of some or all of those features in other papyri, such as the Old Testament pieces, which enables them to be labelled 'Christian' also.

First, the handwriting in many is less professional than the assured, clear forms of most Greek literary rolls. C.H. Roberts observed,

> Almost all the early Christian manuscripts are written in hands which, although those of practised and professional scribes, have some resemblances, e.g. in the use of ligature, to the better documentary hands of the period. They are the work of men who, used to writing, are not accustomed to writing books, and while trying to be as 'literary' as possible betray the documentary practice with which they are more familiar.

In contrast, he stated, clearly Jewish biblical manuscripts 'are written in hands of almost hieratic elegance.'[25]

Since Roberts wrote, publication of more early New Testament papyri (notably nos. 3 and 4 listed above, Chapter 2, p. 45) has led to greater emphasis on the 'literary' elements in their presentation.[26]

---

23. For this situation in other contexts, see A.R. Millard, 'The Small Cuboid Incense Burners: A Note on their Age', *Levant* 16 (1984), pp. 172-73.

24. See also van Haelst, 'Les origines du Codex', pp. 13-35.

25. Roberts, 'P Yale 1 and the Early Christian Book', p. 26, developed in *Manuscript, Society and Belief in Early Christian Egypt*, pp. 12-22.

26. G.N. Stanton, 'The Early Reception of Matthew's Gospel: New Evidence from Papyri?', in D.E. Aune (ed.), *The Gospel of Matthew in Current Study: Essays in Honor of William Thompson S.J.* (Grand Rapids: Eerdmans, 2000). (I am grateful to Graham Stanton for allowing me to read his essay prior to publication.)

Nevertheless, the Christian books are not necessarily the products of a commercial scriptorium where trained copyists created the handsome rolls of Homer and other classics, rather, they are often to be seen as copies which secretaries made as well as they could, for themselves or their friends or their churches, something which any professional scribe might do with any literary work, of course.[27] Certain examples of the third century are described as 'the work of practised scribes writing an ordinary type of hand, but writing it larger than usual', intended, it is thought, for public reading[28]—and it has to be realized that most people would only know the books through hearing them read.

Secondly, numbers are given by ciphers in the current Greek system, A = 1, B = 2, and so on as they are in legal deeds and administrative documents. In copies of classical literary texts, on the contrary, the numbers are spelt out as words.

Thirdly, certain words are abbreviated, the best-known feature of early Christian books, one which continued into later centuries. Scribes invented abbreviations early in the history of writing and in Greek they were frequent for personal names and some other common terms, but they were 'regularly excluded from texts of the classical authors'.[29] The standard method of abbreviation took the initial letters or syllables of the word, or, occasionally, the first and a later syllable, to make a contraction. In the Christian papyri some abbreviations were made in the same way, IH is found for IHΣOYΣ (Jesus, nominative) in the second and third centuries and XP for XPIΣTOΣ (Christ, nominative) in the third century. Yet the majority of the abbreviations were made in a different way, by taking the first and last letters, even when the last letter was a declined case-ending, e.g. IΣ for IHΣOYΣ (Jesus, nominative), IY for IHΣOY (Jesus, genitive). The main words treated in this way are 'God', 'Lord', 'Jesus', 'Christ', with, quite frequently, 'saviour', 'son', 'spirit', 'Israel,' 'Jerusalem', 'David', 'man', 'mother', 'father', 'heaven'. A horizontal line above the letters warned the reader of the abbre-

27. See P. van Minnen, 'Taking Stock: Declarations of Property from the Ptolemaic Period', *Bulletin of the American Society of Papyrologists* 31 (1994), pp. 89-99 (95, 96, for a case in the second century BC).

28. Turner, *Typology*, pp. 84-86.

29. E.G. Turner, *Greek Manuscripts of the Ancient World* (Bulletin of the Institute for Classical Studies, Supplement 46, London: Institute for Classical Studies, 2nd edn, revd P.J. Parsons, 1987), p. 15.

viation.[30] The origin of these *nomina sacra* has long been debated. The proposal that they arose from Jewish ways of writing the sacred name of God in Hebrew, YHWH, lacks evidence to support it. Jewish scribes copying the Greek versions of Old Testament books sometimes inserted the sacred name in Hebrew letters, and when copying the books in Hebrew they sometimes wrote it in the Old Hebrew script; examples of the former stand in the earliest Septuagint papyri (see below, p. 79) and of the latter in the Dead Sea Scrolls. However, there is no trace of abbreviation of the divine name at so early a date in Hebrew and it was not common later. The literary texts among the Dead Sea Scrolls do not have abbreviations, nor do early Jewish copies of the biblical books in Greek from Egypt (see below). To seek the reason in an attempt to disguise the Christian nature of the books is unsatisfactory, for key names such as Peter and Paul and the word 'cross' were not abbreviated. (Although 'crucified' is abbreviated in the Dura fragment of the *Diatessaron* from early in the third century, see Chapter 2, p. 46.) It has been perceived recently that the horizontal line Christian scribes used to mark a contraction was the same as the line used to mark Greek letters which were used as numbers (see p. 70), immediately above the letters. Scribes put the line normally indicating an abbreviation in a slightly different position, hanging over the right hand end of the letters. This has led to the suggestion that Christian scribes marked the abbreviation IH (for Jesus) to draw attention to its numerical value, 18 (I = 10, H = 8), which is the same as the numerical value of the Hebrew word 'life', a significance noted by Christian writers early in the second century. Once that was done, other shortened forms were marked in the same way, although they had no significant numerical values. While attractively accounting for the use of the line marking numbers as distinct from abbreviations, the proposal really only applies to the abbreviation IH and cannot explain the peculiar Christian habit of contracting words to their first and last letters.[31] Another possibility is that Christian scribes may have drawn this method from a Semitic habit, for contractions of proper names to their first and last letters do stand on Phoenician and Palestinian coins of the Hellenistic period and in graffiti from the Punic towns of North Africa.[32]

30. Roberts, *Manuscript*, Chapter 2, '*Nomina Sacra*; Origins and Significance'.
31. L.W. Hurtado, 'The Origin of the Nomina Sacra: A Proposal', *JBL* 117 (1998), pp. 655-73.
32. See Alan Millard, 'Ancient Abbreviations and the *Nomina Sacra*', in C.J.

Figure 14. *Part of Luke 10 from a volume of the Gospels and Acts, Chester Beatty (𝔓⁴⁵), copied in the mid-third century, showing abbreviations, each over-lined: first line, near centre ΘΥ, θεου (verse 9b), 9th line, right end, OB for 72 (verse 17), 10th line, left of centre ΚΕ, κυριε (verse 17), 15th line, right of break, [Π]ΝΑ, πνευματα (verse 20), 17th line, left of break, Π[ΝΙ], πνευματι, 18th line, beginning, ΠΡ ΚΕ, πατηρ κυριε (verse 21). F.G. Kenyon, The Chester Beatty Biblical Papyri. II. Gospels and Acts, Plates (London: Emery Walker, 1934), fol. 11, verso. (Photograph reproduced by courtesy of the Trustees of the Chester Beatty Library, Dublin.)*

The fourth unusual feature is the use of large initial letters to open paragraphs, something not done in formal Greek literary manuscripts, although found in documents (two larger initial letters stand at the start

Eyre, A. Leahy and L.M. Leahy (eds.), *The Unbroken Reed: Studies in the Culture and Heritage of Ancient Egypt in Honour of A.F. Shore* (London: The Egypt Exploration Society, 1994), pp. 221-26. To the coins cited there add some marked *'n* which may belong to Ascalon, indicated by the first and last letters of the name to avoid confusion with coins of Ashdod, marked with the first two letters, which would be the same in West Semitic script, see Y. Meshorer, 'The Mints of Ashdod and Ascalon during the Late Persian Period', *Eretz Israel* 20 (1989), pp. 287-91 [in Hebrew].

of new sections in a file-copy of a legal deed of the second century BC from Dura Europos[33]). Now one of the Greek Bible rolls from the Dead Sea caves displays a Jewish scribe starting sections of the text in that way. More commonly, Greek copyists set a small space between the end of one paragraph and the beginning of the next, inserting a short horizontal line (*paragraphus*) to project slightly above the start of the next line. (Examples are visible in the Oxyrhynchus fragment of three columns from a roll of Esther copied in the late first or early second century AD.[34]) This mark was already current in the fifth century BC among Aramaic scribes at Elephantine in southern Egypt and later among the Jewish scribes who copied the Dead Sea Scrolls. Similarly, spaces to mark the ends of sections, occurring in some Christian papyri, had the same function in those Aramaic and Hebrew manuscripts.[35] These devices broke up the text, helping the reader who would otherwise face a block of writing with no physical indication of major sense boundaries, an even greater problem for readers of Greek because words were not separated from each other as they were in Aramaic and Hebrew.

Christian books in the second and third centuries, therefore, were distinguished from most others by their outward shape and by their style of writing; they do not look like the products of the standard Greek scriptoria, but followed their own conventions. Do these factors tell us anything about the reason Christians adopted what was at the time a peculiar form of book? In lectures delivered in 1953, C.H. Roberts suggested that Mark's Gospel was composed in a parchment notebook in Rome and, when it reached Egypt, the form of book was retained in papyrus copies.[36] Later, he and T.C. Skeat favoured Antioch on the Orontes in Syria, as the birth-place of distinctive Christian scribal tradition, as it was one of the centres of Greek culture where Christians early found a home (see Acts 11.19). Their supporting argument, that Christians might have followed Jewish practice in writing the

33. Welles, Fink and Gilliam, *The Excavations at Dura-Europos*, pp. 84-91, no. 15.

34. K. Luchner, '4443. LXX, Esther E16-9.3', in M.W. Haslam *et al.*, *The Oxyrhynchus Papyri*, LXV (London: Egypt Exploration Society, 1998), pp. 4-8.

35. For details see Millard, 'Ancient Abbreviations', pp. 223, 224.

36. 'The Codex', *Proceedings of the British Academy* 40 (1954), pp. 169-204, especially 187-89.

Oral Law on tablets or notebooks of papyrus and so written the teachings of Jesus on the same material, fails because the Hebrew term they took to mean a papyrus sheet only designates a plain wooden tablet.[37] (See below, Chapter 7 on the question of writing the Oral Law.) However, after studying the use of writing reflected in early rabbinic traditions, S. Lieberman concluded, 'In line with [rabbinic practice, see below, Chapter 7, pp. 204-205] we would naturally expect the *logia* of Jesus to be originally copied in codices.'[38] The comparisons just made with Aramaic and Hebrew writing practices and the type of abbreviations current in Phoenicia and Palestine may point to a Christian scribal tradition arising in the Syria-Palestine area, where Antioch would still be a prime candidate. Although there are no manuscripts from that city to set beside those from Egypt, copies of the Hebrew Scriptures in Greek translations found in the Judaean desert, made in the first centuries BC or AD by Jewish scribes, are said not to be written exactly like texts from Egypt, but to 'belong to a different palaeographic tradition, that of Syria, which they share with some of the Hellenistic texts from Dura'.[39] However, they are also the work of professional copyists. Christian books created in the Levant could have been carried to Egypt and influenced the locally trained clerks who copied them there and whose work survives in fragments to tease us to-day. Antioch has also been signalled as influential in the development of contractions in inscriptions on stone, a custom which could easily be borrowed from the scribes working with other materials.[40]

The Christian Adoption of the Codex

Adolf Deissmann, who investigated extensively the papyri and inscriptions early in the twentieth century, argued that the Christians came

37. See C. Sirat, 'Le livre hébreu dans les premiers siècles de notre ère: le témoignage des textes', in J. Lemaire and E. van Balberghe (eds.), *Calames et Cahiers: Mélanges de codicologie et de paléographie offerts à Léon Gilissen* (Brussels: Centre d'étude des manuscrits, 1985), pp. 169-76, especially 172-74, reprinted in Blanchard (ed.), *Les débuts du codex*, pp. 115-24.

38. S. Lieberman, *Hellenism in Jewish Palestine* (New York: Jewish Theological Seminary, 1962), p. 203.

39. Roberts, 'P. Yale 1 and the Early Christian Book', p. 26.

40. M. Avi-Yonah, *Abbreviations in Greek Inscriptions (The Near East, 200 B.C.–A.D. 1000)* (*Quarterly of the Department of Antiquities of Palestine*, Supplement 9, 1940), p. 27.

predominantly from the lower levels of society and supposed Paul kept copies of his epistles in a notebook of the codex form used by artisans, from which other copies were made,[41] the existence of his authoritative letters in that format might then have influenced the copyists to produce the Gospels in the same manner. L.C.A. Alexander has developed this theme, investigating technical 'handbooks' of Roman times.[42] T.C. Skeat has recently offered a different reason, arising from an analysis of the capacity of the third century Chester Beatty codex ($\mathfrak{P}^{45}$) which contained all four Gospels and Acts on 224 pages. The common form of book at that time would need to be a cumbersome roll 30 metres (nearly 33 feet) long to accommodate the same amount of text. The new book style was adopted, Skeat argued, to assert the superiority of the Four Gospels over all the other gospels circulating in the second century. Although it might be possible to add to the Four, as Acts could be included in the Chester Beatty codex, once the Four were accepted together, they could be less easily separated, and the number four may have had theological value.[43] In a somewhat similar way, H.Y. Gamble surmised that at the end of the first century or early in the second a collection was made of Paul's letters to seven churches (in Corinth, Rome, Ephesus, Thessalonica, Galatia, Philippi and Colossae) which was too long for a convenient roll—he calculated they would have occupied a roll 24m. (80 feet) long—and so the codex form was deliberately adopted, allowing easier reference to specific passages. This codex of Paul's authoritative epistles set the style for other Christian books.[44] In reaction, G.H.R. Horsley pointed out the speculative matter

41. A. Deissmann, *Light from the Ancient East* (trans. L.R.M. Strachan; London: Hodder & Stoughton, rev. edn, 1927; repr. Grand Rapids, MI: Baker Book House, 1980), pp. 245-51; see also G. Cavallo, 'Libro e pubblico alla fine del mondo antico', in G. Cavallo (ed.), *Libri, editori e pubblico nel mondo antico: Guida storica e critica* (Bari: Laterza,1975), pp. 81-132 (83), cited by I. Gallo, *Greek and Latin Papyrology* (trans. M.R. Falviere and J.R. March; London: Institute of Classical Studies, 1986), p. 14.

42. L.C.A. Alexander, *The Preface to Luke's Gospel* (SNTSMS, 78; Cambridge: Cambridge University Press, 1993).

43. T.C. Skeat, 'The Origin of the Christian Codex', *ZPE* 102 (1994), pp. 263-68; *idem*, 'A Codicological Analysis of the Chester Beatty Papyrus Codex of Gospels and Acts (P45)', *Hermathena* 155 (1993), pp. 27-43.

44. H.Y. Gamble, *Books and Readers in the Early Church* (New Haven: Yale University Press, 1995), pp. 58-65; he had set out this idea earlier, 'The Pauline

of the order of the letters and the unanswered question of where the innovation may have taken place. He suggested Asia Minor, without recalling that Paul's *membranae* were left at Troas (2 Tim. 4.13), which might imply currency of the codex there.[45] He then set out his view that the practical advantage of the codex made it the natural choice among the non-literary congregations of early Christians, accustomed to seeing it used in daily life for notes and hardly aware of the roll.[46] To which we may add, if the copyists who produced the early Christian papyrus codices were mostly not professional book copiers but clerks employed in government offices and accountancy duties using notebooks beside rolls, they could well have taken advantage of a form familiar to them, rather than turn to the the book-trade's roll, to which they owed no particular allegiance. However, unawareness of book rolls was not universal in the early Church as there were numbers of converted Jews who would have known of the synagogue rolls. Some evidence points to the custom of Roman writers keeping copies of their letters in codex notebooks and Paul's letter-book, E.R. Richards has suggested, may have stimulated the wider use of the codex amongst early Christians.[47] The everyday nature of the earliest forms of codex has been stressed by M. McCormick, observing that the majority of non-Christian codex fragments from the second century come from educational or medical teaching books and that they were mostly of conveniently portable size.[48] Beside these considerations of practicality and orthodoxy may be brought another reason: in times of persecution what appeared to be notebooks might attract less attention than standard book rolls. G.N. Stanton has recently suggested that early Christians first used codex-notebooks, then adopted that format as their normal 'book', both for convenience and to distinguish them from their roll-using contemporaries.[49] Not only was the codex-form outwardly distinctive, readers

Corpus and the Early Christian Book', in W. Babcock (ed.), *Paul and the Legacies of Paul* (Dallas, TX: Southern Methodist University Press, 1990), pp. 265-80.

45. G.H.R. Horsley, 'Classical Manuscripts in Australia and New Zealand', *Antichthon* 27 (1993), pp. 60-83, see 78-80.

46. Horsley, 'Classical Manuscripts', pp. 80-83.

47. E.R. Richards, 'The Codex and the Early Collection of Paul's Letters', *Bulletin for Biblical Research* 8 (1998), pp. 151-66.

48. M. McCormick, 'The Birth of the Codex and the Apostolic Life-Style', *Scriptorium* 39 (1985), pp. 150-58.

49. G.N. Stanton, 'The Fourfold Gospel', *NTS* 43 (1997), pp. 317-46 (338-39).

would find the presentation of the texts had unexpected features, small, yet different from other 'books'. As already noted, the early Church was subject to continual attack as an illegal religion and, after the persecutions in the first century, there were major ones under the emperors Decius (250) and Valerian (257), culminating in the worst of all, the 'Great Persecution,' of Diocletian beginning in 303, when churches were destroyed in various places and books of Scripture burnt, as the tales of the martyrs describe.

The physical survivors exemplify the work of Christian scribes from the middle of the second century onwards. The unique Rylands fragment of John ($\mathfrak{P}^{52}$) may illustrate their work a little earlier. All these manuscripts display the scribal characteristics outlined already, a common trait which led C.H. Roberts and T.C. Skeat to deduce the existence of a single scribal centre at an earlier date where the conventions were set. They placed that centre at Antioch and put the date before AD 100 in order to allow time for the pattern to spread from the Levant to middle Egypt. Reacting to their work, Joseph van Haelst reached a different conclusion.[50] In his opinion, partly based upon the more conservative dates for the papyri followed here, Christianity did not spread quite so early in Egypt. The Christians in Rome, he suggested, probably adopted the codex because they saw in it a convenient way to circulate the Gospel which was a new sort of technical book, as already noted, a manual for conduct and a liturgical text. They had written their books at first on rolls, the evidence of Luke's work being in two parts, the Gospel and the Acts, implies that, for it was too long to put in a single roll, but could be satisfactorily contained in one codex. However, van Haelst did not discuss the distinctive features of the Christian manuscripts, noted above, and was unaware that they may point to a near eastern scribal tradition.

The tiny number of Christian manuscripts from second-century Egypt contrasts strongly with the number of pagan literary texts of the same

---

50. van Haelst, 'Les origines du codex', pp. 32, 34, 35. See also S.R. Llewellyn's discussion in 'The Development of the Codex', in *idem* (ed.), *A Review of the Greek Inscriptions and Papyri Published in 1982–1982* (New Documents Illustrating Early Christianity, 7; Macquairie University, 1994), pp. 249-56. Note also B.A. Pearson, 'Earliest Christianity in Egypt: Some Observations', in B.A. Pearson and J.E. Goehring (eds.), *The Roots of Egyptian Christianity* (Philadelphia: Fortress Press, 1986), pp. 132- 59.

date, perhaps about 1000. In the third century the number of Christian books increases to approximately 80 (counting those dated second/third century with those dated third century), while the number of Greek literary texts falls to 650 or so. In the fourth century Christian literary texts climb towards 100 while copies of pagan literature fall to little over 200.[51]

Before deducing from the surviving manuscripts the existence of only a small Christian presence in Egypt in the second century and a very much larger one in the third, although other sources may point to that, it is essential to recognize the random element in their survival and the haphazard nature of the discoveries.[52] There are no collections of literary or other papyri from most of the major centres, notably none from Alexandria. If few Christians happened to live in the communities that have supplied us with many Greek literary texts, the small percentage of Christian books cannot be taken as representative for the whole country. Here it is to be noted that many of the papyri still exist because the settlements shrank as their irrigation systems declined in the late third and fourth centuries and the ground dried out. Moreover, Christianity was an illicit religion until 312, so Christians who moved from such settlements are more likely to have taken their books with them than to have thrown old ones on to a public dump, for their books were not on sale at any publishing house, they had to be privately commissioned. The pieces of Christian books found in the rubbish mounds at Oxyrhynchus and other places may equally as well be the products of persecutions and the looting or clearing of martyred Christians' houses as of the normal jettisoning of rubbish by householders.[53] In contrast,

51.　These figures are based upon W.H. Willis, 'A Census of the Literary Papyri from Egypt', *GRBS* 9 (1968), pp. 205-41, with adjustments, and upon Roberts and Skeat, *The Birth of the Codex*. See further, W. Haberman, 'Zur chronologischen Verteilung der papyrologischen Zeugnisse', *ZPE* 122 (1998), pp. 144-60.

52.　On the randomness of the papyrus discoveries, see Turner, *Greek Papyri*, pp. 42-53, and the discussion in Chapter 1 above.

53.　On the Christian papyri of Oxyrhynchus compared with the pagan, see E.J. Epp, 'The New Testament Papyri at Oxyrhynchus in their Social and Intellectual Context', in W.L. Petersen, J.S. Vos and H.J. de Jonge (eds.), *The Sayings of Jesus: Canonical and Non-Canonical. Essays in Honour of Tjitze Baarda* (NovTSup, 89; Leiden: E.J. Brill, 1997), pp. 47-68, and *idem*, 'The Codex and Literacy in Early Christianity and at Oxyrhynchus: Issues Raised by Harry Y. Gamble's *Books and Readers in the Early Church* ', *CR* 10 (1997), pp. 15-37.

the Bodmer collection shows how long Christian books could be kept. This collection, housed in Geneva, contains remnants from the majority of about 38 papyrus rolls and codices which had belonged to a monastic library and were apparently hidden at the time of the Arab invasion in the seventh century. By that time the books in the library were already old. They included classical literature: Greek copies of Homer's *Iliad* and *Odyssey* on rolls, plays of Menander in a codex and, in Latin, Cicero's oration *In Catilinam*. The majority of the books are Christian, many of them books of Scripture in Greek or translations into Coptic. Bodmer Papyrus 2 ($\mathfrak{P}^{66}$), Gospel of John, was the oldest, copied in the first half of the third century.[54]

Sparse as the evidence from the papyri for Christianity spreading through second-century Egypt may be, it is still impressive, especially in comparison with papyrus books left by other religious groups. In Alexandria the long-established Jewish community was greatly reduced after the rebellion of 115–17, but Jews were still to be found there and throughout the country. Papyrus documents and inscribed tombstones are the evidence.[55] Yet no copies of Hebrew books from the last two centuries BC or the first two of our era have been found. A scrap now in Cambridge University Library, the Nash Papyrus, is the sole early Hebrew text, the Ten Commandments in a mixture of Exodus 20 and Deuteronomy 5 followed by the Shema, described as 'perhaps a type of lectionary', dated to the second century BC.[56] The number of copies of Jewish Greek works is very small. Pieces of one papyrus roll of the Greek version of Genesis and three of Deuteronomy are known, the first three dated to the middle of the first century BC, the last to the second century BC. Apart from their ages, the presence of the divine name YHWH written in Hebrew script in the Greek text of one of them and the fact that they are rolls point to their Jewish origin.[57] The frag-

54. See Robinson, *The Pachomian Monastic Library*.

55. See V.A. Tcherikover, A. Fuks and M. Stern (eds.), *Corpus Papyrorum Judaicarum* (3 vols.; Cambridge, MA: Harvard University Press, 1957–64), note the list of 'Places of Jewish Habitation in Egypt', III, pp. 197-209; W. Horbury and D. Noy, *Jewish Inscriptions of Graeco-Roman Egypt* (Cambridge: Cambridge University Press, 1992).

56. See J.A. Duncan, 'Excerpted Texts of Deuteronomy at Qumran', *RevQ* 69 = 18.1 (1997), pp. 43-62.

57. Z. Aly and L. Koenen, *Three Rolls of the Early Septuagint: Genesis and Deuteronomy* (Bonn: Habelt, 1980); C.H. Roberts, *Two Biblical Papyri in the John Rylands Library, Manchester* (Manchester: John Rylands Library, 1936).

ment of an Esther roll mentioned already, a tiny fragment of Job and one piece of a codex of Genesis copied in the second century are the other possible candidates from that period, with only half a dozen from the third and fourth centuries.[58] This rarity of Jewish biblical papyri may be due to the reverence accorded any writing which contained the name of God, old, worn or unwanted books being buried to decay naturally or hidden (exemplified by the Cairo Geniza, see Chapter 7, p. 191), rather than thrown on to a rubbish dump. Moreover, Judaism was a recognized religion in the Roman Empire, so there was no official persecution to cause the owners to hide their books lest they be destroyed, although anti-Jewish agitation did arise from time to time, with riots and massacres, which could have led to that, or to books being discarded by looters. Nevertheless, the difference in quantity between the Christian books and the Jewish is striking and may illustrate both the spread of Christianity and the early Christians' attachment to Scripture, both the Jewish and their own.

Another religious movement of the early centuries which has made a great impact in modern scholarship is Gnosticism. Until 1945 little was known about it except from the writings of Christians who attacked it. The exceptions were two papyrus books, which were obtained in Egypt in the eighteenth century: the Bruce Codex, now in the Bodleian Library, Oxford; the Askew Codex in the British Library and a third acquired by the Berlin Museum in 1896. They were copied in the fourth century. In 1945 the discovery of the Nag Hammadi Codices changed the picture dramatically by making a large collection of Gnostic writings available. Peasants in Upper Egypt seeking fertilizer found a jar which held at least 12 volumes and part of one more—the exact contents are uncertain because the widowed mother of one of the finders burnt some pages. These are Coptic versions of over 50 Greek compositions, all in manuscripts from the fourth century.[59] Of earlier

58. See Roberts, *Manuscript*, pp. 74-78. T.C. Skeat, 'Theological Texts: Job 42.111-12', in P.J. Parsons (ed.), *The Oxyrhynchus Papyri*, pp. 1-3. The divine name is written in Old Hebrew letters in this text.

59. See B.A. Pearson, 'Nag Hammadi Codices', *ABD*, IV, pp. 984-93; K. Rudolph, 'Gnosticism', *ABD*, II, pp. 1033-40. Translations: J.M. Robinson (ed.), *The Nag Hammadi Library* (Leiden: E.J. Brill, 1977); B. Layton, *The Gnostic Scriptures* (London: SCM Press, 1987); C. Schmidt and V. MacDermott, *The Books of Jeu and the Untitled Text in the Bruce Codex* (Leiden: E.J. Brill, 1978); *idem, Pistis Sophia [Askew Codex]* (Leiden: E.J. Brill, 1978).

date are the three Oxyrhynchus fragments of the *Gospel of Thomas* which supply the only first-hand testimony to Gnostics in Egypt before about AD 250. Again, the contrast is notable: if Gnosticism, was popular or its adherents widely scattered across the country already in the second century, more copies of its Greek books might be expected from that and the next century.

Biblical books were not the only ones copied by the Christian scribes or for Christian readers. There were Christian teachers and scholars in the second and third centuries whose compositions circulated in Egypt and continued to be read and duplicated in later centuries. The works of the Apostolic Fathers, Clement of Rome (c. 95), Ignatius of Antioch (martyred in 107), Polycarp of Smyrna (martyred 155 or 168) and Papias (early second century), together with the *Didache*, the *Epistle of Barnabas* and the *Shepherd* of Hermas are the earliest, but Papias's five-volume composition is known only from quotations made by Eusebius 200 years later. Among others there followed the volume *Against Heresies* by Irenaeus of Lyons (c. 130–200)—of which a papyrus fragment copied about AD 200 exists—and the *Refutation of all Heresies* by Hippolytus of Rome (c. 170–236). The culmination is the work of the great scholar Origen (c. 185–254), many of whose books are lost. His *Hexapla*, an edition of the Old Testament in Hebrew with four to seven Greek renderings in parallel columns, was so large that it was almost impossible to copy. A Patriarch of Baghdad, Timothy I, at the end of the eighth century wrote of the difficulty it presented, reporting that it took one dictator and three copyists six months to complete half of it.[60] This productivity testifies to the intellectual and combative life of the church and a readiness on the part of some to write for the benefit of their fellow-believers.

The spread of books from an original source of copying could have been rapid. Travel in the Roman empire was frequent and, if conditions were favourable, relatively swift. Letters from Egypt exist with notes indicating the time taken for them to pass from the sender to the addressee. Examples in the archive of Zenon of the mid-third century BC (see Chapter 1, p. 36) show the 240 km (150 miles) from Alexandria

---

60. P. Petitmengin and B. Flusin, 'Le livre antique et la dictée', in E. Lucchesi and H.D. Saffrey (eds.), *Mémorial André-Jean Festugière: Antiquité païenne et chrétienne* (Geneva: Cramer, 1984), pp. 247-62. (I am indebted to Alison Salvesen for this reference.)

to Philadelphia at the Fayyum within Egypt covered in four or seven days, the journey from Sidon to Alexandria taking two weeks, but letters from Transjordan to Alexandria taking over one month and a voyage from Alexandria to Cilicia suffering delays so that it took about two months.[61]

Books evidently played an important role among Christians in the second century, whether read by individuals or in public. The uniform adoption of non-literary practices in copying Christian books does point to a single, authoritative, source, as Roberts and Skeat observed, laying down conventions for copyists that made them distinctive. Whether or not that included the codex form and where it was located are still debatable. How early the standard was set remains uncertain; the latest possibility would be about AD 130, if the Rylands fragment of John is given the most conservative date of 150 or shortly after. Christian books in the second century were not a novelty, for the New Testament itself shows books serving a vital function from about AD 50 onwards in the form of the letters of Paul and others, some addressed to named persons, some to congregations. They were not oral messages later committed to writing, they were written compositions from the first, although they were substitutes for the presence of the authors. Letters are numerous, too, among the Greek papyri, affording some material for comparison with the epistles in the New Testament.[62] With the Gospels the situation is different. Twentieth century scholarship accepts the existence of up to four decades of mainly oral tradition before the written books were created. A major text-book states 'It is incontrovertible that in the earliest period there was only an oral record of the narrative and sayings of Jesus'.[63] The Gospels are unique; despite many attempts

61. See E.J. Epp, 'New Testament Papyrus Manuscripts and Letter Carrying in Greco-Roman Times', in B.A. Pearson (ed.), *The Future of Early Christianity: Essays in Honor of Helmut Koester* (Minneapolis: Fortress Press, 1991), pp. 35-56 (52-55); M.B. Thompson, 'The Holy Internet: Communication between Churches in the First Christian Generation', in R. Bauckham (ed.), *The Gospels for All Christians: Rethinking the Gospel Audiences* (Grand Rapids, MI: Eerdmans; Edinburgh: T. & T. Clark, 1998), pp. 49-70 and R. Bauckham, 'For Whom Were the Gospels Written', in *idem* (ed.), *The Gospels for All Christians*, pp. 9-48, especially 33-44.

62. See J.L. White, *Light from Ancient Letters* (Philadelphia: Fortress Press, 1986); S.K. Towers, *Letter Writing in Greco-Roman Antiquity* (Philadelphia: Fortress Press, 1986).

63. W.G. Kümmel, *Introduction to the New Testament* (trans. A.J. Mattill; London: SCM Press, rev. edn, 1975), pp. 55, 56.

no-one has succeeded in finding other Greek or Latin books which are truly comparable, although they are most similar to classical 'lives'. The question to be developed is: Were the words and deeds of Jesus preserved by word of mouth alone before AD 70?

Chapter 4

WRITING IN HERODIAN PALESTINE

Inscribed material recovered from most parts of Herodian Palestine is meagre—names scratched, or short notes written in ink, on potsherds, a few formal inscriptions and numerous burial notices. Unspectacular as these specimens may be, they are still very informative.

While the written remains from Palestine are hardly different from those found in most parts of the Roman world, circumstances parallel to those which have preserved perishable materials in Egypt do exist in one region, the southern Jordan Valley and the Dead Sea coasts. There rainfall is minimal and, away from fresh water, aridity almost total. In 1947 the unexpected was realized with the discovery of the Dead Sea Scrolls. Since that first 'lucky strike', books and documents on leather and papyrus have come to light in various caves, protected to a greater or lesser degree from the harmful attacks of moisture, insects and rodents. Occasionally, where the writing material has disappeared, the texts may still survive. Papyrus scrolls had rested on the soil in Cave 7 of the Qumran caves and left their mark, as explained in Chapter 1.

This chapter aims to give an impression of the written material surviving from the period in the languages then current in Palestine, Aramaic, Greek, Hebrew and Latin.[1] Inevitably it will become something

1.   See J.C. Greenfield, 'Languages of Palestine, 200 B.C.E.–200 C.E.,' in H.H. Paper (ed.), *Jewish Languages, Theme and Variations* (New York: Ktav, 1978), pp. 143-54; J. Barr, 'Hebrew, Aramaic and Greek in the Hellenistic Age', in W.D. Davies and L. Finkelstein (eds.), *The Cambridge History of Judaism* (2 vols.; Cambridge: Cambridge University Press, 1989), II, pp. 79-114. The majority of the Aramaic texts cited are presented in J.A. Fitzmyer and D.J. Harrington, *Palestinian Aramaic Texts* (Biblica et Orientalia, 34; Rome: Biblical Institute Press, 1978) (cited by number) and in K. Beyer, *Die aramäischen Texte vom Toten Meer* (Göttingen: Vandenhoeck & Ruprecht, 1984) with *Ergänzungsband* (1994). Other references are only given where further information or illustrations are helpful. For a catalogue of the papyri and other non-literary texts from the first and second cen-

of a catalogue, but that very fact should give a clear impression of the amount that is available, the aspects of life it covers and the uses made of writing.

1. *Aramaic*

'Ephphatha', 'Talitha kum', 'Abba'—these foreign words in the Greek Gospels, retained in modern translations, purport to be the words Jesus spoke, not the Gospel-writers' Greek renderings, but the original Aramaic, the language of Jewish people in Palestine in his day (see Chapter 5).

Aramaean tribes in upper Mesopotamia took power in the towns of Syria at the end of the second millennium BC and their language gradually replaced the other West Semitic languages and the Hittite dialect of the previous inhabitants. Damascus, Arpad, Gozan were some of the principal centres. When the Assyrians deported large proportions of the populace to other parts of their empire, Aramaic became widely used in trade and diplomacy, as accurately depicted in the narrative of Sennacherib's threat to Jerusalem (2 Kgs 18.26).[2] It spread to replace Assyrian and Babylonian in the east and so become the language of administration throughout the empire of the Persians, well illustrated by the Elephantine papyri and other documents from Egypt[3] and the formal letters in the book of Ezra. From Palestine itself there are a few papyri of the fourth century BC, the largest group being those found between 1962 and 1964 in a cave in the Wadi Daliyeh on the west edge of the Jordan valley. Written between 375 and 335 BC, they concern sales of slaves and other property by citizens of Samaria who probably fled to the cave at the time of a revolt against Alexander the Great in 331 BC.[4]

turies, see H.M. Cotton, W.E.H. Cockle, F.G.B. Millar, 'The Papyrology of the Roman Near East: A Survey', *JRS* 85 (1995), pp. 214-35.

2.   The contentions of G. Garbini, *History and Ideology in Ancient Israel* (trans. J. Bowden; London: SCM Press, 1988), pp. 44-47, that Aramaic would not be known in Judah at so early a date are simply wrong.

3.   Now collected by B. Porten and A. Yardeni, *Textbook of Aramaic Documents from Ancient Egypt* (4 vols.; Winona Lake, IN: Eisenbrauns, 1986–99), see also B. Porten, A. Yardeni, *et al.*, *The Elephantine Papyri in English: Three Millennia of Cross-Cultural Continuity and Change* (Documenta et monumenta Orientis antiqui, 22; Leiden: E.J. Brill, 1996).

4.   F.M. Cross, 'A Report on the Samaria Papyri', in J.A. Emerton (ed.), *Congress Volume: Jerusalem 1986* (VTSup, 40; Leiden: E.J. Brill, 1988), pp. 17-26.

Despite the impact of Greek following Alexander's conquests (see pp. 102-107), Aramaic remained the language of the majority of people in the Near East until after the rise of Islam. Dialect differences are already evident in the earliest texts, from the ninth century BC, and by the first century they were strongly marked, variant forms of the alphabet being identified with each, all those forms being lineal descendants of the handwriting of the Persian chancery.

Although Aramaic-speakers mingled with Israelites in the north of the country throughout the history of the kingdom, it was in the Exile in Babylonia that the Jews took up Aramaic as their language for everyday life. Indeed, the Law had to be translated from Hebrew for the people of Jerusalem in the fifth century BC according to the accepted understanding of Neh. 8.8. Within the Bible, Ezra 4.8–6.18 and Dan. 2.4–7.28 are in Aramaic.[5] Government seals bore the name of the area in Aramaic, *Y*^{e}*hud*, and it was stamped on the handles of store jars and, a little later, on small silver coins issued from Jerusalem. At several sites in Palestine ostraca of Persian date have been recovered, dealing with local administrative and private affairs.[6] A collection of over 400 from Idumaea demonstrates the mixture of the population late in the fourth century BC, with personal names of Edomite, Arab, Phoenician and Jewish types.[7]

5.   The authenticity of the letters in Ezra is supported by parallels in language and style from the Achaemenid period; disputes continue over the date of the book of Daniel, but the Aramaic language suits the Persian period well; see K.A. Kitchen, 'The Aramaic of the Book of Daniel', in D.J. Wiseman, *et al.*, *Notes on Some Problems in the Book of Daniel* (London: Tyndale Press, 1965), pp. 31-79; E.Y. Kutscher, 'Aramaic', in T.A. Seboek (ed.), *Linguistics in South-West Asia and North Africa* (Current Trends in Linguistics, 6; The Hague: Mouton, 1970), pp. 347-412; P. W. Coxon, 'Greek Loan-words and the Alleged Greek Loan Translations in the Book of Daniel', *Transactions of the Glasgow University Oriental Society* 25 (1973–74), pp. 24-40.

6.   For examples of these stamps, coins and ostraca see R. Hestrin *et al.*, *Inscriptions Reveal: Documents from the Time of the Bible, the Mishna and the Talmud* (Israel Museum Catalogue, 100; Jerusalem: Israel Museum, 2nd edn, 1973), nos 149-55, 144-47, 156-65.

7.   A. Lemaire, *Nouvelles inscriptions araméennes d'Idumée* (Paris: J. Gabalda, 1996); I. Eph'al and J. Naveh, *Aramaic Ostraca of the Fourth Century BC from Idumaea* (Jerusalem: Magnes Press, 1996).

Aramaic in Public Use in Palestine

The continuance of Aramaic under Greek rule is neatly shown by a dedication found at Dan which carries the main text in Greek with an Aramaic version below: 'to the gods in Dan'.[8] At the other end of the country, ostraca discovered near Hebron include one in Greek and one in Greek and Aramaic, written early in the third century BC (see p. 105), while an ostracon from Maresha (see p. 104) gives the text of a marriage contract drawn up in Aramaic for Edomite inhabitants in 176 BC.[9]

Figure 15. *Coin of Alexander Jannaeus with Greek (left) and Aramaic (right) legends. Diameter 1.55 cm (0.61 in). (Private collection; photograph D.J. Restall.)*

According to the Mishnah, Jewish marriage deeds were customarily composed in Aramaic in the areas of Jerusalem and Galilee, whereas in Judah they were in Hebrew (*M. Ket.* 4.12; the clauses in 7-11 are also in Aramaic). When the Hasmonaeans gained virtual independence, they marked their achievement by striking coins with Hebrew legends in the Old Hebrew script (see p. 121), or with Hebrew and Greek legends, but Alexander Jannaeus (103–76 BC) issued a quantity with Aramaic and Greek legends in his twenty-fifth year (78 BC). The introduction of Aramaic on the coins is explained as the need to communicate to the majority of the population who could read neither Old Hebrew letters

8.   A. Biran, *Biblical Dan* (Jerusalem: Israel Exploration Society, 1994), pp. 221-24.

9.   E. Eshel and A. Kloner, 'An Aramaic Ostracon of an Edomite Marriage Contract from Maresha, Dated 176 B.C.E.', *IEJ* 46 (1996), pp. 1-22.

nor Greek, although no other Jewish coins have Aramaic legends.[10] Inscriptions and other official documents do not survive from the Jerusalem offices of the Jewish kings or the Herodian dynasty, but there can be little doubt Greek and Aramaic were current there side by side (see Chapter 6, pp. 172-73). That appears from eight notices carved in stone blocks around the town of Gezer in the first century BC. They state 'Boundary of Gezer' in Aramaic and '(Authority) of Alkios' in Greek, perhaps marking the limits of a private estate, or of the Sabbath boundary.[11] Two fragments of a monumental inscription found in the ruins of the fortress of Hyrcania may relate to the family of Alexander Jannaeus, but they are too meagre for certainty.[12] One formal inscription from Jerusalem does demonstrate the use of Aramaic in a very Jewish situation. A stone slab from a burial tunnel (*loculus*, Hebrew *kokh*) bears four lines of carefully engraved letters which read 'Hither were brought the bones of Uzziah, king of Judah. Not to be opened!' Uzziah (Azariah) had been buried in the City of David in the eighth century BC (2 Kgs 15.7), so presumably building works as the city expanded and was reconstructed in the first century disturbed his tomb, then still identifiable by an inscription, causing a reverent re-burial under religious or civil authority.[13] In the Temple, according to later reports, the chests for receiving the two drachma Temple-tax, payable annually by every Jew (cf. Mt. 17.24-27) were labelled in Aramaic, 'Old Shekels' and 'New Shekels' for the past and current years

10. J. Naveh, 'Dated Coins of Alexander Jannaeus', *IEJ* 18 (1968), pp. 20-26; Y. Meshorer, *Ancient Jewish Coinage* (2 vols.; New York: Amphora Books, 1982), I, pp. 79-81; Beyer, *Die aramäischen Texte*, pp. 329-30, I3; Hestrin, *Inscriptions Reveal*, nos 203, 204, 234.

11. R.A.S. Macalister, *The Excavation of Gezer 1902–1905 and 1907–1909* (London: Palestine Exploration Fund, 1912), p. 137; Beyer, *Die aramäischen Texte*, p. 339, 1-8; Hestrin, *Inscriptions Reveal*, no. 215. Note the Samaritan dedications in Aramaic found on Mt Gerizim, J. Naveh and Y. Magen, 'Aramaic and Hebrew Inscriptions of the Second Century B.C.E. at Mount Gerizim', *'Atiqot* 32 (1997), pp. 9*-17*.

12. Fitzmyer and Harrington, *Palestinian Aramaic Texts*, no. 37; Beyer, *Die aramäischen Texte*, p. 330, 14.

13. Fitzmyer and Harrington, *Palestinian Aramaic Texts*, no. 70; Beyer, *Die aramäischen Texte*, pp. 343,20; Hestrin, *Inscriptions Reveal*, no. 255; the arguments of Garbini, *History and Ideology*, pp. 42-44, against the authenticity of this inscription are groundless.

respectively.[14] From the excavations outside the Temple wall comes part of the support or leg of a stone vessel with the word 'Qorban' and two birds upside down engraved on it. The term, familiar from Mk 7.11, had the meaning of 'gift given entirely to God' and is also found on an ossuary, warning robbers against pillaging its contents. The same word appears on a stone block found a century ago on the property of the church of St Peter in Gallicantu. The inscription reads 'For the fire, *qorban*' and may indicate the stone marked the place in Herod's Temple where wood was placed ready for the burnt offerings. The stone was reused to cover an ossuary, when the dead man's name was scratched on it.[15]

Jewish Books in Aramaic

The acceptance of Aramaic in Jewish culture is seen most clearly in the amount and type of literature written in that language. In Jewish circles, the Bible was the book par excellence, yet already in the time of Ezra the books existing in Hebrew were partly or largely unintelligible to the people of Jerusalem (see above), so an Aramaic translation had to be provided. In later years, according to the Mishnah, in public worship the Scriptures were read first in Hebrew then rendered into Aramaic. Whereas the sacred texts were written in Hebrew, the Aramaic was not to be read from a written book. The Aramaic versions known in rabbinic literature and preserved in mediaeval manuscripts, the Targums, are far from literal translations, for they introduce all sorts of explanatory phrases and modernizations, applying the text to new circumstances.[16] Targums did exist earlier in written form, for rabbinic sources report the order of Gamaliel I, early in the first century, that a targum book shown to him should be buried under some masonry.[17] The reason

14. Beyer, *Die aramäischen Texte*, p. 360, Pl. 2.

15. B. Mazar, 'The Excavations in the Old City of Jerusalem', *Eretz Israel* 9 (1969), pp. 168-70, Pl. 15.5 (Hebrew); Hestrin, *Inscriptions Reveal*, no. 167; Fitzmyer and Harrington, *Palestinian Aramaic Texts*, no. 69; Beyer, *Die aramäischen Texte*, p. 346; see J.A. Fitzmyer, 'The Aramaic Qorbân Inscription from Jebel Ḥallet eṭ-Ṭûri and Mk 7:11/ Mt 15:5', *JBL* 78 (1959), pp. 60-65, reprinted in J.A. Fitzmyer, *Essays on the Semitic Background of the New Testament* (London: Geoffrey Chapman, 1971), pp. 93-100; *CIJ* 1407-1408; Fitzmyer and Harrington, *Palestinian Aramaic Texts*, nos. 69, 107; Beyer, *Die aramäischen Texte*, pp. 343-44, 19, 21.

16. See J. Bowker, *The Targums and Rabbinic Literature* (Cambridge: Cambridge University Press, 1969) for examples and discussion.

17. *b. Šab.* 115a.

for that is not clear. Some suppose Gamaliel held the view that what was oral tradition should not be written down (see Chapter 7),[18] and that could be especially valid were the rendering quite literal and so might risk being treated as if it were the original. Now the Dead Sea Scrolls have altered the picture considerably, revealing targum-like Aramaic books of the Herodian period which were previously unknown. An Aramaic version of Job among them follows the Hebrew text very closely for the most part.[19] Scraps of another version of Job and one of Leviticus share the same feature, supporting the idea that Gamaliel's concern was for the distinction of the original from the translation. Rather different is the *Genesis Apocryphon*, which gives an expanded paraphrase of parts of Genesis, adding information that an audience might like to know, but which was irrelevant to the biblical narrator, such as the name of Noah's wife and details of the beauty that made Sarah attractive to Pharaoh. Similar to that are fragments about Noah, Esther and Daniel, the third including a prayer put in the mouth of Nabonidus, the last king of Babylon who is not named at all in the biblical work.

Jewish authors were active in creating religious literature in Aramaic for moral instruction and to encourage faith by inculcating hope of future bliss, and the Scrolls yield many fragmentary examples. The book of Tobit, thought by many scholars of the nineteenth and early twentieth centuries to have been written in Greek, is now known in Aramaic and in Hebrew, although which of those is the original is still disputed.[20] Further removed from the biblical text than the targum-like paraphrases is *1 Enoch*, known in its entirety only in mediaeval Ethiopic manuscripts, and related compositions. The patriarch travelled to heaven, then around the world, receiving visions of the future involving contests between powers of good and fallen angels, with God's justice

---

18. S. Lieberman, *Tosefta ki-Fšuṭah: A Commentary on the Tosefta* (8 vols.; New York: 1955–73), III, p. 203 n. 6, cited by M. Sokoloff, *The Targum of Job from Qumran Cave XI* (Ramat-Gan: Bar-Ilan University, 1974), p. 5.

19. J.P.M. van der Ploeg, A.S. van der Woude, *Le Targum de Job de la grotte XI de Qumran* (Leiden: E.J. Brill, 1971); Sokoloff, *The Targum of Job*; Fitzmyer and Harrington, *Palestinian Aramaic Texts*, no. 5; Beyer, *Die aramäischen Texte*, pp. 280-98, Y; F. García Martinez, *The Dead Sea Scrolls Translated: The Qumran Texts in English* (trans. W.G.E. Watson; Leiden: E.J. Brill, 1994), pp. 143-53.

20. The fragments are edited by J.A. Fitzmyer in VanderKam (ed.), *Qumran Cave 4*, pp. 1-76.

and his righteous people ultimately prevailing. Chapters 72 to 82 comprise the Astronomical Book in which Enoch is told how the heavenly bodies and the winds function, based on a 364-day year. This section is partly preserved in Aramaic fragments among the Dead Sea Scrolls, some dated as early as the third century BC, setting the composition among the earliest pieces of Jewish literature in Aramaic. Presentation of the last words of Jacob's sons gave writers opportunity to set out both good advice, prophecies and visions, and pieces among the Scrolls show that these *Testaments of the Twelve Patriarchs*, preserved in mediaeval versions, circulated in earlier forms in Aramaic. Qahat, son of Levi, and his son Amram were also credited with testaments and visions. The Scrolls can only offer a segment of the literature of the time, yet they demonstrate considerable activity in religious circles reading and writing in Aramaic.

Rabbinic literature has preserved a few relics of first-century Aramaic compositions. Most notable are the brief sayings of the teacher Hillel, who lived in the latter part of the first century BC, presented in the tractate 'Sayings of the Fathers' (*Ab.*),[21] although the Mishnah as a whole is in Hebrew (see Chapter 7). There is also a list of festival days commemorating events from the Maccabaean revolt to the beginning of the First Revolt in AD 67, such as the re-dedication of the temple in December, 164 BC, (cf. Jn 10.22) celebrated to-day as Hanukkah. It was forbidden to fast on those days, so the composition is known as 'The Scroll of Fasting' (*Meg. Ta'an.*); it is thought to have been compiled soon after the Fall of Jerusalem.[22]

Aramaic in Everyday Life

The dominance of Aramaic in the everyday life of the Jewish population in Palestine is clear from the number and variety of documents and graffiti recovered. The work of ordinary scribes survives in collections of papyri secreted in caves by the Dead Sea during the Second (Bar Kochba) Revolt. They include legal deeds, which, although mostly written after AD 70, can justifiably be seen as continuing older practices

21. Given in Beyer, *Die aramäischen Texte*, pp. 361-62, xyRH, with other pieces of early Jewish Aramaic preserved in rabbinic books.

22. See Fitzmyer and Harrington, *Palestinian Aramaic Texts*, no. 150; Beyer, *Die aramäischen Texte*, pp. 354-58, xyMT; E. Schürer, G. Vermes, F. Millar, M. Black (eds.), *The History of the Jewish People in the Age of Jesus Christ* (3 vols.; Edinburgh: T. & T. Clark, 1973–87), I, pp. 114-15.

and so reflecting the activities of previous decades.[23] They deal with gifts and sales of property, loans and receipts, marriage and divorce. One text acknowledging a debt, is dated 55/56 (see below), and a couple of others are dated to approximately the same time by the palaeography.[24] Small fragments of similar documents were catalogued among the manuscripts from Cave 4 at Qumran and so may be supposed to date from before AD 67. However, the provenance is doubted, but the date and value of these pieces is clear, for several can be dated by their script in the first century BC and the first century AD. There are deeds of sale in Aramaic and Hebrew, accounts for cereals, an acknowledgment of debt and a letter in Aramaic, supporting the assumption that the types of text more fully known from the second century were being written in the first.[25]

Three texts, although damaged, give a glimpse of the affairs of those days. The first is the deed of loan from Nero's reign:[26]

> [On day X of month Y in the] second year of Nero Caesar, at Soba, Absalom son of Hanin of Soba, living in Cephar Signah, has declared he has borrowed from me, Zechariah son of Jehohanan of [   ], living in Chesalon, twenty (?) silver denarii (*zûzîn*). I (Absalom) [shall repay the money   ] and if not, from what I realize, I shall pay to you

23. Fitzmyer and Harrington, *Palestinian Aramaic Texts*, nos. 38-52; Beyer, *Die aramäischen Texte*, pp. 306-23, M,V, *Ergänzungsband*, pp. 163-66, 188-97; Hestrin, *Inscriptions Reveal*, nos. 190, 192.

24. The 'Nero' deed: P. Benoit, J.T. Milik and R. de Vaux, *Les Grottes de Murabba'ât* (DJD, 2; Oxford: Clarendon Press, 1962), pp. 100-104, Murabba'at 18; Fitzmyer and Harrington, *Palestinian Aramaic Texts*, no. 39; Beyer, *Die aramäischen Texte*, pp. 306-307, *Ergänzungsband*, p. 163; J. Naveh, *On Sherd and Papyrus* (Hebrew; Jerusalem: Magnes Press, 1992), pp. 84-86; Cotton, Cockle and Millar, 'Papyrology', p. 226, no. 224; Llewellyn, 'The Development of the Codex', pp. 230-32; for the other two deeds, see A. Yardeni in H.M. Cotton and A. Yardeni, *Aramaic, Hebrew and Greek Documentary Texts from Nahal Hever and Other Sites* (DJD, 27; Oxford: Clarendon Press, 1997), pp. 38-56, nos 9, 10; Cotton, Cockle and Millar, 'Papyrology', p. 226, nos. 228, 229. The writing of the emperor's name and title in Aramaic, *nrwn qsr*, is notable as a case of these words spelt in such a way that their numerical value is 666, a solution often sought for the 'number of the beast' in Rev. 13.18, but not hitherto found in any first-century text.

25. A. Yardeni in Cotton and Yardeni, *Aramaic, Hebrew and Greek Documentary Texts*, pp. 283-317.

26. See n. 24.

[   ] even if it is a sabbatical year. Now if I do not do so, you may claim repayment from my possessions and satisfaction from whatever I acquire.

> [Zecha]riah son of Jehohanan present in person.
> Joseph son of [   ] wrote it, is witness.
> Jonathan son of Jehohana is witness.
> Joseph s[on of J]ehudan is witness.
> [One name missing.]

Marriages involved ownership of money and property and so the terms were often set out in writing when a couple became man and wife and when they separated. A poorly preserved papyrus which records a contract of marriage can be partly completed from others, from rabbinic sources and from the traditional marriage deed, the *Ketubah*.[27]

> On the 7th of Adar in the el[eventh year of   in Harodna, Judah, son of Jo] son of Manasseh from the descendants of Eliashib, [living in Harodna (?), said to X daughter of Y] you will become my wife according to the law of M[oses and I shall feed and clothe you from to-day for ever. I have received your dowry from you] in good money, X silver denarii (*zûzîn*) [   ] shall be validly yours. If you [want a divorce, I shall repay your dowry.] If you pass into eternity [before me, any sons we have shall inherit your dowry and whatever is rightly theirs.] If there are daughters they shall live in my house and be maintained] until marriage. Now if I should die [you may live in my house and] receive maintenance from my possessions [for as long as] you remain a widow… [All the possessions which I own or shall acquire are] security and guaran[tees to assure your dowry for you] and for your heirs against any [dispute. Whenever you want, I shall renew] this deed for you [if I am still alive].

When a marriage ended, the settlement could be arranged in the way this papyrus written in Masada but found in Wadi Murabba'at exemplifies:[28]

27. Milik in Benoit, Milik and de Vaux (eds.), *Les Grottes de Murabba'ât*, no. 20; Fitzmyer and Harrington, *Palestinian Aramaic Texts*, nos. 8-52; Beyer, *Die aramäischen Texte*, pp. 309-10, *Ergänzungsband*, p. 163; Naveh, *On Sherd*, pp. 92-93. For some aspects of continuing tradition see M. Geller, review of Beyer, *Die aramäischen Texte*, in *BSOAS* 51 (1988), pp. 315, 316. The second-century BC ostracon bearing a marriage deed between two Idumaeans written in Aramaic at Maresha is also akin, see n. 9.

28. Benoit, Milik and de Vaux (eds.), *Les Grottes de Murabba'ât*, no. 19; Hestrin, *Inscriptions Reveal*, no. 189; Fitzmyer and Harrington, *Palestinian Aramaic*

> On the 1st of Marcheswan, year six [i.e. of the First Revolt, A.D. 71/72]
> at Masada. On this day, of my own freewill, I Joseph, son of Naqsan
> from [X] living at Masada, leave and divorce you, my wife, Miriam
> daughter of Jonathan [from X] living at Masada, who was previously my
> wife, so that you are free to go to marry any Jewish man you like. This is
> my deed of renunciation and bill of divorce for you... Whenever you
> ask me, I shall renew this document correctly.

> > Joseph son of Naq[san] present in person.
> > Eliezer [son of] Malka is witness.
> > Joseph son of Malka is witness.
> > Eliezer son of Hanana is witness.

This deed is a double document. The text was written on the upper part
of the sheet and then repeated on the lower part. The upper part was
then rolled over until all the writing on it was concealed, cords were
passed through holes in the sheet and the roll tied and sometimes
sealed. The witnesses signed their names on the back of the paper, one
beside each string. The copy of the text on the lower half remained
visible for anyone to consult; the cords would only be cut should a serious dispute arise.

The scribes wrote letters as well as legal and business documents, but
the only examples in Aramaic on papyrus are from the Second Revolt,
many of them to or from Bar Kochba himself. However, these, too, may
be seen as later examples of a use current in the first century. Beside the
letters on papyrus and some ostraca, the collection contains one written
in ink on a sliver of wood, like those from Vindolanda (see Chapter 1,
p. 29), the sole relic of that writing material from Palestine.[29]

Where neither papyrus nor wood was available or the message was
too unimportant to warrant their use, potsherds were the substitute writing material. A few examples have been uncovered in excavations
across the country. Three from Gezer are dated in the second century
BC. One a man's name and surname, one a list of names, so far as it can
be read, and one indeterminate.[30] The greatest number of ostraca comes

Texts, no. 40; Beyer, *Die aramäischen Texte*, pp. 307-308, *Ergänzungsband*, p. 163; Naveh, *On Sherd*, p. 90.

29. Bar Kochba Letters: Fitzmyer and Harrington, *Palestinian Aramaic Texts*, nos. 53-60; Beyer, *Die aramäischen Texte*, pp. 350-52, ySK1-15 (1 is the wooden tablet); *Ergänzungsband*, pp. 213-16 (fuller text of ySK1).

30. J. Rosenbaum and J.D. Seger, 'Three Unpublished Ostraca from Gezer', *BASOR* 264 (1986), pp. 51-60.

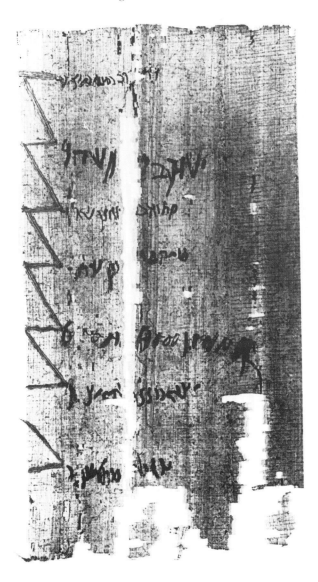

Figure 16. *Early second century 'double' deed with seven witnesses' sig-natures on the back, the first four in Aramaic, fifth in Greek, the sixth and seventh in Nabataean. (Reproduced from N. Lewis,* The Documents from the Bar-Kokhba Period in the Cave of Letters, Greek Papyri *(1989) Pl. 24, no. 20, back, by courtesy of N. Lewis and the Israel Exploration Society.)*

from Masada, all assigned to the time of the First Revolt. They are brief, some extremely brief, messages; over two dozen require the issue of bread on specific days to named individuals, some others are five or six lines long, one pleading for repayment of a debt. In a list of names with amounts beside them stand some familiar from the New Testament, 'the Gadarenes', 'Son of Jesus' (cf. Bar-Jesus, Acts 13.6) and 'Jesus the proselyte'. Names were also painted on pottery vessels to mark ownership, such as Joseph, Johanan (= John), Saul, while on other pots were notes of their contents, 'pressed dates', 'fish', 'dough'. There were jars set aside for religious purposes, labelled 'holy', or 'priest's tithe' and some marked to show they were or were not suitable for consecrated contents, that is, things the priest and Levites could eat.[31]

Outside Masada there are a handful of ostraca from an unknown site about deliveries of foodstuffs, brief notes excavated in Jerusalem and pots labelled with their owners' names, all from the earlier part of the first century, including several from the Qumran region.[32] While weights bearing marks of authority in Greek are not uncommonly found (see pp. 107-108), one from a house in Jerusalem has the name Bar Kathros scratched on it in the square script. The Babylonian Talmud reports a tradition that this was the name of a high priestly family infamous for corruption and for oppressing the people.[33]

Widespread use of Aramaic is evident among the range of fairly wealthy Jewish people who could afford to be buried in rock-cut tombs around Jerusalem and elsewhere. Many contain graffiti, giving the

31. See Y. Yadin, J. Naveh and Y. Meshorer, *Masada. I. The Aramaic and Hebrew Ostraca and Jar Inscriptions. The Coins of Masada* (Jerusalem: Israel Exploration Society, 1989); Beyer, *Die aramäischen Texte, Ergänzungsband*, pp. 209-13,yMS; Cotton, Cockle and Millar, 'Papyrology', pp. 227, nos. 233, 235-39.

32. Baillet, Milik and de Vaux, *Les 'Petites Grottes' de Qumran*, p. 30 (a jar bearing the letters *rwm'* which, although read by some as 'Rome', are best interpreted as a personal name, an abbreviation of 'God X is exalted', as known in Nabataean, see J. Cantineau, *Le nabatéen* [2 vols.; Paris: Leroux, 1932], p. 146); Hestrin, *Inscriptions Reveal*, nos. 244-48; E. Puech, 'The Tell el-Fûl Jar Inscription and the Netînîm', *BASOR* 261 (1986), pp. 69-72. Fragments of jars bearing names in Hebrew, Aramaic and Greek were found at the Hasmonean-Herodian castle of Alexandrium (Sartaba), see Y. Tsafrir and I. Magen, 'Sartaba-Alexandrium', in E. Stern (ed.), *New Encyclopedia*, pp. 1318-20 (1320).

33. N. Avigad, *Discovering Jerusalem* (Nashville, TN: Nelson, 1983), pp. 129-31; Hestrin, *Inscriptions Reveal*, no. 233; Fitzmyer and Harrington, *Palestinian Aramaic Texts*, no. 65; Beyer, *Die aramäischen Texte*, p. 346, yJe34.

Figure 17. *Ostracon from Masada bearing a list of names in Aramaic, including 'the Gadarenes' and Bar-Jesus. (Reproduced from Y. Yadin, J. Naveh,* Masada I, *pl. 24, no. 420, by courtesy of J. Naveh and the Israel Exploration Society.)*

names of the dead or lamenting them. Earliest are the lines scribbled in charcoal on the wall of a fine tomb in west Jerusalem, created early in the first century BC. There are five in Aramaic and one in Greek. The dead man for whom the tomb was built is identified by the Greek name Jason, then another man, Honi, refurbished it for himself. Other lines give dates and a plea for respect for the tomb. The Greek text is reconstructed as 'Eat while you are alive, brothers, and drink, happy ones! No-one is immortal!'[34] In another tomb, seven lines of writing in a form of Old Hebrew letters carved in the rock wall and highlighted in red-brown paint record the piety of a priest, exiled from Jerusalem to Babylon, who brought a compatriot to be buried in Jerusalem.[35]

A year after burial, it was customary to collect and wash the bones, place them in a box, an ossuary, and put it back into the tomb. Wooden ossuaries have almost entirely perished, but stone ones exist in large numbers. Often they carry the dead person's name scratched on them and very many of the names are in Aramaic. Usually they were for identification; they were not epitaphs or tomb-stones, so they only give names, relationships and occupations, or, rarely, other information, and exactly the same information is found in Greek and Hebrew. They 'tend to be carelessly executed, clumsily spaced, and, often, contain spelling mistakes.'[36] Examples are 'Joseph son of Qoppa', 'Judah, son of Eleazar, the scribe', 'Sapphira the wife of Simeon', 'Joseph, Elasa Arthaka's son, has brought the bones of our mother Emma to Jerusalem'.[37] In one tomb near Jericho the details were not limited to

34. N. Avigad, 'Aramaic Inscriptions in the Tomb of Jason', *IEJ* 17 (1967), pp. 101-11; Fitzmyer and Harrington, *Palestinian Aramaic Texts*, no. 89; Beyer, *Die aramäischen Texte*, pp. 328-29, I 1.2; B. Lifschitz, 'Notes d'épigraphie palestinienne. I. L'exhortation à la jouissance de la vie dans une inscription tombale juive à Jérusalem', *RB 73* (1966), pp. 248-57; E. Puech, 'Palestinian Funerary Customs', *ABD*, V, pp. 130, 131.

35. Giv'at ha-Mivtar: E.S. Rosenthal, 'The Giv'at ha-Mivtar Inscription', *IEJ* 23 (1973), pp. 72-81; J. Naveh, 'An Aramaic Tomb Inscription Written in Paleo-Hebrew Script', *IEJ* 23 (1973), pp. 82-91; Fitzmyer and Harrington, *Palestinian Aramaic Texts*, no. 68; Beyer, *Die aramäischen Texte*, pp. 346-47,yJe80; Hestrin, *Inscriptions Reveal*, no. 263.

36. L.Y. Rahmani, *A Catalogue of Jewish Ossuaries in the Collections of the State of Israel* (Jerusalem: Israel Academy, 1994), p. 11.

37. *CII, passim;* see also Fitzmyer and Harrington, *Palestinian Aramaic Texts*, nos 72-131, 133-35, 137-48; Beyer, *Die aramäischen Texte*, pp. 339-48, *Ergänzungsband*, pp. 205-209; Rahmani, *Catalogue*, nos. 893, 871; note that the ossuary

scratching on the ossuaries, they were painted on the inside and outside of a pottery bowl left in the tomb as well.[38] Unusually, a stone coffin has incised on its lid a warning that it is closed and no one else should be buried in it, yet without giving the dead person's name ![39]

In addition to the graffiti in tombs, some were noticed in a cave in the steep Michmash valley (Wadi Suweinit). Refugees at the time of the First Revolt hid there and passed the time scratching on the wall in Aramaic. They left two alphabets, a name, a call for peace and a message, 'Joezer has been taken, the guards have entered !'[40]

Various forms of Aramaic were used throughout the Near East and visitors to Palestine naturally brought texts with them or wrote there in their own style. Traces of some of those languages appear in the handful of Jerusalem ossuaries which have names scratched on them in the distinctive form of the Aramaic square script at home in the trading city of Palmyra, half-way between Damascus and Babylonia.[41] Further east, members of the royal family of Adiabene, the region of Erbil, east of

of 'Joseph son of Qoppa' (Z. Greenhut, 'The "Caiaphas" Tomb in North Talpiyot, Jerusalem', *'Atiqot* 21 [1992], pp. 63-71, with R. Reich, 'Ossuary Inscriptions from the "Caiaphas" Tomb', *'Atiqot* 21 [1992], pp. 72-77) has no connection with the High Priest Caiaphas of the Gospels, whose name would be written *qyp'*. See Beyer, *Die aramäischen Texte, Ergänzungsband*, pp. 207-208, 243; E. Puech, 'Inscriptions funéraires palestiniennes: tombeau de Jason et ossuaires', *RB* 90 (1993), pp. 482-533; W. Horbury, 'The "Caiaphas" Ossuary and Joseph Caiaphas', *PEQ* 126 (1994), pp. 32-48. Other examples Hestrin, *Inscriptions Reveal*, pp. 256-61.

38. R. Hachlili, 'A Jerusalem Family Tomb in Jericho', *BASOR* 230 (1978), pp. 45-56; Beyer, *Die aramäischen Texte*, pp. 347,yJR2.3; cf. A. Killebrew, 'Jewish Funerary Customs During the Second Temple Period in the Light of Excavations at the Jericho Necropolis', *PEQ* 115 (1983), pp. 109-32; R.A. Kearsley, 'The Goliath Family at Jericho', in S.R. Llewellyn (ed.), *A Review of the Greek Inscriptions and Papyri Published in 1980–1981* (New Documents Illustrating Early Christianity, 6; Macquarie University, 1992), pp. 162-64.

39. E. Puech, 'Une inscription araméenne sur un couvercle de sarcophage', *Eretz Israel* 20 (1989), pp. 161*-65*; Beyer, *Die aramäischen Texte, Ergänzungsband*, p. 207, yJE42, interprets 'Closed' as the owner's name, Sakar.

40. J. Patrich, 'Inscriptions araméennes juives dans les grottes d'el-Aleiliyât', *RB* 92 (1985), pp. 265-73; Beyer, *Die aramaischen Texte, Ergänzungsband*, pp. 222-23, ySW 3-5.

41. F.-M. Abel, 'Chronique: Tombeau et ossuaires juifs récemment découverts', *RB* 10 (1913), pp. 262-77 (271, nos. 10, 11); *CII* nos. 1217, 1222; E. Puech, 'Ossuaires inscrits d'une tombe du Mont des Oliviers', *Liber Annuus* 32 (1982), pp. 355-72; Rahmani, *Catalogue*, no. 579.

the Tigris, converted to Judaism and came to live in Jerusalem. Josephus reports some were buried in a magnificent sepulchre constructed north of the city by Helena, one of their queens. A large tomb north of the Old City, now called 'The Tombs of the Kings', is probably the place and in it lay a stone sarcophagus bearing the words 'Queen Saddan' (or 'Saran') written both in a letters similar to those used for Aramaic (early Syriac) texts in upper Mesopotamia, and in the square script.[42]

Much of Transjordan and the Sinai was ruled by the Nabataeans from their capital at Petra in ancient Edom. They spoke an Arabic dialect but wrote a form of Aramaic in their own cursive adaptation of the Aramaic alphabet, both language and writing derived from the chancellery of the Achaemenid empire. When their king Aretas III (84–71 BC) issued coins for use in Damascus, where he had control, he had his name and title engraved in Greek as was usual in most of the states in the Levant, but all his successors had the legends in Nabataean. That may be seen as an assertion of identity parallel to that of the Hasmonaean kings having Hebrew or Aramaic legends on their coins (see p. 87), except that the Nabataeans went further and eschewed the engraving of parallel versions in Greek in the way the Jewish die cutters had done.[43] Scores of Nabataean inscriptions on stone are known from sites in Jordan and western Arabia, and thousands of graffiti scratched on cliffs along the trade routes through Edom, the Negev and Sinai or by sacred places. The caves west of the Dead Sea have yielded Nabataean legal texts on papyrus which add a new dimension to knowledge of the language and society. The archive of Babatha (see p. 115) includes six documents in Nabataean, which is not surprising since her family lived near Zoar at the southern end of the Dead Sea, an area under Nabataean rule. Other Nabataean documents were recovered that may be related, but a few are older, one a contract written between AD 59 and 69, another a piece of a letter.[44] Outside Palestine, it is worth noting how

42. See Schürer, *History of the Jewish People*, III, p. 164 n. 66; *CII*, no. 1338; Fitzmyer and Harrington, *Palestinian Aramaic Texts*, no. 132; Beyer, *Die aramäischen Texte*, pp. 342, yJe18b; see J. Naveh, *Early History of the Alphabet* (Jerusalem: Magnes Press, 1982), p. 149 for the script.

43. See Y. Meshorer, *Nabataean Coins* (Qedem, 3; Jerusalem: Hebrew University, 1975).

44. The contract: J. Starcky, 'Un contrat nabatéen sur papyrus', *RB* 61 (1954), pp. 161-81; Fitzmyer and Harrington, *Palestinian Aramaic Texts*, no. 64; see

Figure 18. *Nabataean graffito on a rock face in Petra, 'May Aslah be safe and sound'. (Photograph by courtesy of M.C.A. Macdonald.)*

some of the Arab tribes in Transjordan scratched graffiti on rocks and boulders in the desert in their own forms of the South Arabic alphabet (Safaitic, Thamudic). Dated to the first centuries of the present era, thousands of these have been catalogued, thousands are yet to be studied. Rare examples identify stone vessels as votive offerings. Limited in content to epitaphs, prayers and brief reports of an individual's activities, these are remarkable relics of people who are best described as 'literate shepherds'.[45] In the Yemen, where the South Arabian alphabet was current, hundreds of inscriptions on stone monuments, metal objects and seals are known, as well as graffiti, and dozens of sticks have come to light in recent years with texts scratched on them. The sticks, up to 30 cm in length (12 in) carry scribal exercises, lists, genealogies, business documents and letters of all sorts. They are dated to the first centuries AD[46] and open the possibility that the Thamudic and Safaitic tribesmen could also use documents written on perishable materials.

F. Millar, *The Roman Near East 31 BC–AD 337* (Cambridge, MA: Harvard University Press, 1993), pp. 403-405; the letter: Yardeni in Cotton and Yardeni, *Aramaic, Hebrew and Greek Documentary Texts*, pp. 286-88, no. 343.

45. See M.C.A. Macdonald, 'Inscriptions, Safaitic', *ABD*, III, pp. 418-23.

46. See Y. Abd-Allâh and I. Gajda, *Yémen, au pays de la reine de Saba* (Paris: Flammarion, 1997), pp. 115-17.

Figure 19. *'Thamudic' inscriptions written vertically on a rock in Wadi al-Leyyah, on the east side of Wadi Ramm. From right to left, 'By Aun son of Sa'd'; 'By Nahab son of Wasit son of Ha-Rabb (= 'the lord')', tribal marks; 'By Aun son of Sa'd' again; one further text. For the first two, see G. Lankester Harding and E. Littmann,* Some Thamudic Inscriptions from the Hashemite Kingdom of Jordan *(Leiden: E.J. Brill, 1952), nos. 462, 461. (Photograph courtesy of the Department of Antiquities of Jordan (no. A825) and M.C.A. Macdonald.)*

All of these texts show that Aramaic was the dominant written language for the people of the land, for affairs of daily life and death and was also actively used for literature.

2. *Greek*

Greek was the imposition of of Alexander the Great and his successors in the Near East. However, their arrival was not the first appearance of Greek speakers in the Fertile Crescent. Already, early in the sixth century BC, Ionians served in the court of Nebuchadnezzar of Babylon, for lists of rations issued to them were recovered in the ruins of a palace there. The Greeks' names stand beside Lydians, Phoenicians and others, and the exiled king Jehoiachin of Judah.[47] At the end of the same century, other Ionians worked for Persian kings, in building and decorating their palaces at Pasargadae and Persepolis.[48] Some Greeks reached the Levant even earlier, for a potsherd from Al Mina, near the mouth of the Orontes river in Syria, had Greek words scratched on it in the eighth century BC.[49] In this context a Greek band for entertaining Nebuchadnezzar and his nobles easily takes its place (Dan. 3). The custom of ornamenting the royal court with exotic foreign craftsmen and the products of their skills was ancient. Babylonian kings in the fourteenth century BC asked the pharaohs of Egypt for models of Egyptian animals,[50] and Assyrian kings delighted in the strange creatures they caught when their armies reached the Mediterranean, even making images of them in stone to stand at the doorways of their palaces.[51] Those kings also had singers from east and west to entertain them.[52] Nebuchadnezzar was following the tradition of Mesopotamian royalty with his musicians from the far west.

Those were restricted and haphazard displays of Greek language and craft in the Near East. When Alexander conquered the area, they became universal. He settled his veterans in cities across his realm from

47. A.L. Oppenheim, 'Nebuchadnezzar II (c) Varia', in *ANET*, p. 308. Original publication by E.F. Weidner, 'Jojachin, König von Juda, in babylonischen Keilschrifttexten', in *Mélanges syriens offerts à M. René Dussaud* (Paris: Geuthner, 1930), pp. 923-35.

48. C. Nylander, *Ionians in Pasargadae* (Uppsala: Almqvist and Wiksell, 1970); for a summary see E. Yamauchi, *Persia and the Bible* (Grand Rapids, MI: Baker Book House, 1990), pp. 389-94.

49. J. Boardman, 'An Inscribed Sherd from Al Mina', *Oxford Journal of Archaeology* 1 (1982), pp. 365-67; A.L. Jeffery, *Local Scripts of Archaic Greece* (Oxford: Clarendon Press, revd A.W. Johnston, 1990), p. 426; for the significance of Greek pottery in the Levant, see J.C. Waldbaum, 'Greeks *in* the East or Greeks *and* the East? Problems in the Definition and Recognition of Presence', *BASOR* 305 (1997), pp. 1-17.

50. El-Amarna Letter 10, see W.L. Moran, *The Amarna Letters* (Baltimore: The Johns Hopkins University Press, 1982), pp. 19, 20.

51. Tiglath-pileser I (c. 1114–1076 BC): A.K. Grayson, *Assyrian Rulers of the Early First Millennium B.C. I.* (Royal Inscriptions of Mesopotamia, Assyrian Periods, 2; Toronto: University Press, 1991), pp. 44, 62-63; *idem, Assyrian Royal Inscriptions* (2 vols.; Wiesbaden: Otto Harrassowitz, 1976), §§103, 156-58.

52. See J.V. Kinnier Wilson, *The Nimrud Wine Lists* (London: British School of Archaeology in Iraq, 1972), pp. 76-78.

Anatolia to India, and the cities he founded or refounded were built and governed in Greek fashion. After his death, his generals divided the empire between them and, even where local strong men seized control in the eastern parts, many subsequent rulers continued to erect monuments and strike coins with Greek inscriptions. In India, for example, Greek was the formal language until the beginning of the Christian era, while in Babylonia the Parthian kings stamped their names in Greek until the Sassanian conquest in the third century AD and statues were set up bearing Greek dedications in Nineveh and Babylon.[53]

Greek speakers permeated near eastern society. In Palestine the coastal towns—Gaza, Azotus (ancient Ashdod), Ascalon, Joppa, Dor, were largely Greek. Herod settled his foreign veterans at Gaba on the north-east of Mt Carmel and rebuilt Strato's Tower on the coast as Caesarea in a wholly Hellenistic-Roman style. Samaria had became a Greek city when Alexander settled some of his Macedonian troops there; it was conquered and destroyed by Jewish forces of the Hasmonaeans, then reconstructed after Pompey's invasion and rebuilt by King Herod who settled some of his troops there. East of the Jordan lay nine towns of the Decapolis, among them Pella, Abila, Jerash and Philadelphia ('Amman), with one, ancient Beth-Shan, Greek Scythopolis, on the west bank. These ten places were among those established as Greek colonies following Alexander's time and enjoyed some degree of autonomy, although Syrian, Jewish and Nabataean rulers tried to control them. As shown by architecture, inscriptions and coins, their culture, language and religion, were thoroughly Greek.[54]

A very fine example of Hellenization is seen in the town of Marisa (biblical Maresha) in the Judaean foothills, north-north-east of Lachish. The upper city was laid out in the third century BC on a typical Greek grid plan and later decorated with statues and inscriptions honouring Ptolemy IV of Egypt (221–203 BC), who won a victory over the Seleucids of Syria near Gaza. The population of Marisa was a mixture of Idumaeans, descendants of the Edomites who occupied southern Judah after the Nebuchadnezzar's conquest, and who spoke Aramaic, of

53. See P.M. Fraser, *Cities of Alexander the Great* (Oxford: Clarendon Press, 1996).

54. See Schürer, *History of the Jewish People*, II, pp. 125-58; J.-P. Rey-Coquais, 'Decapolis', *ABD*, II, pp. 116-21. In general see M. Hengel, *The 'Hellenization' of Judaea in the First Century after Christ* (trans. J. Bowden; London: SCM Press, 1989), who discusses much of the material presented here.

Greeks and of people from Sidon. The last became wealthy and were buried in rock-cut tombs around the town. Their burials were frequently identified by Greek inscriptions and graffiti. Two graffiti, one in very literary style, imply one tomb served as a lovers' trysting place.[55] Hunting scenes painted on the walls of the tomb of a leading family of the Sidonian community had names of the animals written beside them in Greek. The members of the family intermarried with local people, some of them bearing Idumaean names, but Greek names came to dominate. That dominance is reflected in the collection of magical texts found in the town. The names of those whom the gods were asked to curse are principally Greek, with a few Semitic, Egyptian and Roman ones. The place was destroyed by the Parthians in 40 BC.[56] At Gezer a curse was scribbled on a wall: 'Pampras. May fire follow up Simon's palace'. The words are thought to be directed against Simon the Maccabee who seized and fortified the town in about 142 BC.[57]

A group of ostraca found at Khirbet el-Kôm in the Hebron hills to the south-east of Marisa includes the oldest pieces of Greek writing yet found in the country. One is entirely in Greek, the other a bilingual, in the Edomite/Idumaean language and Aramaic script and in Greek. The latter, a receipt, is dated 'year 6', a date which the editor argues is 277 BC, the sixth year of Ptolemy II. The mixture of peoples here is similar to that at Marisa, with personal names of both Semitic and Greek origin and languages from both sources in use.[58]

In Syria-Palestine Greek replaced Aramaic as the language of administration and law. The coins of the Ptolemies who controlled Palestine

55. See recently J. Hordern, 'An Erotic Inscription from Marisa, Judaea (I.U. Powell, Collectanea Alexandrina 184)', *ZPE* 126 (1999), pp. 81-82.

56. J.P. Peters and H. Thiersch, *Painted Tombs in the Necropolis of Marissa* (London: Palestine Exploration Fund, 1905); E.D. Oren and U. Rappaport, 'The Necropolis of Mareshah-Beth Govrin', *IEJ* 34 (1984), pp. 114-53; M. Avi-Yonah and A. Kloner, 'Mareshah (Marisa)', in E. Stern (ed.), *New Encyclopedia*, III, pp. 948-57.

57. Macalister, *The Excavation of Gezer*, pp. 210-13; F.-M. Abel, 'Topographie des campagnes machabéennes', *RB* 35 (1926), pp. 510-33 (515-17); *CII*, no. 1184.

58. L.T. Geraty, 'The Khirbet el-Kôm Bilingual Ostracon', *BASOR* 220 (1975), pp. 55-61; *idem*, 'The Historical, Linguistic, and Biblical Significance of the Khirbet el-Kôm Ostraca', in C.L. Meyers and M. O'Connor (eds.), *The Word of the Lord Shall Go Forth: Essays in Honor of David Noel Freedman* (Winona Lake, IN: Eisenbrauns, 1983), pp. 545-48; *idem*, 'Kom, Khirbet el-, Ostraca', *ABD* IV, pp. 99-100.

from Egypt until 200 BC and of the Seleucids of Antioch, who wrested it from them, all bear Greek legends, as do many struck by the independent cities such as Tyre and Sidon. A fascinating archive of papyrus documents unearthed in Egypt illustrates the role of Greek well. The papers come from the office of Zenon, agent for Apollonius, the finance minister of Ptolemy II (283–46 BC). Zenon travelled in Palestine about 260 BC, on his master's business, corresponding and, we may assume, speaking in Greek, and receiving letters in Greek from his staff in Palestine after he had returned to Egypt. Most of the papyri deal with financial affairs, among them a small group concern Tobias, who was probably the governor of the region which had been the kingdom of Ammon, centred on Amman. The man himself was almost certainly descended from that Tobiah the Ammonite who opposed Nehemiah in the fifth century BC (Neh. 2.19-20, etc.). These texts give incidental information about the activity of a government office and the wide-ranging affairs of its staff.[59]

Palestine has not yielded such papyrus texts from so early a date, but an inscribed stone slab found near Beth-Shan in the Jordan valley in 1960 witnesses the same official use of Greek. The monument brings together two letters from Ptolemy son of Thraseas, governor of part of Syria and Phoenicia to his master, the Syrian king Antiochus III (223–187 BC), with the royal replies. Ptolemy proposed various measures concerning the movement of goods, the security of titles to property and the protection of villages from the demands of travellers. He set out the case, then the king gave his approval and ordered copies of the documents to be inscribed on stone and erected in the villages affected. In an incomplete text from a coastal settlement Antiochus V, in 163 BC, responds to a group of Sidonians who had appealed to him for tax concessions. A number of epitaphs and dedicatory inscriptions have been found at Samaria, Beth-Shan (Greek Scythopolis) and coastal sites like Accho (Greek Ptolemais) and a piece of a decree setting prices may also come from second century Palestine. A second-century BC inscription from Jerusalem appears to be a pagan dedication.[60]

59. See above, p. 36 n. 38.

60. Y.H. Landau, 'A Greek Inscription Found near Hefzibah', *IEJ* 16 (1966), pp. 54-70; Hestrin, *Inscriptions Reveal*, no. 214; cf. H.W. Pleket and R.S. Stroud (eds.), *Supplementum Epigraphicum Graecum* 41 (Amsterdam: J.C. Gieben, 1994), no. 1574; B. Isaac, 'A Seleucid Inscription from Jamnia-on-the-Sea: Antiochus V Eupator and the Sidonians', *IEJ* 41 (1991), pp. 132-44; cf. *Supplementum Epi-*

By the end of the second century BC, therefore, when the Jews had their own state based on Jerusalem, Greek was firmly entrenched. The little bronze coins of the four Hasmonaean priest kings, starting with Alexander Jannaeus (103–76 BC), show that clearly. The smaller coins bear the name and titles in Hebrew alone, but the larger types struck by Jannaeus and his last successor, Mattathias Antigonus (40–37 BC) carry the legend in Greek as well. Patriotism dictated the Hebrew texts, the need to identify the issuing authority more widely may have required the Greek ones, but these low value coins did not circulate in quantity outside the Jewish state, so the need for the Greek wording was evidently felt within the realm. When King Herod took power, he had his name and title stamped in Greek only on the coins he issued, and his sons did the same for the different parts of Palestine they ruled. When Rome took control in Judaea, Greek only was stamped on the small bronze coins the Roman governors issued.[61] Coins of self-governing cities in the Levant which reached Palestine through trade all had Greek legends by the time of King Herod, so made their contribution to spreading the language. That was particularly the case with the coins in which the Jerusalem priests required every Jew to pay the annual temple tax of two drachmae or two denarii (cf. Mt. 17.24-27). They were silver two and four drachma pieces of Tyre, carrying the head of the god Melqart on one side and an eagle surrounded by the words 'Of Tyre, holy place and sanctuary' on the other.[62]

As well as coins, weights were officially regulated. Jerusalem shop-keepers in the street beside Herod's temple measured out their wares against stone weights marked in Greek with a date. Several examples have 'year 5', sometimes with a royal title, both perhaps referring to Herod Agrippa I, whose fifth year was AD 41; a similar weight was found at Khirbet Qumran.[63] Another bears the name and titles of Herod

graphicum Graecum 41 (1994), no. 1556; I.L. Merker, 'A Greek Tariff Inscription in Jerusalem', *IEJ* 25 (1975), pp. 238-44; S. Applebaum, A. Oppenheimer, U. Rappaport and M. Stern (eds.), *Jerusalem in the Second Temple Period. Abraham Schalit Memorial Volume* (Jerusalem: Yad Izhak ben-Zvi, 1980), pp. 56-59, cf. *Supplementum Epigraphicum Graecum* 30 (1980), no. 1695.

61. See Meshorer, *Ancient Jewish Coinage*.

62. Y. Meshorer, 'One Hundred Ninety Years of Tyrian Shekels', in A. Houghton, *et al.* (eds.), *Studies in Honor of Leo Mildenberg* (Wetteren: Editions NR, 1984), pp. 171-79.

63. Mazar, 'The Excavations in the Old City of Jerusalem', pp. 161-76, pl. 46. 12-14 (Hebrew); *idem*, 'The Excavations in the Old City of Jerusalem near the

(the Great) in Greek and is dated c. 9 BC: 'Year 32 of Herod the king, pious and loyal to Caesar. Inspector of markets, 3 minas.' More elaborate weights were made of lead, cast in moulds.[64] One, found in the Tiberias district, was issued in the reign of Herod Antipas in AD 29–30. It reads 'Under Herod the Tetrarch, 34, Gaius Julius the inspector of markets, 5 talents'. Greek circulated in another way, also, incised on bone counters made as tickets for entry to the theatre.[65]

Trade also brought amphorae of wine from the Aegean in the third to first centuries BC. Their handles carried factory stamps in Greek which could have brought the script and language to the attention of porters and labourers as they loaded, unloaded or opened the jars. Numerous examples have been discovered in Jerusalem and other sites.[66]

Apart from royal authority, Greek was used for public notices even in the Temple at Jerusalem. Warnings to foreigners against entering the sacred enclosure were posted, appropriately, in Greek and Latin, according to Josephus. One complete specimen in Greek on a stone block was identified in 1871, a fragment of another was unearthed in 1935.[67] The letters of the latter still have traces of the red paint that made them stand out against the creamy-white stone so that no one

Temple Mount, Preliminary Report of the Second and Third Seasons, 1969–1970', *Eretz Israel* 10 (1971), pp. 1-33 (17, 21, Pl. 23 [Hebrew]); Avigad, *Discovering Jerusalem*, pp. 94, 203; Hestrin, *Inscriptions Reveal*, nos. 229-232; R. de Vaux, *Archaeology and the Dead Sea Scrolls* (London: Oxford University Press, 1973), pp. 67-68. For another stone weight from year five of Agrippa I or II, see B. Overbeck, *Das Heilige Land: Antike Münzen und Siegel aus einem Jahrtausend jüdischer Geschichte* (Munich: Staatliche Münzsammlung, 1993), p. 13.

64. Y. Meshorer, 'A Stone Weight from the Reign of Herod', *IEJ* 20 (1970), pp. 97, 98; cf. A. Kushnir-Stein, 'An Inscribed Lead Weight from Ashdod: A Reconsideration', *ZPE* 105 (1995), pp. 81-84; Hestrin, *Inscriptions Reveal*, no. 228.

65. Weight: S. Qedar, 'Two Lead Weights of Herod Antipas and Agrippa II and the Early History of Tiberias', *Israel Numismatic Journal* 9 (1986–87), pp. 29, 30; cf. *Supplementum Epigraphicum Graecum* 38 (1988), no. 1646. Counters: Avigad, *Discovering Jerusalem*, pp. 193-94.

66. Mazar, 'Excavations in the Old City...Second and Third Seasons', Pl. 21; Hestrin, *Inscriptions Reveal*, nos. 219-23; D.T. Ariel, *Excavations at the City of David 1978–1985 Directed by Yigal Shiloh*. II. *Imported Stamped Amphora Handles, Coins, Worked Bone and Ivory, Glass* (Qedem, 30; Jerusalem: Hebrew University, 1990), pp. 13-98; Avigad, *Discovering Jerusalem*, p. 79.

67. Hestrin, *Inscriptions Reveal*, no. 169; Schürer, *History of the Jewish People*, II, pp. 284, 285.

Figure 20. *Stone weight inscribed in Greek 'year 32 of king Herod, benefac-*
tor, friend of Caesar; market-inspector, 3 minas'. Diameter: 11.6
cm; weight 1233 gm. Y. Meshorer, 'A Stone Weight from the Reign
of Herod', IEJ 20 (1970), pp. 97, 98. (Israel Antiquities Authority,
68-119; photograph by courtesy of the Israel Antiquities
Authority.)

could avoid their message: 'No Gentile may go beyond the partition
and boundary around the Temple. Whoever is caught will be responsible for his own ensuing death'. Part of a stone slab found outside the
Temple area records a gift made by a resident of Rhodes for laying a
pavement, perhaps in the Temple, apparently in Herod's twentieth
year.[68] The first book of Maccabees records the text of a national reso-
lution made in honour of Simon Maccabee which was 'engraved on
bronze tablets and set up in a prominent position within the precincts of
the temple' (1 Macc. 14.25-49). Whether the text was in Hebrew, Aramaic or Greek is not stated; Greek is a real possibility, for this was a
Greek mode of honouring distinguished men.

68. Isaac, 'A Donation for Herod's Temple, pp. 86-92; *Supplementum Epi-*
graphicum Graecum 33 (1983), no. 1277.

Under Roman rule Greek remained the normal language for official texts, although Latin might be used in certain circumstances (pp. 125-31). Most of the Greek inscriptions of the Roman emperors known from Palestine were erected after the Fall of Jerusalem, with one possible exception. That is the 'Nazareth Decree', a stone slab now in the Louvre with an inscription headed 'Ordinance of Caesar', prohibiting the disturbance of burials and imposing the death penalty for tomb-robbery. Its date is uncertain, the Caesar is not named, nor is its origin known. Nazareth is the place from which it was sent to a French collector. Although intensively discussed as a possible imperial counter to the Christian claim that Jesus rose from the grave, this stone stands in its own right as an example of the use of Greek in the Galilee region, probably in the first century AD.[69]

Longest of the Greek inscriptions from Jerusalem is one known as the Theodotus Inscription. It states

> Theodotus, son of Vettenus, priest and synagogue ruler, son and grand-son of a synagogue ruler, (re-)built the synagogue for reading the law and teaching the commandments, also the guest room and upstairs rooms and the water supplies as an inn for those from abroad in need, which his ancestors and the elders and Simonides founded.

The stone block was found during excavations directed by the French archaeologist R. Weill in 1913. At some time it had been taken from its position and placed in a disused cistern with other masonry blocks and column drums at the south end of the hill called 'The City of David'. The whole area had served as a quarry for the workmen building the Roman city of Aelia Capitolina in the second century AD, and nothing can be said of the building to which the block belonged, although ritual baths and fragments of walling uncovered nearby have been taken to be parts of the structure Theodotus refurbished. The archaeological indications that the area was unoccupied after the Fall of Jerusalem suggest

---

69. See B.M. Metzger, 'The Nazareth Inscription Once Again', in E.E. Ellis and E. Grässer (eds.), *Jesus und Paulus: Festschrift für Werner Georg Kümmel zum 70. Geburtstag* (Göttingen: Vandenhoeck & Ruprecht, 1975), pp. 221-38; recently E. Grzybek and M. Sordi, 'L'édit de Nazareth et la politique de Néron à l'égard des chrétiens', *ZPE* 120 (1998), pp. 279-91, argued that it was a decree of Nero against Christians in Judaea, while A. Giovannini and M. Hirot, 'L'inscription de Nazareth: nouvelle interprétation', *ZPE* 124 (1999), pp. 107-32, made a case for its origin in Asia Minor about 30 BC.

Figure 21. *Greek inscription recording the rebuilding of a synagogue and associated rooms by Theodotus, son of Vettenus, found in Jerusalem. First century* AD. *R. Weill,* La cité de David *(Paris: Geuthner, 1920), Pl. xxv. (Israel Department of Antiquities S842; photograph courtesy of the Israel Antiquities Authority.)*

the inscription belonged to an earlier building. In the circumstances, that cannot be certain; the block may even have been carried from another place. Comparison of the style of lettering with inscriptions that contain dates, found in Egypt and other countries, points to the first half of the first century AD as the most likely time for the engraving of this text. Furthermore, the donor commemorated had only two names, Theodotus Vettenus, whereas men named later in the first century would normally have had three. As realized soon after the discovery, the second name, the name of Theodotus's father, belongs to Etruria and was probably the name given to him as a freed slave. Overall, an early first-century date for this monument has strongest support, despite continuing proposals to place it later, in the second, which seems unlikely on historical grounds, or even in the fourth century AD.[70]

70. R. Weill, *La cité de David* (Paris: Geuthner, 1920), pp. 130, 186-96, Pl. xxv; recently discussed by R. Riesner, 'Synagogues in Jerusalem', in R. Bauckham (ed.), *Palestinian Setting: The Book of Acts in its First Century Setting* (5 vols.; Carlisle: Paternoster Press, 1995), IV, pp. 179-211, especially 192-200, and by K. Atkinson, 'On Further Defining the First-Century CE Synagogue: Fact or Fiction?', *NTS* 43

Figure 22. *Stamps on handles of amphorae imported from Greece, 2nd cen-*
tury BC, found in the Samaria region. The upper one bears the
name of the responsible official, Eucratides, the lower the name of
the potter, Aristion. (Private collection; photograph D.J. Restall.)

Palestinian Jewish Literature in Greek

Beyond the realm of royal and formal inscriptions, there is evidence for
Greek as a language for literature, both secular and sacred. Jews living
outside Palestine in the Mediterranean area wrote in Greek regularly,
the most prolific being Philo of Alexandria (c. 20/10 BC–AD 40/50). A
smaller number active in Palestine wrote in Greek, among the most
important being the historian Jason of Cyrene, whose five part history
of Antiochus Epiphanes' attack on Judaism was summarized in 2 Maccabees, late in the second century BC. Only short sections of other
works have survived, in quotations made by later authors. (One is
Eupolemus who retold the biblical narrative in an imaginative way in
the second century BC.[71]) The historian Josephus composed the first

(1997), pp. 491-502 (499); Dr W.E.H. Cockle kindly advised me on the palaeographic and onomastic aspects and Dr Irina Levinskaya reported that Dr Joyce
Reynolds considered the first century date probable.
    71. B.Z. Wacholder, *Eupolemus: A Study of Judaeo-Greek Literature* (Cincin-

version of his Jewish *War* in Aramaic, then the final form in Greek.[72] Religious books, written in Greek or translated from Hebrew or Aramaic, circulated in Palestine, for among the Dead Sea Scrolls are fragments of Greek renderings of books of the Pentateuch and of other works, some little known, like the Epistle of Jeremiah,[73] parts of the book of Enoch and others not yet identified, while a Greek version of the Minor Prophets, copied, it is thought, late in the first century BC, was found in a cave further south.[74] There are also small pieces of unidentified Greek literary texts beside the Hebrew literary manuscripts from caves occupied during the Second Revolt, some in late first century script. Whether they are local compositions or imports cannot be said.[75] While these Greek texts are very much in the minority among the Hebrew and Aramaic scrolls, they indicate an awareness of Greek and, presumably, the presence of people who could read them, even if they were not copied in the Qumran region but had been brought into the country from outside.

Greek in Daily Life
Those were the products or possessions of the educated who read books. Recognition of Greek is implicit in the range of fairly wealthy Jewish people who could afford to be buried in rock-cut tombs around Jerusalem and elsewhere. The stone ossuaries (see above, p. 96) often carry the dead person's name scratched with greater or lesser skill in Greek letters. Usually they were for identification; they were not epitaphs, tomb-stones, so they only give the name, either Greek ones, such as Ariston or Berenice, or Semitic ones in Greek form, like Simon or

nati: Hebrew Union College, 1974). For him and other authors, see Schürer, *History of the Jewish People*, III.1, pp. 470-704.

72. See T. Rajak, *Josephus: The Historian and his Society* (London: Gerald Duckworth, 1983), Chapter 7.

73. Baillet, Milik and de Vaux, *Les 'Petites Grottes' de Qumrân*, p. 143.

74. See P.W. Skehan, E. Ulrich and J.E. Sanderson, *Qumran Cave IV.4: Palaeo-Hebrew and Greek Biblical Manuscripts* (DJD, 9; Oxford: Clarendon Press, 1992), nos. 119-27, pls xxxviii-xlvii; E. Tov, *The Greek Minor Prophets Scroll from Nahal Hever (8HevXIIgr)* (DJD, 8; Oxford: Clarendon Press, 1990). A valuable discussion of the significance of these pieces is A.R.C. Leaney 'Greek Manuscripts from the Judaean Desert', in J.K. Elliott (ed.), *Studies in New Testament Language and Text: Essays in Honour of George D. Kilpatrick* (NovTSup, 44; Leiden: E.J. Brill, 1976), pp. 285-300.

75. Benoit, Milik and de Vaux, *Les Grottes de Murabba'ât*, pp. 234-38.

Joannes (= John) or Jesus.[76] A few ossuaries have more information. Some give a father's name, for example 'Maria daughter of Thenas', or place of origin, like 'Maria, wife of Alexander, from Capua', or add some other detail of interest, as 'Judah, son of Laganion, a proselyte'.[77] For Gospel studies the most interesting is an ossuary marked 'Alexander of Cyrene' in Hebrew and 'Alexander son of Simon' in Greek, a burial which may reasonably be identified as that of one of the sons of Simon of Cyrene who carried Jesus' cross (Mk 15.21). In one case a reason for fame is noted: 'Bones of the sons of Nicanor the Alexandrian who made the doors' in Greek, the names Nicanor and Alexas being written also in Hebrew script. The reference is almost certainly to the magnificent doors embellished with Corinthian bronze which the Mishnah reports Nicanor of Alexandria presented to the Temple.[78] (For the bilingualism indicated, see Chapter 5.)

Figure 23. *Ossuary inscribed with the name John in Greek, Herodian period. (Israel Museum; photograph David Townsend and Lion Publishing.)*

76. For this material see *CII*; J.P. Kane, 'The Ossuary Inscriptions of Jerusalem', *JSS* 23 (1978), pp. 268-82; Rahmani, *Catalogue, passim.*

77. *CII*, nos. 1284, 1385.

78. For the Cyrenaican and the Nicanor ossuaries, see Kane, 'The Ossuary Inscriptions'.

Discoveries in caves in the Judaean desert and excavations at Masada have produced the clearest examples of Greek in everyday use in Jewish communities. From the caves near the Dead Sea south of Qumran scores of papyrus documents have been recovered, most of them dating from the end of the first century and the early decades of the second, having been hidden during the Bar Kochba or Second Revolt (132–35). Noteworthy is the archive of a lady named Babatha, containing 35 papyri, written between 93 and 132, of which two dozen are in Greek. There are deeds of gift, purchase and sale, marriage and court documents, letters and a copy of an extract from the minutes of Petra city council.[79] Another group of documents of the same date belonged to a second lady.[80] Although none of the Greek papyri carries a date before AD 70, there is no reason to suppose a major change occurred then that would greatly affect the styles of legal deeds, so the material can be taken as a good reflection of documentary activity throughout the Herodian period.

At Masada it was difficult to tell whether objects found belonged to the time when Herod's palace flourished, to the following decades, to the years of the Jewish Revolt when the Sicarii occupied the fortress, or to the Roman garrison that took it over from them. A few pieces are clearly dated to Herod's reign (see below, p. 128). There are some five dozen pots or pieces of pots with notes painted on them which are more likely to come from Herod's reign than from later years. Mostly they bear owners' names, both Greek (among them Simon, Zenon, Diodotos, Beryllos) and Jewish (examples are Shimeon, Eleazar, Hillel, Johanan), some with words describing the jars' contents as of good quality. One group of jars has the owner's name in both Greek and Hebrew (see Chapter 5, pp. 136-37). Slightly later may be a piece of a letter on papyrus concerning the despatch of goods, including lettuces, and a scrap of a deed on leather apparently carrying a date between 25 and 35. This scrap may relate to the same person as the sender of the letter.

---

79. For these Greek texts see Cotton, Cockle and Millar, 'The Papyrology of the Roman Near East'; N. Lewis and J.C. Greenfield (eds.), *The Documents from the Bar Kokhba Period in the Cave of Letters*. I. *Greek Papyri* (Jerusalem: Israel Exploration Society, 1989).

80. H.M. Cotton, 'The Archive of Salome Komiase, Daughter of Levi: Another Archive from the "Cave of Letters" ', *ZPE* 105 (1995), pp. 171-208 and Cotton and Yardeni, *Aramaic, Hebrew and Greek Documentary Texts*, pp. 60-64, no. 12, pp. 158-237, nos 60-65.

The contents of other fragments of Greek papyri, written by the inhabitants of Masada before its capture, perhaps by its Jewish defenders, are too small to identify. Ostraca may withstand the elements better than papyri, although the ink may be washed off, and, in fact, some 20 Greek ostraca were uncovered on Masada and attributed to the period of the First Revolt (66–73/4). They are brief orders for supplying wheat or barley, such as 'Give seven measures of wheat to the donkey drivers, for baking' (or 'for the kitchen'), lists of names with sums of money beside them, single names and letters of the alphabet in order. A large number of small sherds were marked with both Greek and Hebrew letters, apparently serving as tokens (see Chapter 5, p. 137).

Figure 24. *Greek ostracon from the Jewish garrison on Masada, 'Give to Kosmas for baking(?), each(?), one kabos, baking(?) two'. (Reproduced from H.M. Cotton and J. Geiger,* Masada II, *Pl. 13, no. 773, by courtesy of H.M. Cotton and the Israel Exploration Society.)*

People scratched their names on pots and pans elsewhere and examples in Greek were unearthed in Jerusalem,[81] and craftsmen used Greek letters as numerals to ensure that structural elements were erected in the correct order.[82]

81. Avigad, *Discovering Jerusalem*, pp. 202, 203.
82. Avigad, *Discovering Jerusalem*, p. 165, a Greek letter on masonry; for other

To summarize, the attested presence of Greek in Palestine from the third century BC onwards and the variety of texts available from the Herodian period implies that there were few parts of the country where some knowledge of the language could not be found. The land is small and there was a lot of travel—as the Gospels alone illustrate—so Aramaic-speaking Jews easily met and mixed with people who used Greek, in many cases living side by side. In the towns and villages the activities of pedlars and merchants, tax-collectors and government officials, Herod's foreign troops and Roman legionaries would often demand enough Greek from the local people for market-place negotiations. Even where there were determinedly Hebrew or Aramaic speaking communities, they could not isolate themselves from all contact with Greek, as the Greek books belonging to the strictly religious community who owned the Dead Sea Scrolls demonstrates.[83]

3. *Hebrew*

The language of many books of the Bible reflects the Hebrew used in Judah during the eighth and seventh centuries BC. Books from the fifth century BC and after, such as Ezra, Nehemiah, Esther and Chronicles, display a clearly later form with shifts in grammar, syntax and vocabulary, some of them being the consequences of continuous exposure to Aramaic. Despite the dominance of Aramaic, Hebrew did not die out. A major book, the Wisdom of Ben Sira, produced in the first quarter of the second century BC, proves that Hebrew was still being written and evidently understood in Palestine then. When, near the end of the century, the author's grandson published a Greek translation that was done in Egypt. The translation was included in the Septuagint as Ecclesiasticus and so passed into early Christian Bibles, whereas the Hebrew text

references see S. Gibson and J.E. Taylor, *Beneath the Church of the Holy Sepulchre* (London: Palestine Exploration Fund, 1994), pp. 21-23.

83. Discussions about the use of Greek in first century Palestine over the past century have been hampered by lack of information; the enormous increase of first hand material over the past thirty years has enabled this study to reach a clearer view, one already appearing in more recent works, notably J.N. Sevenster, *Do You Know Greek? How Much Greek could the First Jewish Christians Have Known?* (NovTSup, 19; Leiden: E.J. Brill, 1968) and J.A. Fitzmyer, 'The Languages of Palestine in the First Century A.D.', in *idem, A Wandering Aramean: Collected Aramaic Essays* (Missoula, MT: Scholars Press, 1979), pp. 29-56, reprinted from *CBQ* 32 (1970), pp. 501-31.

did not gain scriptural status in Jewish circles and, although current in the early Middle Ages, eventually ceased to be copied. It was lost until the end of the nineteenth century when some pages of mediaeval date were found in Cairo, among the discarded writings which had accumulated in the Genizah or store-room of an old synagogue (see Chapter 7, p. 191). More recently, fragments have been identified among the Dead Sea Scrolls and parts of a copy were recovered at Masada.[84] Other books composed in Hebrew but preserved only in the Septuagint in Greek and in later translations include the apocryphal or deutero-canonical books Baruch and the Letter of Jeremiah, Judith, Susanna, Bel and the Dragon, the Prayer of Azariah and 1 Maccabees, with others surviving outside any Scriptural canon, the *Martyrdom of Isaiah*, the *Assumption of Moses*.

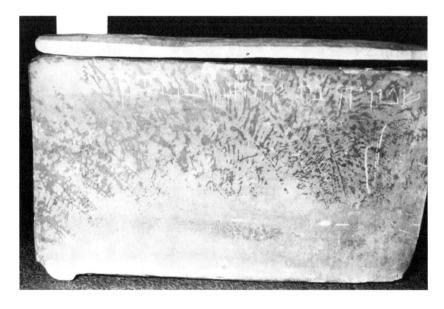

Figure 25.   *Ossuary inscribed with the name of Shitrat, daughter of Jehohanan (= John) in Hebrew, Herodian period. (Israel Museum; photograph David Townsend and Lion Publishing.)*

84. See P.W. Skehan and A.A. Di Lella, *The Wisdom of Ben Sira* (AB, 39; New York: Doubleday, 1987).

The Dead Sea Scrolls have shown that there was a great deal more literary activity in Hebrew during this period than had been thought before their discovery. They have yielded pieces of several books otherwise known only in translation, such as some of the *Testaments of the Twelve Patriarchs* and the book of *Jubilees*. More significantly, they have provided a variety of works lost for almost 2000 years.

The Scrolls belonged to a puritanical Jewish sect which drew recruits from all over the world, hence the manuscripts may stem from various places, not all were necessarily written or copied in Palestine or at Qumran. It is likely, however, that many of the Hebrew ones were produced in Judaea, mostly at Qumran. The biblical manuscripts kept ancient Hebrew before the sectaries' eyes and so they tried to imitate it in some of their own writings, coming close to the later stage of biblical Hebrew, although there are clear differences.[85] Beside those books, one composition in particular, 'Some Precepts of the Law' (abbreviated as *MMT = Miqṣat Ma'aśeh Ha-Torah*, see below, Chapter 8), is written in another style which may be closer to the Hebrew actually spoken in the sect and, perhaps, by other Jews. The rabbinic compilation of oral law, the Mishnah, is also written in Hebrew (Mishnaic Hebrew), but a type of Hebrew markedly different from the biblical and distinct from the literary language of the Scrolls. At one time scholars thought Mishnaic Hebrew was an artificial language, an attempt to resurrect Hebrew for teaching purposes by Hebraizing Aramaic. Before the Dead Sea Scrolls were found that hypothesis had been disproved.[86] Now, the Scrolls, and the documents deposited during the Second, Bar Kochba, Revolt, demonstrate that Hebrew was a living language, in use for literary and everyday documents, and in more than one dialect, with *MMT* and the list of hidden treasure engraved on the Copper Scroll sharing many features with Mishnaic Hebrew.

The books of the sect cover a wide range, although all are religious works. Application of biblical law to daily life resulted in compilations of rules for behaviour (Hebrew *halachâ*) and a special regulations for

85. See E. Qimron, *The Hebrew of the Dead Sea Scrolls* (Harvard Semitic Studies, 29; Atlanta: Scholars Press, 1986).

86. See M.H. Segal, *A Grammar of Mishnaic Hebrew* (Oxford: Clarendon Press, 1927); E.Y. Kutscher, 'Hebrew Language, Mishnaic', *EncJud* XVI, cols. 1590-1607 and *A History of the Hebrew Language* (Jerusalem: Magnes Press, 1982), Chapter 6.

the community (the *Manual of Discipline* or *Rule of the Community and the Damascus Document*). Biblical exegesis in the light of current events produced sentence by sentence commentaries (Hebrew *peshārîm*) and rewritings of the sacred texts explaining obscurities or elaborating on the simple original, while some compositions are an amalgam of biblical passages and sectarian ideas, such as the *Temple Scroll*, effectively new 'Scriptures', although their status in the community is not clear. These writers also composed poetry, hymns and prayers for worship on general occasions and on particular festivals, on the lines of the Psalms and prayers for protection. The tradition of giving wise advice, seen in Ben Sira, was continued and there are fragments of horoscopes and calendars to show when the festivals would fall and which priestly families should serve in the temple. In all about 800 manuscripts were recovered from 10 caves, the majority of them in small pieces and very far from complete, nevertheless, relics of a library unexpectedly large for an association of exclusive and strict first century Palestinian Jews.[87] The Ben Sira pieces and other fragments of Hebrew scrolls excavated at Masada hint at the books available in other circles. They include biblical books (Genesis, Leviticus, Deuteronomy, Ezekiel, Psalms), 'Songs for the Sabbath Sacrifice' also present in the Dead Sea Scrolls, one like the book of *Jubilees* and others apparently on biblical topics, too fragmentary to identify.[88]

Hebrew kept a role as a nationalistic symbol. Bronze coins issued by the Hasmonaean kings bore their names and titles in Hebrew. The earliest, coins of Alexander Jannaeus (103–76 BC), bear the words 'King Jonathan' or 'Jonathan the High Priest and the Council of the Jews' and his successors' are similar. For Jannaeus a chance find has produced impressions on clay of two seals, one reading 'Jonathan, the king', the

---

87. Eleven caves were found to contain ancient manuscripts, but one, Cave Seven, had only Greek papyri in it, see Ch. 1, p. 38, Ch. 2, p. 54. For translations of the major texts see G. Vermes, *The Dead Sea Scrolls in English* (Harmondsworth: Penguin Books, 1995); for a more comprehensive translation see García Martínez, *Dead Sea Scrolls Translated*.

88. See C. Newsom, *Songs of the Sabbath Sacrifice: A Critical Edition* (Harvard Semitic Studies, 27; Missoula, MT: Scholars Press, 1985); S. Talmon, 'Fragments of Scrolls from Masada', *Eretz Israel* 20 (1989), pp. 278-86 (Hebrew) and 'Hebrew Written Fragments from Masada', *Dead Sea Discoveries* 3 (1996), pp. 168-77.

other 'Jonathan the High Priest, Jerusalem'.[89] On the coins and on the seals, the texts are written with the letters of the Phoenician or Old Hebrew alphabet, a legacy from the time of the Monarchy, not in the 'square' script from which mediaeval and modern Hebrew writing developed, and which grew out of the handwriting of the Persian imperial administration adopted for Hebrew during the Exile. Most of the Dead Sea Scrolls are in the 'square' script, but the divine name (YHWH, Jehovah) is written in the old letters in some, and a few whole books were copied and, presumably, read in the Old Hebrew letters as shown by a lengthy section of Leviticus and other pieces of the Bible.[90] One fragment of papyrus recovered at Masada, inscribed on both sides in this script, the writing on the back being a reuse, mentions Mt Gerizim and may be of Samaritan origin.[91] In fact, the Samaritans have maintained a form of this script as their own to this day.

Hebrew Inscriptions

Perhaps it is not surprising that there were notices in Hebrew in the Temple in Jerusalem, the heart of Jewish identity. The excavations outside the southern and western sides recovered small fragments of carefully engraved slabs, but the letters remaining are too few to give the sense. There is also one piece of an inscription in the Old Hebrew script, again, too little to show its content, except that someone son of someone was named.[92] More intelligible is a large block which lay among fallen masonry at the south-west corner of the temple. It originally belonged at the top of a wall, most likely at that corner, for it bears the words, in the square script, 'To the place of trumpeting, for x[…]' and Josephus recorded that the signal for the start of the Sabbath

89. For the coins see Meshorer, *Ancient Jewish Coinage*, I; for the impressions see N. Avigad, 'A Bulla of King Jonathan', *IEJ* 25 (1975), pp. 245-46 and 'A Bulla of Jonathan the High Priest', *IEJ* 25 (1975), pp. 8-12, and *Discovering Jerusalem*, p. 77.

90. Baillet, Milik and de Vaux, *Les 'Petites Grottes' de Qumran*, pp. 105, 106; Skehan, Ulrich and Sanderson, *Qumran Cave IV.4*; D.N. Freedman and K.A. Matthews, *The Paleo-Hebrew Leviticus Scroll* (Winona Lake, IN: Eisenbrauns for the American Schools of Oriental Research, 1985).

91. Talmon, 'Fragments of Scrolls', pp. 283-84, no. 320-1039.

92. B. Mazar, 'The Archaeological Excavations near the Temple Mount', in Y. Yadin (ed.), *Jerusalem Revealed* (trans. R. Grafman; Jerusalem: Israel Exploration Society, 1976), pp. 25-40.

Figure 26.   *Hebrew letters and numerals to guide builders in erecting columns*
           of Herod's palace at Masada. Above M1 = 41, below M4 = 44.
           (Reproduced from G. Foerster, Masada V, *90, no. 142, 91 no. 143,*
           by courtesy of G. Foerster and the Israel Exploration Society.)

was a trumpet blast from the Temple roof (*War* 4.580-83).[93] Whatever
other monuments stood in Herodian Jerusalem bearing dedications or
instructions in Hebrew have disappeared.

Opposite the temple, near the foot of the Mount of Olives, wealthy
priests constructed three fine tombs early in the first century BC. The

---

93. B. Mazar, 'Herodian Jerusalem in the Light of the Excavations South and
Southwest of the Temple Mount', *IEJ* 28 (1978), pp. 230-37 (234); A. Demsky,
'When the Priests Trumpeted the Onset of the Sabbath', *BAR* 12.6 (1986), pp. 50-
52.

two outer ones are called Zechariah's Tomb and Absalom's Tomb to-day. In the centre one the owners ensured the dead would not be forgotten by having the names of six brothers and two of their cousins, all members of the Hezir family (see 1 Chron. 24.15), engraved above the entrance:

> This is the tomb and memorial of Eleazar, Hania, Joezer, Judah, Simeon, Johanan, sons of Joseph son of Obed. Joseph and Eleazar, sons of Hania, priests of the Benei Hezir.[94]

Hebrew in Daily Life

As they did in Aramaic and in Greek, so members of families in Jerusalem scratched the names of their dead relatives in Hebrew on ossuaries. Scores have been unearthed, bearing names alone, or with relationships, 'Jehohanan (= John) son of Hezqiel', 'Judith daughter of Nadab',[95] or with other particulars, 'Judah, the scribe',[96] but the Hebrew notices are less informative than those in Aramaic and Greek, perhaps because they refer to local people only.

As with Aramaic, so with Hebrew, we may assume legal and business documents were being written in the first century, although only a few scraps may attest them (see above, p. 92). Apart from the examples from Masada (see Chapter 5, p. 136), there are also a few ostraca from the first century in Hebrew. Excavations at Khirbet Qumran in 1996 recovered two broken pieces of an ostracon lying against the outside of the enclosure wall. Enough remains of the Hebrew text to show it records a deed of gift made in the second year (of a missing period) by a man named Honi in Jericho. It seems he gave an estate, including house, fig trees and perhaps palm trees and a slave, to another man, Eleazar son of N... whose title is lacking.[97] This ostracon, whether written as a draft or as the deed itself, is a significant example of the currency of Hebrew for a legal purpose in the first century AD. At Herodium an ostracon was found which was an exercise, bearing two complete alphabets on one face and part of another on the back. An

---

94. Hestrin, *Inscriptions Reveal*, no. 173.
95. See Rahmani, *Catalogue*, nos. 218, 572.
96. *CII*, no. 1308
97. F.M. Cross and E. Eshel, 'Ostraca from Khirbet Qumrân', *IEJ* 47 (1997), pp. 17-28, re-edited, with different readings, A. Yardeni, 'A Draft of a Deed on an Ostracon from Khirbet Qumran', *IEJ* 47 (1997), pp. 233-37.

alphabet and a list of personal names occur on another sherd acquired through the antiquities trade and dated late in the century.[98] Two jar fragments, also from Herodium, have incomplete Hebrew texts painted on them, referring, apparently to hiding places, and there are jars from the Qumran building and nearby caves with words on them in ink, either personal names or short messages.[99]

Various pots and pans, vessels of clay and of stone bear words or names in the square script, so may be either Aramaic or Hebrew, thus an inscribed potsherd found in the Galilaean town of Jotapata is listed as 'an ostracon with a brief inscription in Jewish script' of the first century BC or AD.[100] The presence of the Hebrew words for 'son', *bēn* and 'wife of', *'ēsheth*, may distinguish some as Hebrew, for example, a pot-stand dug up in Jerusalem belonged to a Ben Jason. The lid of one of the ossuaries found in a tomb at Bethphage carries a list of names mostly in the form 'son of X' (*ben* x), each followed by amounts thought to be their pay for a day's work, possibly in making the ossuaries. The majority of the men are listed by surname, for example 'son of Jehohanan', a few by their own names, such as 'Joseph', one by both, 'Simeon son of Shaltu' and a few are described as 'Galilean' or, in one case, 'Babylonian'.[101]

Greek letters had long been used as numerals and, probably from the second century BC. Hebrew letters were employed in the same way.[102]

98. E. Testa, *Herodion*, IV. I, *Graffiti e gli ostraca* (Jerusalem: Franciscan Printing Press, 1972), no. 53; E. Puech, 'Abécédaire et liste alphabétique de noms hébreux du début du IIe s. A.D.', *RB* 87 (1980), pp. 118-26.

99. J. Naveh, 'The Inscriptions', in E. Netzer (ed.), *Greater Herodium* (Qedem, 13; Jerusalem: Hebrew University, 1981), p. 71; R. de Vaux and J.T. Milik, *Qumrân Grotte 4.II (Archéologie et 4Q128-4Q157)* (DJD, 6; Oxford: Clarendon Press, 1977), p. 15.

100. D. Adam-Rayewitz, M. Aviam and D.R. Edwards, 'Yodafat 1992', *IEJ* 45 (1995), pp. 191-97 (195).

101. For vessels unearthed in Jerusalem, see Mazar, 'The Excavations…Second and Third Seasons', p. 17, Pl. 25; 'Ben Jason' sherd: Avigad, *Discovering Jerusalem*, p. 202; others Hestrin, *Inscriptions Reveal*, nos. 244-47; Bethphage lid: J.T. Milik, 'Le couvercle de Bethphagé', in A. Caquot and M. Philonenko (eds.), *Hommages à A. Dupont-Sommer* (Paris: Adrien-Maisonneuve, 1971), pp. 75-94; see also Naveh, *On Sherd*, pp. 68, 69 (sherds), 50 (lid).

102. A. Millard, 'Strangers from Egypt and Greece: The Signs for Numbers in Early Hebrew', in K. van Lerberghe and A. Schoors (eds.), *Immigration and Emigration within the Ancient Near East: Festschrift E. Lipiński* (Orientalia Lovaniensia Analecta, 65; Leuven: Peeters, 1995), pp. 189-94.

At Masada Herod's masons marked column drums so that they should be correctly assembled. They usually carry a single letter in the square script followed by vertical strokes for numbers up to eight, and the practice is attested elsewhere.[103] In a tomb outside Jerusalem the slabs covering a burial were kept in order in the same way.[104]

4. *Latin*

'Pilate had a notice prepared and fastened to the cross. It read JESUS OF NAZARETH, THE KING OF THE JEWS…and the sign was written in Aramaic, Latin and Greek' (Jn 19.19, 20).

The presence of Latin, the official language of the ruling power in Palestine, beside Aramaic, Greek and Hebrew, has received less attention, for there has been little evidence for its currency in comparison with the other three.[105] If the ordinary citizens of Judaea, Samaria and Galilee knew of Latin, few are likely to have learnt to speak or read it actively. It is often assumed educated Roman government officials and military commanders commonly spoke and wrote Greek, Latin had little role in their work. Thus a standard textbook states, 'in Palestine… Latin made no major inroads until the later period of the empire', then shows how it might appear occasionally in notices set up by imperial authorities.[106] Three cases are reported in Josephus' *Antiquities*, edicts of Caesar and of Mark Antony, all with parallel Greek versions. To them is to be added the famous notice at the Temple enclosure in Jerusalem, which warned Gentiles against entering the sacred area (see above, p. 109). None of these monuments has survived. There is, however, the well-known inscription of Pilate found at Caesarea in 1961,

---

103. G. Foerster, *Masada* .V. *Art and Architecture* (Jerusalem: Israel Exploration Society, 1997), pp. 80-99, with references to examples from other sites.

104. G. Avni and Z. Greenhut, *The Akeldama Tombs* (Jerusalem: Israel Antiquities Authority, 1996), pp. 12, 13; S. Gutman, *Gamla: A City in Revolt* (Jerusalem: Ministry of Defence, 1994), pp. 61, 126 (Hebrew).

105. This section is an adaptation of an essay 'Latin in First Century Palestine', in Z. Zevit, S. Gitin and M. Sokoloff (eds.), *Solving Riddles and Untying Knots: Biblical, Epigraphic and Semitic Studies in Honor of Jonas C. Greenfield* (Winona Lake, IN: Eisenbrauns, 1995), pp. 451-58, used by courtesy of the publisher.

106. See Schürer, *History of the Jewish People*, II, p. 80. For a summary account of Latin in first-century Palestine see Fitzmyer, 'The Languages of Palestine in the First Century A.D.'.

which originally bore a dedication in honour of Tiberius by PONTIUS PILATUS PRAEFECTUS IUDAEAE, 'Pontius Pilate, prefect of Judaea'.[107] 'But the spread of Latin in Palestine in the early period of Roman rule did not extend far beyond official uses of this kind.'[108] In 1997 archaeologists uncovered a mosaic pavement in a room forming part of the administrative quarters of the governor's seat at Caesarea. In the centre of the floor is a simple frame enclosing the words SPES BONA AD VIORIBUS OFFICI CUSTODIAR. 'Good prospects to the assistants of the prison office'.[109] All these display Latin as the language of the ruling power, and that, presumably, was the governor's intention in writing the title for Jesus' cross in Latin (Jn 19.19, 20). In daily life the most familiar occurrence of Latin was the legends on imperial coins, mainly the silver *denarius* and, for the wealthy, the gold *aureus*. The 'tribute penny' shown to Jesus at his request (Mt. 22.19-21) was such a *denarius*, with the emperor's titles in Latin around his bust, TI. CAESAR DIVI AUG. F. AUGUSTUS and on the reverse, PONTIF. MAXIM. 'Ti(berius) Caesar, son of divine Aug(ustus), Augustus, High Priest'.

Roman soldiers, it might be thought, would speak Latin. This was true for many, but before the Jewish Revolt of AD 67–73, the garrisons in Palestine were drawn mainly from local non-Jewish residents, with some from nearby territories. They would have spoken Greek or Aramaic. Only after the Fall of Jerusalem was the Tenth Legion Fretensis stationed in the land, stamping its name on tiles made for its forts and using Latin more generally. Before that time the number of Latin speakers in the land was small. While the governors, who came from the educated equestrian class, certainly knew and used Latin, they probably spoke Greek and read Greek as freely and easily. If we could uncover the private bookshelves of Pilate or one of his colleagues, it might hold a few scrolls of Homer, Plato or Euripides, as well as Latin works. Among the latter might be a copy of the recently published patriotic work which Vergil had finished about 19 BC to honour the emperor Augustus, the *Aeneid*. All this is speculation; the only place where books belonging to high officials might be found today is Egypt, but even there the great stores of papyrus manuscripts do not come

107. Hestrin, *Inscriptions Reveal*, no. 216.
108. Schürer, *History of the Jewish People*, II, p. 80.
109. Reported in *Jerusalem Post*, 20 September 1997, with reading of the text in a letter from R.F. Harper, 27 September 1997.

from the main centre of government, Alexandria, their provenances are outlying provincial centres and villages, so they only reveal the books lesser officials were reading. The Latin works among them are very few.

Figure 27. *Latin inscription from Caesarea naming Pontius Pilate. (Israel Museum 61-529; photograph courtesy of the Israel Museum.)*

Yet there were some humbler people who had knowledge of Latin in first-century Palestine. They were servants in the household of Herod. Evidence for this surprising fact comes from the excavations at Masada. A large number of inscribed potsherds came to light, the majority with Aramaic, Hebrew or Greek on them.[110] Some were pieces of large wine jars. These amphorae were specially labelled: C. SENTIO SATURNINO CONSULE PHILONIANUM DE L. LAENI FUNDO REGI HERODI IUDAICI, 'In the consulate

110. Y. Yadin, J. Naveh and Y. Meshorer, *Masada*. I. *The Aramaic and Hebrew Ostraca and Jar Inscriptions. The Coins of Masada* (Jerusalem: Israel Exploration Society, 1989); H.M. Cotton and J. Geiger, *Masada*. II. *The Latin and Greek Documents* (Jerusalem: Israel Exploration Society, 1989). The pieces mentioned here are *Masada*, II, pp. 140-58, nos. 804-816 and 166-167, no. 826; 139, no. 800; 163-164, no. 822.

of C. Sentius Saturninus, Philonian wine from the estate of L. Laenius, for Herod the Jewish king.' The wine merchants or shippers in Italy naturally wrote in their own language. When the wine reached King Herod's cellars, his butler, at least, would need to know enough Latin to select the vintage his master demanded or liked. Jars labelled with consular dates for four years were found: Saturninus's of 19 BC, others from 27, 26 and 14 BC. The same need faced others in Herod's kitchens, for one jar was found marked GARUM, 'salt fish sauce,' followed by 'of the king' in Greek. Bones of small herring and some anchovy found in another jar seem to be the residue from making *garum*, added as a paste to some dishes.[111] Another jar was marked ME, probably for *mel*, 'honey,' and a third MAL, for *mala,* 'apples,' with CUM in the next line, thought to denote CUMANA, i.e. 'from Cumae'. It is not hard to imagine the servant's terror if, unable to distinguish the words, he served the tyrant the sweet or the fruit when he expected the savoury! Masada was only one of Herod's many castles, so similar supplies almost certainly went into the stores and cellars in Caesarea, Jerusalem, Herodium and the others, requiring servants there to recognize their labels. Trade and migration brought some Latin speakers to Judaea who died there. One ossuary bears the name MARION in Latin letters, another IOHANA.[112]

Latin, then, could be seen written in early first-century Palestine in very formal, Roman contexts, in the more well-to-do areas of the markets, or where expensive luxuries were imported from Italy—for Herod's life-style was not restricted to him alone, as the imported pottery and glassware found in houses of wealthy citizens in Jerusalem reveal. They drank foreign wines, too, for amphora handles were unearthed bearing stamps in Latin, one 'from the imperial potteries' being evidence of trade with Italy.[113]

After AD 70, Roman soldiers conducted business in Latin and might read books in Latin. At Masada, papyrus fragments indicating both activities lay in the ruined buildings which belonged to the Roman garrison.

---

111. On *garum* see R.L. Curtis, *Garum and Salsamenta: Production and Commerce in Materia Medica* (Studies in Ancient Medicine, 3; Leiden: E.J. Brill, 1991). H. Cotton, O. Lernau and Y. Goren, 'Fish Sauces from Herodian Masada', *Journal of Roman Archaeology* 9 (1996), pp. 123-28, describe the bone deposit.

112. Rahmani, *Catalogue*, nos. 202, 497.

113. Avigad, *Discovering Jerusalem*, pp. 202, 203.

Figure 28. *Roman amphorae found at Masada, labelled in Latin with the vintage of wine 'for Herod the Judaean king'. (Reproduced from H.M. Cotton and J. Geiger,* Masada II, *pl. 19, nos. 804, 805 by courtesy of H.M. Cotton and the Israel Exploration Society.)*

Figure 29. *Part of an amphora from Masada, labelled 'garum' (fish sauce). (Reproduced from H.M. Cotton and J. Geiger,* Masada II, *pl. 24, no. 826, by courtesy of H.M. Cotton and the Israel Exploration Society.)*

They included a legionary's note of pay received and expenses paid, parts of four letters, a piece listing sick men, bandages and medicaments, and fragments bearing only a few words or characters. Beside those mundane papers was a strip of papyrus with a line of Vergil's *Aeneid* on one side and a line of an unidentified work on the other.[114]

Masada's manuscripts can be studied today because of the accidents of their preservation in the arid climate and their discovery; even so, they are surely only a small part of the documents that once existed there. When only a single find is made like this, it is impossible to draw general conclusions. The garrison at Masada was not unique in its day, writing of the same sort could have been commonplace among all first-century Roman garrisons, as, indeed, probability suggests it was. For

114. Cotton and Geiger, *Masada*, II, pp. 31-35, no. 721.

the next centuries discoveries in other parts of the empire, notably Vindolanda in Britain and Mons Claudianus in Egypt, assure us that this was indeed the case, even to lines of Vergil.[115]

Herodian Palestine was host, it is now clear, not only to indigenous Semitic, Hebrew and Aramaic, writing, with some Nabataean, but also to books and documents in Greek and Latin. Leather and papyrus rolls, wooden tablets, waxed tablets and potsherds were all brought into service as writing materials, the last being freely available.

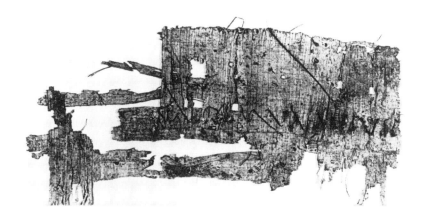

Figure 30. *Papyrus fragment bearing part of line 9 from Vergil's* Aeneid, *Book 4, found at Masada, dated about AD 70. (Reproduced from H.M. Cotton and J. Geiger,* Masada II, *pl. 1, no. 721, by courtesy of H.M. Cotton and the Israel Exploration Society.)*

115. Bowman and Thomas, *The Vindolanda Writing-Tablets*, pp. 65-67; W.E.H. Cockle, 'Writing and Reading Exercises', in J. Bingen *et al.*, *Mons Claudianus: Ostraca Graeca et Latina I (O. Claud. 1 à 190)* (Cairo: Institut français d'Archéologie orientale, 1992), pp. 179-90 (no. 190).

Chapter 5

A POLYGLOT SOCIETY

The writings described so far illustrate the use of Aramaic and Hebrew, Greek and Latin in Herodian Palestine. In some societies languages may mark off one sector from another, intercourse being restricted to a few people who can interpret. That situation may have arisen from time to time in Palestine, for example between the Roman governors and some of their subjects, but there is evidence for a great amount of bilingualism in this period. Greek and Aramaic stand side by side on the dedication from Dan (Chapter 4, p. 87), Greek and Hebrew or Greek and Aramaic on the coins of Alexander Jannaeus (Chapter 4, pp. 87, 120), although those legends may have been aimed at different populations within his realm. Readers of the Dead Sea Scrolls could move between Hebrew and Aramaic and some to Greek. While that may be dismissed as part of the Jewish literary heritage and an aspect of an élite, exclusive sect, there are more mundane signs of bilingualism in the speech of daily life.

Although compiled after the fall of Jerusalem, the archive of the lady Babatha (see Chapter 4, p. 115) contains several deeds written in Greek with endorsements added in Aramaic or Nabataean or with summaries in either language, in one case itself translated into Greek. Some witnesses signed their names in Aramaic at the end of Greek texts, and some in Nabataean, as well as Greek. In one case, the earliest text, from year two of Nero (see Chapter 4, p. 92), two of the witnesses are titled 'witness' in Aramaic, the third in Hebrew. Here the mixture of the languages is patent in legal contexts.

The inscriptions on ossuaries discussed earlier are not in Aramaic or Hebrew or Greek alone, a number are bilingual. One has the same text in Hebrew and in Aramaic, for example, 'Simon the temple-builder'.[1]

1.   J. Naveh, 'The Ossuary Inscriptions from Giv'at Ha-Mivtar', *IEJ* 20 (1970), pp. 33-37; Fitzmyer and Harington, *Palestinian Aramaic Texts*, no. 85; Beyer, *Die aramäischen Texte*, p. 344, yJE25.

Figure 31. *Greek deed concerning the sale of a date crop, endorsed in Aramaic and Nabataean, AD 130. (Reproduced from N. Lewis,* The Documents from the Bar-Kokhba Period in the Cave of Letters, Greek Papyri *(1989) Pl. 27, no. 22 by courtesy of N. Lewis and the Israel Exploration Society.)*

On the ossuary of the sons of Nicanor (Chapter 4, p. 114), below the main epitaph in Greek are the names 'Niqanor' and 'Alexas' in the Hebrew or Aramaic square script. Another has the names followed by a curse in Greek and above that the names alone in Hebrew. Names belonging to one language could be written in another, thus many Hebrew names occur in Greek forms and script, like ΙΗΣΟΥΣ for Jeshua or Jehoshua, 'Jesus, Joshua' or ΑΝΑΝΙΑΣ for Hananiah. Greek names like Athenagoras, Papias and Theophilos appear in square script and Latin names, like Julia, are written in Greek letters. A lady called Salona had her name on her ossuary in Greek followed by a description which is not Greek but a Semitic word written in Greek letters, *katana* (ΚΑΤΑΝΑ) 'little'.[2] The Greek name of one man, Theodotion, was cut in square script on one side of his ossuary, with his title 'teacher' in Greek on the other (ΔΙΔΑΣΚΑΛΟΣ).[3] The place of origin may be given in Semitic and Greek, as in the case of the lady whose ossuary is inscribed 'Julia of Asia' in Greek which is balanced by 'Johanna from Saba'a' in square script.[4] Similarly, one 'Ammiya' is described in Aramaic as 'a woman of Beth-Shan' but in Greek as 'from Scythopolis', the Hellenistic name for the only city of the Decapolis west of the Jordan river, illustrating neatly the parallel use of the languages and the place names.[5] The bones of a man from Beth-Shan were put in an ossuary with notices in Hebrew and Greek, 'Hanin of Beth-Shan' and 'Anin of Scythopolis' then, later, a note was added in Aramaic, 'Joseph son of Hanin, made it, our father is buried herein'.[6] One tomb near Jericho held 22 ossuaries, only eight of them nameless. The notices on the rest indicate the burials cover three generations of one family, two members, father and son, with the nickname Goliath. One man's ossuary had painted on it twice in Greek the information that he was a freedman of queen Agrippina, the mother of Nero, thought to be the wife and murderess of Claudius, thus giving an approximate date for the burial. (Nero had Agrippina assassinated in AD 59.) Although the reason why that and five other notices were written in Greek and four others only in

2.   Rahmani, *Catalogue*, no. 871.

3.   *CII*, no. 1266.

4.   Rahmani, *Catalogue*, no. 559; Puech, 'Inscriptions funéraires palestiniennes, pp. 522-23; Beyer, *Die aramäischen Texte, Ergänzungsband*, p. 207, yJE41.

5.   *CII*, no. 1372.

6.   Fitzmyer and Harrington, *Palestinian Aramaic Texts*, no. 145, with a different reading; Beyer, *Die aramäischen Texte*, p. 342, yJE16c.

Figure 32. *Inscriptions on an ossuary found on French Hill, Jerusalem. 'Mariam wife of Matyah' is painted in black in Hebrew. The same name is inscribed in Greek, followed by a curse that anyone who removes her bones be struck blind. The word for blindness is Hebrew, written in Greek letters,* ouroun *for* 'iwwarôn. *L.Y. Rahmani,* A Catalogue of Jewish Ossuaries in the Collections of the State of Israel *(1994), no. 559. (Photograph by courtesy of the Israel Antiquities Authority.)*

Aramaic while three are both in Aramaic and in Greek, cannot be discerned, this tomb presents the bilingual situation clearly.[7] A consequence of bilingualism is interference from one language to another and that is apparent on certain ossuaries. One, found north-east of Jerusalem, was marked for Johanna. Her name was repeated with the addition 'daughter of Johanan, son of the High Priest Theophilos'—her father held office from 37 to about 41 and was son of the High Priest Annas, familiar from the Gospels. His title is given in Hebrew although the words 'daughter' and 'son' are in Aramaic.[8]

The site that has contributed most to this topic is Masada. The Latin, Greek, Aramaic and Hebrew documents found there could come from separate groups of people, indeed, the Roman military papyri in Latin are distinct from the relics of the Jewish defenders. On the other hand, the Latin graffiti on jars in Herod's palace stores were hardly read by servants who habitually used Latin. It is the ostraca and labels on jars left by the rebels that demonstrate multilingualism most clearly. There are ostraca in Greek, Aramaic and Hebrew, as already described. Several large jars were marked in Hebrew, probably to indicate which rows in the store-room held contents approved as ritually pure, suitable for priests to use, and which did not. A few were marked 'holy' in Aramaic and one labelled 'A[nani]as the High Priest. Aqavia his son' in Aramaic. (The High Priest, Ananaias, who served from c. 47–59, was murdered in 66 as the First Revolt began; his son evidently escaped to Masada and took advantage of his father's title there.) Many jars are marked with their owners' names, such as 'Shimeon son of Joseph' in Aramaic, 'Joseph son of Eleazar' in Hebrew, where only the words for 'son' indicate the difference. With single names the distinction cannot be made in most cases. One group of jars has the name 'Zenon' painted on them in Greek letters and some of them have 'Shabyo' or 'Bar Jason' beside it in square script. A few other jars also had words in both scripts, but one or other is now illegible. The greatest excitement in the excavations at Masada was caused when 11 small sherds were uncovered lying near the gate to the water supply. Each bore a single name, Hebrew or Aramaic, one of them being 'Ben Yair' whom the excavator,

7.   R. Hachlili, 'The Goliath Family Tomb in Jericho: Funerary Inscriptions from a First Century A.D. Jewish Monumental Tomb', *BASOR* 235 (1979), pp. 31-65; Beyer, *Die aramäischen Texte, Ergänzungsband*, p. 348, yJE4.

8.   Rahmani, *Catalogue*, no. 871; Beyer, *Die aramäischen Texte, Ergänzungsband*, p. 206, yJE39.

Figure 33. *Part of a storage jar inscribed 'Zenon' in Greek and 'Shabyo' in Hebrew, from Masada. (Reproduced from H.M. Cotton, J. Geiger, Masada II, Pl. 35, no. 886 by courtesy of H.M. Cotton and the Israel Exploration Society.)*

Yigael Yadin, identified with Eleazar ben Yair, leader of the Zealots holding Masada against the Romans. As Josephus reports the last of the rebels drew lots to kill the remaining defenders, then themselves, Yadin concluded that the sherds were those lots. Further study in the light of all the inscribed potsherds from Masada throws great doubt on that imaginative idea. More sherds were found with names on them, in some cases followed by numerals, and these were almost certainly a sort of token. That is the explanation best fitting two other collections of sherds. One, with 80 sherds, has multiple examples of a single name, Jehohanan, Judah or Shimeon, followed by a letter in the Old Hebrew script and one in Greek, or one in the square script and one in the Old Hebrew. The second group has over 280 pieces, each carrying one or more letters in the square script, 16 with Old Hebrew letters and four with Old Hebrew and Greek letters. In the circumstances of the siege, where scores of families were confined, an equitable system of food distribution would be essential and these sherds would serve very well as ration coupons. The fact that many were found near the doorways of the store-houses adds strength to the argument.[9]

9. See J. Naveh in Yadin, Naveh and Meshorer, *Masada*, I, pp. 28-31, for these texts and their interpretation.

On Masada there were people who could use three scripts and write in three languages. Although it is impossible to be sure that a single man could write in Aramaic, Hebrew and Greek, bilingualism in the first two is certain, given the Jewish milieu, and bilingualism in Aramaic and Greek is hardly to be questioned.

The haphazardly preserved inscriptions and manuscripts of Herodian Palestine leave no room for doubt that all three languages were current, with Hebrew more widely used than many have allowed, and the documents from the second century add their support. Within the country's small area, with military garrisons posted in various strongholds, tax-collectors and customs officers active in many towns and with a high proportion of the population making a pilgrimage to Jerusalem at least occasionally, if not as often as the Evangelist states the Holy Family did (Lk. 2.41-52), the exposure of Aramaic-speakers to Greek would be unavoidable. If travel from Galilee to Jerusalem usually involved a detour to avoid Samaria (Mk 10.1), there would be contact with the Greek region of the Decapolis, where there is no reason to suppose everyone spoke Greek, despite the high degree of Hellenization, and where there were considerable numbers of Jewish inhabitants.

Beside these three principal languages of Herodian Palestine, other languages were spoken by foreigners who came to Jerusalem to settle there, or visited for trade or for worship. The presence of numerous pilgrims from Jewish communities throughout the world, especially at Passover time, brought a great variety of languages and consequent demand upon shopkeepers and guides to have some ability in some of them—a situation characteristic of the city still. (Estimates of the size of the population of Jerusalem and the number of pilgrims going there in the first century vary widely. Josephus alleged 2,500,000 came for Passover, a figure now considered far too high. The city's inhabitants may have numbered 100,000, according to a recent investigation, with as many as 1,000,000 arriving for the three major festivals during each year.[10]) The list of those present at Pentecost in Acts 2.5-11 gives some idea of the places pilgrims came from, covering most of the Diaspora,[11]

10. W. Reinhardt, 'The Population Size of Jerusalem and the Numerical Growth of the Jerusalem Church', in R. Bauckham (ed.), *Palestinian Setting: The Book of Acts in its First Century Setting* (5 vols.; Grand Rapids, MI: Eerdmans; Carlisle: Paternoster Press, 1995), IV, pp. 237-65.

11. See B.M. Metzger, 'Ancient Astrological Geography and Acts 2: 9-11', in W.W. Gasque and R.P. Martin (eds.), *Apostolic History and the Gospel: Biblical*

Figure 34. *Masada tokens or 'coupons', bearing two Hebrew letters, left* gb,
right šq, *below, left, a name 'Simeon' and two Hebrew letters, the
latter in Old Hebrew script,* šm'wn gd, *and, right, part of a jar
labelled 'fig cake'. (Reproduced from Y. Yadin, J. Naveh,* Masada
I, *pl. 1, no. 24, pl. 12, no. 274, pl. 19, no. 366, pl. 40, no. 524 by
courtesy of J. Naveh and the Israel Exploration Society.)*

and the different groups claim they heard the apostles' words in their
own languages. Very many of them from Asia Minor and Mesopotamia

and Historical Essays Presented to F. F. Bruce (Exeter: Paternoster Press, 1970),
pp. 123-33, reprinted in B.M. Metzger, *New Testament Studies: Philological, Versional, and Patristic* (Leiden: E.J. Brill, 1980), pp. 46-56.

probably spoke dialects of Aramaic, yet that need not detract from the marvel, for the dialects had distinctive features which would have made mutual intelligibility difficult, especially with differences of accentuation and pronunciation, matters that made Galilean speech strange to Jerusalemites according to Lk. 22.59, Acts 2.7 and rabbinic sources. If the 'seven different Western Aramaic dialects' which 'can be distinguished at the time of Jesus' were mutually understandable,[12] speakers of Eastern Aramaic dialects from Elymais (ancient Elam in western Iran), for example, probably found them almost incomprehensible.

The Language of Jesus

With such a variety of languages, what was the ordinary language of daily life which Jesus would have spoken? Each of the Gospels includes some words that are not Greek, some of them placed on Jesus' lips, and they had to be explained in Greek for the audience. They are:

abba	'father'	Mk 14.36
Ēloi, ēloi lama	'My God, my God,	Mk 15.34,
sabachthani	why have you forsaken me?'[13]	cf. Mt. 27.46
ephphatha	'be opened'	Mk 7.34
kēphas	'Rock'	Jn 1.42
messias	'the Christ'	Jn 1.41; 4.25
qorban	'a gift'	Mt. 27.6; Mk 7.11
rabbûni	'Master'	Mk 10.51; Jn 20.16
talitha qûm	'Little girl, rise up'	Mk 5.41.

There are other non-Greek words which stand without explanations:

amēn	'truly'	Mt. 5.18, etc., Mk 3.28, etc., Lk. 4.24, etc., Jn 1.51, etc.
Gehenna	'Hell'	Mt. 5.22*, 29, 30; 10.28; 18.9*; 23.15, 33; Mk 9.43*, 45, 47; Lk. 12.5 (* 'of fire' is added).
Hōsanna	'Save us!'	Mt. 21.9 = Mk 11.9 = Jn 12.13; Mt. 21.9bis = Mk 1.10; Mt. 21.15.

12. K. Beyer, *The Aramaic Language* (trans. J.F. Healey; Göttingen: Vandenhoeck & Ruprecht, 1986), p. 38.

13. The textual variants for the 'Cry from the Cross' do not obscure its clearly Aramaic nature.

mamōnas	'wealth'	Mt. 6.24 = Lk. 16.13; 16.9, 11.
pascha	'Passover'	Mt. 26.2, etc.; Mk 14.1, etc.; Lk. 2.41; 22.1, etc.; Jn 2.13, etc.;
raka	'Fool'	Mt. 5.22;
rabbi	'Master'	Mt. 23.7, etc.; Mk 9.5, etc.; Jn 1.38, etc.;
sabbaton	'the Sabbath day'	Mt. 12.1, etc.; Mk 1. 2, etc.; Lk. 4.16, etc.; Jn 5.9,etc.;
satana	'Satan'	Mt. 4.10, *cf.* Mk 1.13; Mt. 12.26 = Mk 3.26; 16.23 = Mk 8. 33; Mk 3.26 = Lk. 11.18; Lk. 22.3 = Jn 13. 27; Mk 3.23; 4.15; Lk. 10.18; 13.16; 22.3 = Jn 13. 27; Lk. 22. 31.
saton	'a measure'	Mt. 13.33 =Lk. 13.21.

All these words are certainly Aramaic.[14] The personal names Barabbas, Barjona, Bartimaeus and Bartholomew begin with the Aramaic word for 'son of' (*bar*), not the Hebrew (*ben*).[15] The Gospels also contain place names in Aramaic forms. The cases of Gabbatha and Golgotha (Jn 19.13, 17) reveal the answer to a problem sometimes seen in the description of some words as 'Hebrew' in the New Testament (the others are Jn 5.2, of Bethesda; Rev. 9.11 of Abaddon, 16.16 of Armageddon). The ending *-tha'*, in these two, is distinctively Aramaic, a form of the definite article. As John states that Gabbatha is the *Hebrew* equivalent of Greek *lithostraton*, 'pavement', and Golgotha of 'place of the skull', he demonstrates that for Greek speakers there was no need to distinguish between the languages the Jews spoke, 'Hebrew' applying to both. Josephus followed the same path.[16]

14. The analysis of *ephphatha* as Hebrew, which a few scholars have maintained, has not been strong enough to overcome the alternative analysis as Aramaic; see J.A. Emerton, '*Maranatha* and *Ephphatha*', *JTS* NS 18 (1967), pp. 427-31 (428-31); S. Morag, 'εφφαθα (Mark vii.34): Certainly Hebrew not Aramaic?', *JSS* 17 (1972), pp. 198-202; K. Beyer accepted it as Aramaic, *Die aramäischen Texte*, p. 130. The term *abba* may not be distinctively Aramaic rather than Hebrew, but common to both, see J. Barr, ''Abba isn't "Daddy" '', *JTS* NS 39 (1988), pp. 28-47.

15. See also Barjesus, Barnabas and Barsabas in Acts. Hebrew *ben* may occur in Mk 3.17, Boanerges, usually explained as *bᵉnê regeš* for 'sons of thunder', but this is uncertain.

16. The New Testament material gives stronger ground for understanding 'Hebrew' to include Aramaic than the uses in Josephus, discussed by T. Rajak, 'The Native Language of Josephus', in *idem, Josephus the Historian*, pp. 230-32. The REB's rendering of ἑβραΐδι, *hebraidi*, 'in the Jewish language' at Acts 21.40; 26.14,

Each of the Evangelists has Aramaic words, John fewer than the other three. The following table sets out the principal occurrences, showing parallel passages for all rare words and passages where a Greek term is substituted.

Aramaic (Greek substitute)	*Matthew*	*Mark*	*Luke*	*John*	*Other NT books*
abba (*patēr*)	(26.39)	14.36	(22.42)		Rom. 8.15; Gal. 4.6
ēloi, ēloi	27.46 =	15.34			
ephphatha		7.34			
kēphas				1.42	1 Cor. 1.12+3×; Gal. 2.9
korban	27.6	7.11			
messias				1.41; 4.25	
rabbûni (*kyrie*)	(20.33)	10.51	(18.41)	20.16	
talitha kûm		5.41			
amēn introducing, frequent in all					Only as concluding word.
geenna 11×	18.9 10.28 =	9.46	12.5		Jas 3.6
hōsanna	21.9 = 21.9 =	11.9= 11.10		12.13	
mamōnas	6.24 =		16.13 16.9, 11		
pascha 26×	26.2 =	14.1 =	22.1	13.1	Acts 12.4; 1.Cor. 5.7; Heb.11.28
rabbi 15×	26.49 =	14.45		1.38	
raka	5.22				
sabbaton 55×	12.1 =	2.23 =	6.1	5.9	Acts 10×, Epistles 2×
sata	13.33 =		13.21		
satana (*diabolos*) 14×	(4.1)	1.13	(4.2)		Acts 2× Epistles 9×
		4.10	22.3 =	13.27	Revelation 8×

The simplest explanation for the presence of these foreign terms in the Greek text is accurate reporting. Before that can be accepted, other reasons have to be explored. Would an audience for the Greek Gospels

rather then 'Hebrew' or 'Aramaic', is apt, but the distinction of ἑβραϊστὶ, *hebraisti* as 'Hebrew' in Jn 5.2; 19.13, 17, 20; Rev. 9.11, 16.16, seems odd when the words so described are also Aramaic!

expect to meet a few foreign words from the mouth of a Levantine Jewish teacher ? In modern English novels, even in biographies, foreign characters may utter a word or two in their own languages, such as a greeting, 'Bonjour', or an expression of gratitude, 'Danke schön', with the remainder of their speeches in the narrator's tongue. Do these Aramaic terms serve that purpose, to remind the audience they are facing a foreigner, to give verisimilitude? It is hard to suppose so, for they are not the phrases that might be expected. The cry 'Save me!' could have been presented in Aramaic to give immediacy in Mt. 14.30, or the command to dead Lazarus, 'Come out' in Jn 11.43, as 'Hosanna' is at the Triumphal Entry in Matthew, Mark and John and *ephphatha*, 'Be opened!' in Mk 7.34, yet they are not. When Jesus hailed his disciples after the Resurrection, for example, with the Semitic salutation, 'Peace!', the Aramaic is not given in Greek letters, *salam*, with a translation, as it could easily have been, but only the Greek greeting, 'Hail!' (Mt. 28.9).[17] The Aramaic terms interpreted in Greek were obviously expected to be unintelligible to the audience, yet they were retained. Their rarity and distribution, therefore, speak in favour of their origin in very early traditions, for a novelist might be expected to use more Aramaic words in more ordinary situations. Of the ten words in the second list, which have no explanatory phrase, *amēn*, *pascha*, *sabbaton*, *satana* and *saton* occur in the Septuagint, with *sabbaton* already in the non-Jewish Zenon papyri of the third century BC (see Chapter 4, p. 106), so they may have gained sufficient currency in Greek to be accepted without interpretation, as was the case with the Phoenician names for letters of the alphabet, including *iōta*, 'jot' in Mt. 5.18, and various weights, like the *mina* in Lk. 19.13-25. Of the other five words there is no trace in Greek writings older than the Gospels. Unless the audience of the Gospels had some familiarity with Aramaic, although Greek was obviously their normal language, they could not have fully understood the passages containing them. Josephus gave explanations of Semitic terms he used in his Greek books in a similar way, but they are fewer in proportion and often in particular contexts. He tells his readers, for example, that *pascha* is the Jewish term for the Feast of Unleavened Bread (*War* 2.10; *Ant.* 2.313, etc.), the temple treasure he says is called

---

17. In the first century BC Meleager of Gadara spoke Greek, Aramaic and Phoenician and gives greetings in each, including *salam*, in *The Greek Anthology* (trans. W.R. Paton; 5 vols.; LCL; London: Heinemann, 1916–18), 7.419.

korban in one passage (*War* 2.175), while in another he says *korban* means 'gift' (*Ant.* 4.73).

As the lists show, the Gospels do not always have the same Aramaic words in parallel passages. All four share *amēn*, *pascha* and *sabbaton*, Matthew, Mark and John share 'Hosanna' and 'rabbi', the three Synoptic Gospels 'Gehenna', while 'three *sata*' is in both Matthew and Luke. 'Satan' occurs in the Temptation narratives of Mark and Matthew, but not at the same points: Mt. 4.1 having 'being tempted by the devil' (*diabolos*) whereas Mk 1.13 has 'being tempted by Satan'; then Mt. 4.10 'depart, Satan'. In other cases Mark has an Aramaic word, Matthew and Luke the Greek equivalents (for *abba*, *rabbûni* and *Satan*). Mark has the largest number of different Aramaic terms, Luke the smallest.

These differences between the Gospels point to a common source, or to several sources. Matthew, it is usually argued, drew heavily from Mark and so they have words in common, Matthew and Luke share *mamōnas* and *saton* which Mark lacks. Matthew alone has *raka*, John alone has *Messias*; but *abba* and *Kēphas*, found in Mark and John respectively, were known in Christian circles, occurring in the Epistles of Paul.[18] In those circles another Aramaic expression was acceptable, too, *Maran atha*, 'Our Lord, come!' (1 Cor. 16.22). These observations may be held to favour the antiquity in Christian tradition of the Aramaic words of the Gospels, words believed to be those Jesus himself and those around him spoke, words worth preserving even in Greek writings.

On this evidence we can assume that Jesus spoke Aramaic as a matter of course. That leads to the inquiry, 'Can we reconstruct his sayings in Aramaic and so hear, in effect, the words he uttered?' In addition to the Aramaic words, scholars find many hints at Aramaic underlying the Gospels. There are grammatical constructions and expressions which seem odd in Greek but can be explained as Semitic.[19] A translation process is highly likely, but it has to be remembered that many of the

---

18. On Kephas, see J.A. Fitzmyer, 'Aramaic Kepha' and Peter's Name in the New Testament' in E. Best and R.McL. Wilson (eds.), *Text and Interpretation: Studies in Honour of M. Black* (Cambridge: Cambridge University Press, 1979), pp. 121-32.

19. See the balanced study by C.F.D. Moule, *An Idiom Book of New Testament Greek* (Cambridge: Cambridge University Press, 2nd edn, 1959), pp. 171-91.

early Christians had strong Jewish backgrounds and were familiar with the Greek Bible which displays similar features. Hellenized Semitisms may have been natural to them, whatever the form of the original. The quest for the Aramaic of the Gospels has fascinated and frustrated scholars throughout the twentieth century. The frustration lies in the fact that hardly anything has been known about first-century Aramaic. As shown in Chapter 4, there were no texts or documents available before the discovery of the Dead Sea Scrolls, except for graffiti on ossuaries and the texts preserved in later rabbinic books, where they were possibly subject to linguistic change, so the Aramaic words in the Gospels were a prime source. They are so meagre that attempts have been made to reconstruct first-century Aramaic, or to render the sayings of Jesus into Aramaic, by taking the Aramaic of the Targums, especially the Palestinian Targums, as a base. This was the best that could be done and it could not give any certainty, yet some scholars made far-reaching claims. Gustav Dalman was the pioneer of these studies, providing valuable linguistic reference books as well as investigating the Aramaic background to Jesus' words.[20] C.F. Burney tried first to prove John's Gospel had been composed in Aramaic, then to show that Jesus' sayings could be recognized as poetry when read in Aramaic, primarily seeking basic Semitic elements such as the parallelism in 'Whoever wants to save his life will lose it, but whoever loses his life for me and the gospel will save it' (Mk 8.35).[21] C.C. Torrey even re-translated the Gospels on the basis of a hypothetical Aramaic text which, he argued, had been misunderstood when put into the Greek of the Gospels.[22] In fact, the Targums these scholars used to reconstruct the language cannot be dated earlier than the third century. In many cases they are several centuries later and they are mostly known from mediaeval manuscripts where the language may have been affected by scribal

---

20. G. Dalman, *Die Worte Jesu* (Leipzig: J.C. Hinrichs, 2nd edn, 1930 [1898]), ET *The Words of Jesus Considered in the Light of Post-Biblical Jewish Writings and the Aramaic Language* (Edinburgh: T. & T. Clark, 1902); *Grammatik des jüdisch-palästinischen Aramäisch* (Leipzig: J.C. Hinrichs, 2nd edn, 1905 [1894]); *Aramäische Dialektproben* (Leipzig: J.C. Hinrichs, 1927).

21. C.F. Burney, *The Aramaic Origin of the Fourth Gospel* (Oxford: Clarendon Press, 1922); *The Poetry of our Lord* (Oxford: Clarendon Press, 1925).

22. C.C. Torrey, *The Four Gospels: A New Translation* (London: Hodder & Stoughton, 1934).

modernizations. Despite its clear descent from earlier forms of the language, biblical Aramaic and the Aramaic of the Persian Empire, the stages of development are not at all clear and retrojection of the targumic forms to the first century cannot be justified by any external evidence. Matthew Black pursued the study in his *Aramaic Approach to the Gospels and Acts*,[23] emphasizing the value of targumic, Christian and Samaritan Aramaic texts originating in Palestine, in contrast to *Targum Onkelos* and its kin used by Dalman and others which have Babylonian elements. The distinction is necessary, but the same objection applies, for these texts show signs of being at the very least two centuries later than the time of Jesus.[24] The Dead Sea Scrolls have supplied extensive examples of literary Aramaic current in the first century, including some poetry, and the legal texts and letters from the first century and the Bar Kochba period are beginning to yield information about the more colloquial language.[25] However, all attempts to render the Greek sayings of Jesus back into Aramaic have to remain hypothetical.

As a well-taught, observant Jewish boy, Jesus would also have learnt to read the Scriptures in Hebrew (see Chapter 6, pp. 157-58). Was that the language he spoke? The few scholars who have tried to make that case have not convinced many others.[26] The presence of the Aramaic words just discussed is very difficult to explain if the normal language was Hebrew. Although the two languages are closely related, they are not identical and some of the words are clearly not Hebrew, notably *talitha kum* and the *Eloi, eloi* rendering of Ps. 22.1. The texts from the Dead Sea area and from Masada reveal that Hebrew was written and

23. (London: Oxford University Press, 1946, 2nd edn, 1954, 3rd edn, 1967). See also M. Wilcox, 'Semitisms in the New Testament', *ANRW*, II, 25.2 (Berlin: W. de Gruyter, 1984), pp. 978-1029.

24. For an extensive critique, see J.A. Fitzmyer's review of the 3rd edition of Black's work, *CBQ* 30 (1968), pp. 417-28.

25. See Yardeni in Cotton and Yardeni, *Aramaic, Hebrew and Greek Documentary Texts*, pp. 11-13. See also J. Naveh, 'On Formal and Informal Spelling of Unpronounced Gutturals', *Scripta Classica Israelitica* 15 (1996), pp. 263-67.

26. J. Carmignac, *La naissance des évangiles synoptiques* (Paris: O.E.I.L., 1984) gives examples of passages which he believed demonstrated underlying Hebrew texts, but the linguistic situation described above may explain their presence equally well. The same applies to R.L. Lindsey's *A Hebrew Translation of the Gospel of Mark* (Jerusalem: Dugith Publishers, 2nd edn, 1973 [1969]).

spoken in Herodian Palestine in both religious and secular situations. How widespread that was is impossible to define. At present it seems the people who wrote the documents in Hebrew—letters and legal deeds, notes and marks of ownership—may have come from a relatively small area around Jerusalem and from a small number of families connected with the Temple. However, there is nothing to suggest they used Hebrew exclusively, in fact, the evidence already cited reveals a society where Greek, Hebrew and Aramaic mixed, so it is unlikely Jesus taught regularly in the language a localized minority favoured, for his message is presented as one all could understand; there is no evidence for much Hebrew being spoken in Galilee at the time.

Galilee was an area of trade and development under the Herods, as we have seen, so there is a real possibility that Jesus understood and occasionally used Greek.[27] Indeed, an argument has been advanced in favour of him speaking in Greek the words 'You say so' to Pilate, which stand in all four Gospels (Mt. 27.11; Mk 15.2; Lk. 23.3; Jn 18.37), 'You are Peter…' in Mt. 16.17-19 and of his words to the Syro-Phoenician woman when he was in the region of Tyre, to the 'Greeks' and, perhaps, to the centurion at Capernaum (Mk 7.26; Jn 12.20-28; Mt. 8.5-13).[28] Were it the case that he did speak in Greek on some occasions, there would be no way to tell whether we read in the Gospels what are presented as his own words in the Greek he used, or Greek translations of his Aramaic sayings. Attempts to reconstruct Aramaic originals would have less point, although they could still be applied to passages which contain the most recognizable Semitic forms of expression (e.g. 'son[s] of' as in 'sons of the banquet' for 'guests', Mt. 9.15; Mk 2.19; Lk. 5.34).[29]

27. Fitzmyer, 'The Languages of Palestine in the First Century AD', pp. 32-38.

28. See, e.g., Fitzmyer, 'Did Jesus Speak Greek?', pp. 60, 61; S.E. Porter, 'Did Jesus ever Teach in Greek?', *TynBul* 44 (1993), pp. 199-235. Note, however, J.A. Fitzmyer's opinion that to insist Jesus' actual words may be preserved in Greek presses the evidence beyond legitimate bounds, 'Did Jesus Speak Greek', pp. 62, 63 and 'The Languages of Palestine', p. 37.

29. For a clear and up-to-date survey, see M.O. Wise, 'Languages of Palestine', in J.B. Green, S. McKnight and I.H. Marshall (eds.), *Dictionary of Jesus and the Gospels* (Leicester: InterVarsity Press; Downers Grove, IL: InterVarsity Press, 1992), pp. 434-44.

Spoken Latin in Herodian Palestine?[30]

The first-hand testimonies to written Latin in early Roman Palestine imply readers, not necessarily speakers. Signs of the presence of some Latin speakers outside the governor's court may be perceived in an unexpected place, the Gospels. It is appropriate to notice the presence of Latinisms in the Gospels, concentrating on the lexical material which is less disputable than possible cases of grammatical or syntactical elements. There is a long history of comment on the phenomenon of Latinisms in the Gospels.[31] The material is conveniently displayed in the standard Blass-Debrunner Grammar.[32] Several of the words are terms for measures or money, others refer to military matters, while some are less easily explained. Their presence distinguishes the Gospels from the Hebrew and Aramaic books among the Dead Sea Scrolls, which have no Greek or Latin loanwords,[33] and from the first-century Jewish writers Philo and Josephus, whose extant writings in Greek rarely exhibit the same Latin loanwords as the Gospels.[34] Of the 18 Latin words in the Gospels, 10 occur in Mark, which has more Latinisms 'than any other original Greek literary text', lending support to the long-standing suggestion that Mark's Gospel was written in Rome.[35] Either the number of Latinisms in the Gospels may indicate that they were all composed in an area of strong Latin influence, like Rome, or the Latin elements may reflect the linguistic situation of the eastern Mediterranean littoral early in the first century, or of Palestine itself. If the first possibility were true, then the difference between the Gospels

30. This section is revised from 'Latin in First Century Palestine', in Zevit, Gitin and Sokoloff (eds.), *Solving Riddles and Untying Knots*, pp. 451-58, reproduced by courtesy of the publisher.

31. For example, J.H. Thayer, 'Language of the New Testament', *HDB*, III, pp. 36-43 (40); F.F. Bruce, 'Languages (Latin)', *ABD*, IV, pp. 220-22 (221); A.T. Robertson, *A Grammar of the Greek New Testament in the Light of Historical Research* (London: Hodder & Stoughton, 3rd edn, 1919), pp. 108-11.

32. F. Blass, A. Debrunner and F. Rohrkopf, *Grammatik des neutestamentlichen Griechisch* (Göttingen: Vandenhoeck and Ruprecht, 14th edn, 1975), pp. 6-9.

33. Qimron, *The Hebrew of the Dead Sea Scrolls*, p. 117.

34. See A. Schlatter, *Der Evangelist Matthäus* (Stuttgart: Calwer, 1929), p. 816; *Der Evangelist Johannes* (Stuttgart: Calwer, 1930), p. 393; *Das Evangelium des Lukas* (Stuttgart: Calwer, 1931), p. 710.

35. M. Hengel, *Studies in the Gospel of Mark* (London: SCM Press, 1985), pp. 28, 29, with references to earlier studies.

and the rest of the New Testament in this feature is very striking, for there are only nine additional Latin words in the remaining books. (They are: *colonia*, Acts 16.12; *forum*, Acts 28.15; *libertinus*, Acts 6.9; *macellum*, 1 Cor. 10.25; *membrana*, 2 Tim. 4.13 [see Chapter 3, p. 63]; *paenula*, also 2 Tim. 4.13; *semicinctium*, Acts 23.35, Phil. 1.13; *sicarius*, Acts 21.38; *taberna*, Acts 28.15.)

The distribution of the Latin words within the Gospels is interesting. M. Hengel has drawn attention to Mark's explanations in Latin at two points, κοδράντης, *quadrans* to elucidate the widow's 'two mites' at 12.42 and πραιτώριον, *praetorium* for the governor's hall at 15.16.[36] Yet Matthew has both terms without any qualifying phrases (5.26; 27.27), the former in a passage without parallel in Mark, 'until you have paid the last *quadrans*'. While Mark's Latinisms are the most striking, Latin words in Matthew are as many and not all occur in parallel passages. In addition to *quadrans* in 5.26, he has κουστωδία, *custodia* for the guard on Jesus' tomb (27.65, 66; 28.11) and μίλιον, *milia*, 'mile' in 5.41. His Gospel shares no Latin words with Luke or John, except the frequent *denarius,* which is common to all (14 times). Luke has the fewest Latin words, often giving a Greek equivalent where parallel passages have a Latin word. Thus Lk. 8.16 has σκεῦος where Mk 4.21 and Mt. 5.15 have μόδιος, *modius,* for a measuring vessel; he has φόρος (20.22) where they have κῆνσος, *census* (Mk 12.14; Mt. 17.25; 22.17); he has παιδεύειν (23.16, 22) where they have φραγελλοῦν, *flagellare,* 'to whip' (Mk 15.15; Mt. 27.26). For Matthew's κοδράντης, *quadrans,* (5.26) Luke has λεπτὸν, 'mite' (12.59). On one occasion Luke writes a Greek word where John has a Latin: the accusation placed on the cross is ἐπιγραφὴ in Lk. 23.38, while John terms it τίτλος, *tit(u)lus* (19.19, 20). Luke shares with John the scarf, σουδάριον, *sudarium* (Lk. 19.20; Jn 11.44; 20.7), which reappears in Acts 19.12. Luke's preference for Greek words may accord with his style, generally considered to be the most polished of the New Testament narrators. In this respect he can stand with Philo and Josephus, all concerned to write good Greek to gain favour with their educated patrons or audiences, although the Acts of the Apostles contains six of the nine Latin words found outside the Gospels. The Gospel of John has four Latin words absent from the Synoptic Gospels: λέντιον, *linteum,* 'towel' (13.4, 5), λίτρα, *libra,* 'pound weight' (12.3; 19.39), τιτλος,

36. Hengel, *Studies in Mark*, pp. 28, 29. Note that the second word stands without explanation also in Acts 23.35 and Phil. 1.13.

tit(u)lus, 'title' (19.19, 20), φραγέλλιον, *flagellium*, 'whip' (2.15).

Checking these words in the LSJ and through the *Thesaurus Linguae Graecae*,[37] reveals the remarkable fact that several do not occur in any Greek texts earlier than the first century AD and some of them occur only in the Gospels. They are:

'census'	*census*	κῆνσος:	only in Mark and Matthew;
'small coin'	*quadrans*	κοδράντης:	in Heron (first century BC), Mark and Matthew;
'guard'	*custodia*	κουστωδία:	in Oxyrhynchus Papyrus 294.20 (AD 22) and Matthew;
'measure, cup'	*sextarius*	ξέστης (as a cup):	only in Mark;
'governor's residence'	*praetorium*	πραιτώριον:	only in Mark, Matthew Acts and Philippians;
'towel'	*sudarium*	σουδάριον:	in the Life of Aesop (first century AD), Luke, John and Acts;
'member of governor's staff, executioner'	*speculator*	σπεκουλάτωρ:	only in Mark;
'title'	*tit(u)lus*	τίτλος:	only in John;
'whip'	*flagellium*	φραγέλλιον:	only in John;
'to whip'	*flagellare*	φραγελλοῦν:	only in Mark and Matthew

As noted, several of these words relate to military and administrative activities (*census, custodia, flagellium, flagellare, praetorium, speculator, tit(u)lus*) and so could have become familiar wherever Rome ruled, as would coins and measures (*as, denarius, libra, milia, modius*). The occurrence of all these words, and others, in unofficial writings concerning events in a marginal region of Rome's empire is a surprise. This is all the more so when the words are seen to be distributed across the four Gospels, and where two use the same word in different passages. Seventeen words in 42 occurrences provide insufficient basis for any firm conclusion (leaving aside the 14 cases of *denarius*). They do indicate a milieu for the Gospel writers where Latin words were taken into Greek without great hesitation. That might be anywhere in the Eastern Mediterranean, but the only country to give a large collection of comparable material, Egypt, shows a strong resistance to accepting

37. The check with the Ibycus computer programme was made for me by Tim Freeman at Tyndale House, Cambridge.

either Latin or native words into Greek. In reviewing a study of the subject, the papyrologist J.G. Keenan observed, 'the penetration of Latin terms into everyday Egyptian Greek was limited, artificial and superficial' except for clothing, weights and measures and coins, 'clothing was, as so often, an object of concern in a military context'.[38] The two Latin words for clothing in the Gospels, *linteum* and *sudarium*, do not have a strong military association, but might be supposed to have been imported by military personnel.[39] Texts from Palmyra display a similar range of military and administrative words taken from Latin, including *centurion, qntryn'* and *legio, lgywn'*, while *qntryn'* occurs in a Nabataean tomb inscription from Mada'in Salih in the Hijaz at the beginning of the first century.[40] An inscription of AD 51 thanks a Palmyrene for gifts worth 150 and 120 *denarii*, revealing that the Roman coin was already circulating there. The famous Tariff of Palmyra, issued in 137, refers to an edict from the time of Germanicus, about AD 18, mentioning the *denarius* and the *as* (*dnr* and *'sr = assarion*).[41] In Palestine the Bar Kochba period documents reveal no resistance to loanwords there then (see below), and the epigraphic evidence from Herod's palace at Masada displays some Latin presence a hundred years earlier, as noted above. With its particularly mixed population and its small area, Palestine was perhaps more open to foreign influences in its languages. That applies to Hebrew as well as to Greek. Latinisms are absent from Jewish literary works like the Dead Sea Scrolls and relatively rare in rabbinic works put into writing from the end of the second century AD onwards.[42] On the other hand, some found their way through Greek into

38. J.G. Keenan, review of *Il lessico latino nel greco d'Egitto* (Barcelona: Institut de Teologia Fondamental, Seminario de Papirologia, 2nd edn, 1991) by S. Daris, in *Bulletin of the American Society of Papyrologists* 29 (1992), pp. 219-20. For the evidence supplied by the recent finds, see J.N. Adams, 'The Language of the Vindolanda Writing Tablets: An Interim Report', *JRS* 85 (1995), pp. 86-134: the tablets give new or first attestations for five words.

39. *sudarium* appears in an account of clothes and other items at Vindolanda, Bowman and Thomas, *The Vindolanda Writing Tablets*, no. 184.

40. J.F. Healey, *The Nabataean Tomb Inscriptions of Mada'in Salih* (JSS Supplement, 1; Oxford: University Press, 1993), p. 209. Note the possible occurrence of *census* there in a tomb of similar date, pp. 154, 162 (*qns*).

41. See J. Teixidor, *Un port romain du désert: Palmyre et son commerce d'Auguste à Caracalla* (= *Semitica* 34, Paris, 1984), pp. 49-50 for the dedication to Bel, pp. 80-81 for the Tariff referring to the earlier edict.

42. Lieberman, *Hellenism in Jewish Palestine*, p. 17, observed, 'The Palestinian

ordinary life and after the Fall of Jerusalem, as Roman rule was more firmly imposed, the presence of Latin grew. The Aramaic and Hebrew papyri from the 'Cave of Letters', written during the first quarter of the second century, make that clear. The degree of Latin influences apparent surprised the scholars who edited them, for it is more marked there than in any other of the Eastern provinces. The Latinisms are both syntactical and lexical, the latter including βασιλίκα (*basilica* 16.2, 4), ἀπό ἄκτων (*ab/ex actis* 12.1, 4), πραισίδιον (*praesidium* 11.6, 19), τριβουνάλιον (*tribunal* 14.12-13, 31). There are also Latin terms for money, the most common being δηνάριον (*denarius*), and for dates.[43] Not surprisingly, *denarius* is in several of the 'Cave of Letters' documents, with a Hebrew plural ending, *dînarîn*, and that is found in the Mishnah and other rabbinic texts of the third century beside *quadrans*, *as* and various measures (*qodrantis*, *'issar* in Tosefta, *B. Bat.* 5.12, the latter already in *m. Qid.* 1.1; *môdyâ'* in the Mishnah, *lîṭrâ'* in the Tosefta). More noteworthy are the appearances of *porgal*, *flagellium*, 'whip', in the Tosefta and Mekhilta of the third century and of *sᵉp̄iklator*, *speculator* in Sifre 91 and the midrashim of the same and later centuries, with the sense of 'executioner'. Apart from Mk 6.27, the second word is not found in Greek writings;[44] the former is found after the Gospels in a second-century papyrus and in the works of Origen. In addition, Mishnaic Hebrew *sûḏarîn*, 'towel', is surely *sudarium*.[45]

Latin words apparently entered the Greek and local languages of Palestine in a larger quantity than can be seen in other areas, if the language of the Gospels can be taken as typical. Although their numbers

Rabbis certainly did not know Latin. Except for military and judiciary terms (as well as names of objects imported from Latin speaking countries) which are usually also extant in Syriac and later Greek, Latin words are less than scarce in rabbinic literature.'

43. Lewis and Greenfield, *The Documents from the Bar Kokhba Period*, pp. 16-19.

44. The word does occur on a Greek tombstone of perhaps the third century AD. See J. Robert and L. Robert, 'Bulletin Epigraphique', *Revue des Etudes Grecques* 72 (1959), pp. 149-283 (214, no. 260).

45. M. Jastrow, *A Dictionary of the Targumim, Talmud Babli, Yerushalmi and the Midrashic Literature* (New York: Choret; London: Shapiro Vallentine, 1926), p. 962a disagreed. For the 140 or so Greek and Latin loanwords in rabbinic Hebrew see now Z. Ben Ḥayyim (ed.), *The Historical Dictionary of the Hebrew Language: Materials for the Dictionary, Series I 200 BCE–300 CE* (Jerusalem: Academy for the Hebrew Language, 1988) (on microfiche).

are small and the sources unevenly scattered in time, they seem to allow us to suggest that the presence of Latin words in the Gospels reflects the linguistic picture of Palestine in the first century AD. The Latinate explanations Mark supplies, κοδράντης, *quadrans*, and πραιτώριον, *praetorium*, could indicate an origin in Rome, as Hengel and others argued; yet the use of the same words by Matthew, who has Greek equivalents for some of Mark's Aramaic words (see above pp. 142-44), may imply they were more widely known and that Mark was simply helping the general reader outside Palestine by adding greater precision. Since it is generally agreed the Gospels were written shortly after AD 70, Mark possibly before that date,[46] it would be hard to argue for the authors making a special feature of introducing Latin terms which might alienate Jewish readers, Christian or not, terms used by the conquerors of Jerusalem. We may, therefore, deduce that there was sufficient Latin current to enable such Latin words as stand in the Gospels to pass into the Greek spoken in Palestine early in the first century AD, even in the lifetime of Jesus of Nazareth.

46. See the opinions gathered in standard works such as Kümmel, *Introduction to the New Testament.*

Chapter 6

WHO READ AND WHO WROTE

Reading and writing are almost indivisible to us, but in many societies they are separate; people who read do not necessarily have the ability to write, their lives do not lead them into situations where writing is required, occasionally they may need, or want to read, but that need may never arise. Throughout the Hellenistic and Roman world the distinction prevailed in that there were educated people who were proficient readers and writers, less educated ones who could read but hardly write, some who were readers alone, some of them able to read only slowly or with difficulty and some who were illiterate. What the proportion of literate people was to illiterate in the writing cultures of the ancient world has been discussed often. There are optimists who have assumed a high level of literacy existed from early times in Greece, for example 'archaic Greece was a literate society in a modern sense', and 'in the Near East in the first century of our era writing was an essential accompaniment of life at almost all levels to an extent without parallel in living memory'.[1] As with any estimates about ancient societies, a strong reservation has to be entered: people who did not produce the sort of material under discussion will be poorly represented by it. Currently, more sober conclusions have come to the fore, based on thoroughly sifting information gleaned from classical authors and from excavated texts. After making his extensive inquiry, W.V. Harris argued for 15 per cent of adult males in Athens of the fifth century BC having some literacy, that is about 5 per cent of the total population, a figure rising to

1. O. Murray, *Early Greece* (London: Fontana, 1993), pp. 94, 96, cited, from an earlier edition, by W.V. Harris, *Ancient Literacy* (Cambridge, MA: Harvard University Press, 1989), p. 9, who also cites part of the next quotation from C.H. Roberts, 'Books in the Graeco-Roman World and in the New Testament', in Ackroyd and Evans (eds.), *The Cambridge History of the Bible*, I, pp. 48-66 (48).

10-15 per cent overall by the mid-fourth century and growing to per-haps 30-40 per cent of free-born men in some Hellenistic cities, then declining from the first century BC. Among Greeks of the Roman empire, he deduced,

> It remained unthinkable that a man of property...or a man with any claim to distinction in city life could be illiterate. That of course leaves the mass of the population unaccounted for... There are hints in the evidence that literacy was limited, at best, among artisans. Small farmers and the poor will have been generally illiterate...

although earlier he had observed the economy of Greece and Rome gave 'some incentive...to an artisan or shopkeeper to read and write'.[2] Examples of these last are seen in graffiti at Pompeii made by a fuller, a weaver and other craftsmen, while a papyrus from Egypt lists a scribe and a short-hand writer beside a cook and a barber as slaves in a house-hold of the second century BC. The situation is well described in a study of education in Graeco-Roman Egypt:

> Literacy and writing were not indispensable skills in the ancient Mediter-ranean world, and they neither determined nor limited socio-economic success. Writing was rather a useful, enabling technology that people cared to exhibit even when they possessed it only to a limited degree. Greek and Roman men and women were proud to be numbered among the literates, but esteem for writing was not enough to spread the skill itself to the mass of the population. Writing depended on need, but those who lacked the skill could resort to various strategies to cope with the demands that need imposed upon them.[3]

Far more pessimistic is the assertion of W.H. Kelber, author of *The Oral and Written Gospel*, 'Throughout antiquity writing was in the hands of an élite of trained specialists, and reading required an ad-vanced education available only to a few'.[4] In this chapter I shall seek to establish a more positive view, adopting references from Graeco-Roman texts of all sorts already adduced by Harris, supplemented by those presented in a volume of essays by eight specialists who have

---

2. Harris, *Ancient Literacy*, pp. 13, 328-330.

3. R. Cribbiore, *Writing, Teachers and Students in Graeco-Roman Egypt* (Atlanta, GA: Scholars Press, 1996), p. 6.

4. W.H. Kelber, *The Oral and Written Gospel* (Philadelphia: Fortress Press, 1983), p. 17.

developed or responded to his work.[5] Jewish sources and the discoveries in Palestine described earlier bring additional testimonies which are often overlooked, despite their relevance.

Ignorance of writing, its purposes and power, is not a concomitant of a lack of ability to read or to write; coinage, if no other means, brought writing to the eyes of much of the population of the Roman empire—from Augustus's reign onwards, imperial coins universally bore the emperor's 'image and superscription' which would presumably have become widely recognized, even if the propagandistic legends about military triumphs and political arrangements did not.[6] Every householder would experience the census, every owner of a plot of land would know about the tax-collectors' ominous records, whether they were written in his own language or the language of the administration.

The situation in the Roman empire varied from region to region. Administrators who followed the legions when they annexed effectively illiterate areas such as Gaul or Britain introduced Latin, stimulating some local literacy in that language, and very little was written in local languages and scripts, so that next to nothing may survive. When there was an already established writing system, the Romans might introduce Latin beside it, as in the Punic areas of North Africa where a dialect of Phoenician was spoken and written in a form of the Phoenician alphabet and brief records in the local Berber languages were written with a derivative of the same alphabet.[7] In the East Mediterranean where Greek was at home, they often used that, as it was part of the educated Roman gentleman's accomplishments, with Latin circulating in the army. In Egypt, Greek and then Latin were overlaid upon the ancient Egyptian language and scripts. The complex hieroglyphs and their shorthand form, demotic, were the preserve of the professional scribes and priests who had been thoroughly trained; literacy in ancient Egypt was extremely low, at the highest estimate not more than 1 or 2 per cent of the population, although only the smallest places were likely to be without a scribe of any sort.[8] Greek papyri

5.   Humphrey (ed.), *Literacy in the Roman World.*

6.   See B. Levick, 'Propaganda and the Imperial Coinage', *Antichthon* 16 (1982), pp. 104-16.

7.   See O. Rössler, 'Die Numider: Herkunft—Schrift—Sprache', in H.G. Horn and C.B. Rüger (eds.), *Die Numider: Reiter und Könige nordlich der Sahara* (Cologne: Rheinland Verlag, 1979), pp. 79-89.

8.   J. Baines, 'Literacy and Ancient Egyptian Society', *Man* 18 (1983), pp. 572-

supplant Egyptian ones almost entirely by the first century AD, according to the discoveries made so far, but the Egyptian language continued to be spoken, in the form known as Coptic and by the third century was being written in the Greek alphabet with six added signs. Most examples of Coptic come from Christian or related sources. When Greek papyri designate individuals as 'illiterate', they may mean they could not read or write Greek, without relating to their ability in Egyptian, although complete illiteracy is doubtless intended in many cases.[9] A papyrologist can sketch the picture:

> The government documented all its activities, overseeing and controlling the daily lives of individuals and their communities... Under the Ptolemies, and even more so under the Romans, Egyptian society was profoundly literate in the sense that most people were familiar with literate modes in some way. Written documents proved ownership of property, tax receipts guaranteed that a tax had been paid, petitions provided a means of redress for grievances, and the sending of letters kept channels of communication open. Although literacy and writing penetrated to most circles, most of the population was still illiterate or semi-literate... The pool of literates was extensive enough to help the illiterates respond to official demands for Greek documents and for their everyday writing needs.[10]

Who Read?

The literacy situation in Jewish society differed from that in the Graeco-Roman in a notable way because there was a strong tradition of education in order that men, at least, should be prepared to read from the Scriptures in synagogue services. In theory, every Jewish male was expected to do so. The Palestinian Talmud reports the rule of Simeon ben Shetach about 100 BC that all children should go to school (*y. Ket.* 8.32c), and instruction in the Torah started early, according to both Philo and Josephus (*Leg. Gai.* 210; *Apion* 2.178).[11] How widely that

99; J. Baines and C.J. Eyre, 'Four Notes on Literacy', *Göttinger Miszellen* 61 (1983), pp. 65-96.

9. H.C. Youtie, 'ΑΓΡΑΜΜΑΤΟΣ: An Aspect of Greek Society in Egypt', *Harvard Studies in Classical Philology* 75 (1971), pp. 161-76 and 'Βραδέως γράφων: Between Literacy and Illiteracy', *GRBS* 12 (1971), pp. 239-61, both reprinted in *Scriptiunculae* II (Amsterdam: Hakkert, 1973), pp. 611-27, 629-51.

10. Cribbiore, *Writing, Teachers and Students*, p. 4.

11. Schürer, *History of the Jewish People*, II, pp. 417-21, 450.

was in force is unknown and it is likely that many who learnt to read the Scriptures learnt by heart and never read any other book. The Synoptic Gospels make an interesting contrast between those who read and those who heard the Scriptures. They assume Jewish teachers read the Scriptures by the words 'Have you never read' with which Jesus introduced biblical texts when replying to the Pharisees' criticism of his disciples for plucking corn on the sabbath (Mt. 12.3, 5; Mk 2.25; Lk. 6.3) and to their question about divorce (Mt. 19.4), to the Sadducees on the question of the resurrection (Mt. 22.31; Mk 12.26), to a lawyer asking about eternal life (Lk. 10.26) and to priests and scribes in the Temple (Mt. 21.16, 42; Mk 12.10). This reading was clearly more intensive than the sabbath lesson, implying these men had access to the sacred books. On the other hand, addressing a large, mixed audience in the Sermon on the Mount, Jesus introduced citations from the Law with the words, 'You have heard it was said' (Mt. 5.21, 27, 33, 38, 43; note also Jn 12.34 where the people say, 'We have heard from the Law'). At the same time, the reference to the jot and tittle of the Law expects some familiarity with the smallest features of the written texts on the part of that audience (Mt. 5.18; cf. Lk. 16.17). Deeply engrained religious belief, therefore, affected the attitude to books in Jewish society.

Who Owned Books?

Biblical rolls were kept in the Temple in Jerusalem, a custom reaching back to the days of the kings (2 Kgs 22.8-13). When the Hebrew Bible was to be translated into Greek at royal command in Egypt, the priests in Jerusalem sent a very special copy of the Torah to Alexandria as the exemplar, 'in which the laws were written in letters of gold,' according to the Letter of Aristeas cited by Josephus (*Ant.* 12.29 = Aristeas §176). Rabbinic records tell of three rolls of the Law which differed slightly from each other and were held in the Temple as models. If there was uncertainty about the exact reading of a text, then the three could be consulted and the reading two of them supported was deemed correct. (The types of variation the rabbinic memory preserved from these rolls is noteworthy, for they revolve around very small matters and do not echo the larger differences the Dead Sea Scrolls or the Septuagint reveal.)[12] Josephus refers several times to books preserved in the

---

12. S. Talmon, 'The Three Scrolls of the Law that Were Found in the Temple Court', *Textus* 2 (1962), pp. 14-27.

Temple containing information about Israel's history (see *Ant.* 3.38; 4.303; 5.61). The Roman soldiers in Titus's army who sacked Jerusalem in AD 70 took an enormous booty as the Temple burned. With the golden table for shewbread, the trumpets and the candelabrum (*menorâ*) paraded triumphantly in Rome and carved on the Arch of Titus were other treasures, including a roll of the Law which was kept in the palace (*War* 6.150, 162). When Titus offered his Jewish friend Josephus a choice of keepsakes from the spoils, the historian selected 'a gift of sacred books' (*Life* 418). One roll of the Law taken from Jerusalem was preserved in Rome for some time. A rabbi saw it a century or so later in 'the synagogue of Severus' and minor variant readings from it were cited by an eleventh-century scholar.[13] Since the Temple had been turned into a fortress, it is likely that very many more rolls were destroyed as the fighting progressed and the fires raged.

There were synagogues all over the country. While the word 'synagogue' often means 'an assembly' rather than a structure, there is good reason to assume buildings stood in many places to serve as meeting-places for the local populace, both for religious and for secular affairs. Although physical traces from the first century are few, the building at Gamla[14] and the Theodotus Inscription from Jerusalem (see Chapter 4, pp. 110-11) give strong testimony, independently of such Gospel statements as Lk. 7.5.[15] Those synagogues owned copies of the Scriptures on rolls which were read and studied weekly, according both to Josephus (*Apion* 2.175) and to Philo (*Vit. Mos.* 2.216). Some of the copies were probably paid for by the community, some presented by pious worshippers. A splendid roll is recalled in rabbinic writings which had the name of God written in gold letters, reminiscent of the one sent

13. J.P. Siegel, *The Severus Scroll and 1QIs^a* (Missoula, MT: Scholars Press, 1975).

14. Gutman, *Gamla*, pp. 99-103; H. Syon, 'Gamla—Portrait of a Rebellion', *BAR* 18.1 (1992), pp. 20-37.

15. See R. Hachlili, 'The Origin of the Synagogue: A Re-assessment', *JSJ* 28 (1997), pp. 34-47; Atkinson, 'On Further Defining the First-Century CE Synagogue', pp. 491-502, see above Ch. 4, p. 110 n. 69. Arguments against the existence of synagogue buildings in first-century Palestine appear to ignore the paucity of any evidence from the land. That an inscription at Cyrenaica of AD 56 is the earliest undoubted epigraphic reference to a building called a synagogue does not mean it was at that moment that the word was first used in that sense, contra R.A. Horsley, *Archaeology, History and Society in Galilee* (Valley Forge, PA: Trinity Press, 1996), p. 146.

Figure 35. *View of the 'synagogue' at Gamla, destroyed in* AD *67. (Photograph by the author.)*

to Alexandria (see above, p. 158),[16] and there may have been other elaborate copies, but most were plain. On sabbath days attendants removed them from the cupboard, the 'Ark', and opened them at the passages set for reading. If a small place like Nazareth had a copy of Isaiah (Lk. 4.17), and so as a matter of course a Torah roll and most likely an Esther roll for the festival of Purim, then we may deduce most synagogues had collections of biblical books, even if not a complete set of the Scriptures. The book of Acts suggests that was the case in a synagogue of the Diaspora, at Antioch in Pisidia by specifying 'after the readings from the law and the prophets' (Acts 13.15), and assumes it was so as the Scriptures were read everywhere (Acts 13.27; 15.21; cf. 2 Cor. 3.15). Remembering that the whole collection of books of the Hebrew Bible would occupy 15 to 20 rolls, there would have been literally hundreds of biblical rolls stored for public reading and study in the synagogues of first-century Palestine, therefore. A report by Josephus supports that conclusion. About AD 50, when Cumanus was the Roman governor, brigands robbed a Roman slave in the Beth-Horon

16. J.P. Siegel, 'The Alexandrians in Jerusalem and their Torah Scroll with Gold Tetragrammata', *IEJ* 22 (1972), pp. 139-43.

district, north-west of Jerusalem so the governor sent his forces to punish the people of the area. In the pillage, one soldier openly tore up a roll of the Law he found in a village and burnt it; the resultant public outcry forced Cumanus to execute him (*War* 2.229). Later, when Josephus was commander in Galilee, a rebel confronting him had 'a copy of the law of Moses in his hands' as he harangued the crowd (*Life* 134). Relics of a synagogue's store may be provided by Masada where the excavators clearing the defensive wall came upon a room which the Zealot defenders had apparently remodelled to serve as a synagogue. Hidden in pits in the floor were parts of rolls of Deuteronomy and Ezekiel. Pieces of other biblical books and non-biblical works lay in a room in the wall a few metres to the south (including Psalms, Genesis, Leviticus) and they may all be considered remnants of the synagogue collection (see Chapter 4, p. 120 n. 87).

If Josephus could take former Temple rolls for himself, did other Jews have their own copies of the Scriptures? Affluent men, kings like Herod, could collect books to make libraries as part of the trappings of wealth, following the example of Ptolemy, founder of the Library at Alexandria which reputedly held over 700,000 books in the first century BC (see Chapter 1, p. 18). Herod's court philosopher, Nicolaus of Damascus, wrote numerous books, including a lengthy history of the world and the surviving fragments suggest at least 44 Greek authors were represented in Herod's library.[17] Scholars, rarely rich, then as now, could and did own rolls. In Alexandria the Jewish philosopher Philo, who discussed the Greek Scriptures in detail, surely had his personal copies of the sacred books and that was probably the case for privileged men in Palestine, for all who claimed to be educated, for some of the Pharisees and for teachers like Nicodemus. Their reading was clearly more extensive than the sabbath lesson, implying they had access to the sacred books. As noted already, the Gospels assume they had some familiarity with the text of the Hebrew Scriptures. At the time of Antiochus Epiphanes' attempt to suppress Judaism in 168 BC there were people who owned biblical rolls, for 1 Maccabees relates, 'Every scroll of the law that was found was torn up and consigned to the flames, and anyone discovered in possession of a Book of the Covenant or conforming to the law was by sentence of the king condemned to die' (1.56, 57).

17. B.Z. Wacholder, 'Greek Authors in Herod's Library', *Studies in Bibliography and Booklore* 5 (1960), pp. 104-109.

The Dead Sea Scrolls and related finds are the only surviving specimens of Jewish manuscripts read in the first century. The term 'ancient library' has been applied to them, although there is no sign that they belonged to a single collection organized in any way. While they appear to have been the property of the unusual Qumran Community, the collection undoubtedly contained books owned by individuals coming from outside which they pooled, with their other possessions, on joining the community, beside books composed or copied by members within the community for their own study and meditation, or possibly for despatch to other branches of the sect, or even for sale. Some of the Scrolls bear letters and enigmatic marks in their margins which may be signs of private study and the recurrence of particular marks in several manuscripts might be the traces of one student's personal reading, while a single scribe or copyist can be identified as responsible for producing or correcting different books.[18] It is unlikely the majority of the books were the autograph copies of the authors, thus there were many more copies in the country than the Scrolls represent and the 'multiplicity of [scribal] hands argues overwhelmingly that they must represent, to a greater or lesser extent, a cross section of the trade in books'.[19] On the other hand, the commentaries (*pesharim*) and extracts from biblical books give the impression of being singular productions; so far none is apparently known in more than one exemplar. (In the fragments of five commentaries on Isaiah which have been identified, no duplicate interpretations are preserved.[20]) The extraordinary survival and sectarian parentage of the Scrolls, therefore, do not make them such a special case that they may not be taken as a sample of the books read in the towns and villages of Palestine. Insofar as the biblical and non-sectarian works are concerned, they encourage the supposition that similar rolls could be found throughout the land in the hands of studious or pious individuals. If credence is given to the reports of Essenes living in towns throughout Judaea and they were following the requirement of the Rule of the Community, they, too, would have had books of the Law to study. At a slightly later date, the fragments of Hebrew

18. Tov, 'Scribal Markings', pp. 41-77.

19. M.O. Wise, 'Accidents and Accidence: A Scribal View of Linguistic Dating of the Aramaic Scrolls from Qumran', in T. Muraoka (ed.), *Studies in Qumran Aramaic* (Abr Nahrain Supplement, 3; Leiden: E.J. Brill, 1992), pp. 124-67, (140-43).

20. M. Allegro, *Qumran Cave 4 I (4Q158-4Q186)* (DJD, 5; Oxford: Clarendon Press, 1968), pp. 11-30.

biblical rolls found in caves in the Judaean wilderness where refugees hid during the Second Revolt may indicate such private ownership rather than concern to save synagogue rolls; nothing implies their owners were priests. They are fragments of a roll containing Genesis, Exodus and Numbers, perhaps once a complete torah-scroll, of another of Deuteronomy, of one of Isaiah and a roll of the Minor Prophets.[21] Its language suggests the roll of the Minor Prophets in Greek found there is less likely to have belonged to a synagogue than been private property (unless it came from a synagogue in a Greek town).[22] The reports of the 'Ethiopian eunuch' travelling from Jerusalem towards Gaza reading a copy of Isaiah, perhaps bought in Jerusalem (Acts 8.28), and of the targum of Job brought to Gamaliel (see Chapter 4, p. 89) which was evidently found in private hands point in the same direction. The Mishnah tells a story of a Levite who fell ill on the way to Zoar and died at an inn where his friends had left him. When they returned, the woman inn-keeper gave them his belongings, 'his staff, his bag and the scroll of the Law that had belonged to him'.[23] In the second century AD the famous Rabbi Meir, a scribe, made his own copy of the Torah, with variants that later tradition preserved, although whether he copied from a public or a private exemplar is not stated. On one occasion when in Asia, having no exemplar, as custom required, he wrote the book of Esther from memory.[24] The Talmud accepts books could be in private possession, left on deposit, given in payment of a marriage settlement, or received as a legacy, each case suggesting the books had financial value, although copies of the Law worn out by studious scholars had to be buried.[25]

Not all the owners of books need have been scholars, as the Greek papyri show. The strength of Greek culture in Egypt and demands of government produced a considerable class of officials, tax collectors and clerks who read Greek. When their papers from the early centuries of this era are reconstituted, occasionally a few works of literature occur in them, so that E.G. Turner could write, 'Yet in the villages, too, Greek literature maintained itself, though in ill-written, sometimes mis-

---

21. Benoit, Milik and de Vaux, *Les Grottes de Muraba'ât*, nos. 1-3, 88.
22. See p. 169 n. 42 below.
23. *m. Yeb.* 16.7.
24. *b. Meg.* 18b.
25. *b. Meg.* 27a.

spelled copies…'[26] Contrariwise, another papyrologist has asserted, 'in all periods the ownership and enjoyment of literature was the prerogative of the top stratum of society',[27] which is possibly too general a statement. In the second century BC the similarity of handwriting in documents and book rolls

> suggests that some of the Ptolemaic scribes who wrote administrative documents also wrote the literary texts found in mummy cartonnage. In fact, the very presence of such texts in mummy cartonnage—which as a rule yields very few personal documents—points to scribes in the administration as (at least) the owners of literary papyri. Reading literary papyri was their recreational activity 'on the job'.[28]

Greek culture was equally strong in the Levant, mixing more easily with local habits than in Egypt, except where strict Jewish observance prevailed. In the Greek towns of Palestine, on the coast, in the Decapolis, the picture would be similar, with some high officials owning, reading and perhaps commissioning or importing copies of standard literature, lower levels having fewer but still owning some. Here we are speaking of Greek works, which could include Greek Bible texts, but in the strongly bilingual society of Palestine, there may have been people of the same status who owned Hebrew or Aramaic books also (see above, p. 162). One scholar has asserted 'fair numbers of Semitic and Greek literary works circulated in the outlying villages of Judaea', noting that there was a 'steady flow of literate people to and from Jerusalem' including priests serving their rotas and pilgrims.[29] The translation of books from Hebrew or Aramaic into Greek indicates the extended interest in works of all sorts (see Chapter 4, p. 113).

Books were costly because each one was written by hand. The copyist's time had to be paid for, in addition to the writing materials, leather or papyrus and ink. One man in Egypt in the middle of the first century gave two drachmae for a copy of a letter. That seems a large sum, but there is no indication of the length of what was probably an official

---

26. Turner, *Greek Papyri*, pp. 78, 81, cf. his 'Roman Oxyrhynchus', *JEA* 38 (1952), pp. 78-93 (90-93).

27. R.S. Bagnall, *Reading Papyri, Writing Ancient History* (London: Routledge, 1995), p. 15.

28. van Minnen, 'Taking Stock', pp. 95, 96.

29. Wise, 'Accidents and Accidence', p. 160.

communication, nor of its accessibility.[30] A standard roll of papyrus in mid-first century Egypt cost four drachmae and the wages for workmen varied from half a drachma for an unskilled man to one drachma for a skilled, according to the sparse evidence available.[31] It is very difficult to estimate the price of a book, but if a roll of Isaiah, a long one (see Chapter 1, p. 26), took two to three days to complete, then a little over three days' wages might be an appropriate figure, plus the cost of the roll. As the casual workman's wage in Palestine was one denarius or drachma according to Matthew's Gospel (20.2), and that may be an exemplary rather than a real figure, and we may suppose a scribe might expect a slightly higher rate, we can guess at a price of six to ten denarii for a copy of Isaiah.[32] While that is not cheap, it would not put books out of the reach of the reasonably well-to-do. Comparison with the Roman book trade of the first century BC and the first century AD, of which something is known, is not very helpful because the information comes from the leading literary men, from Cicero, Martial and their companions, and tells nothing about any wider circles of readers. Roman booksellers made copies to order, apparently, unless a writer requested multiple copies for gifts to his friends. If the bookseller did not have a copy of a book a customer wanted, he or the customer had to try to find one.[33] Jewish scribes worked in a different milieu, for they were not slaves, as were copyists often in Rome, but free craftsmen, and their principal task was to copy the well-known standard texts of Scripture. Further, they were not allowed to copy from dictation, as happened in Roman scriptoria. Whether they made copies of the sacred books speculatively, or only to order is unknown. Other books were

30. H.C. Youtie, 'P.Mich.Inv.855: Letter from Herakleides to Nemesion', *ZPE* 27 (1977), pp. 147-50.

31. Harris, *Ancient Literacy*, p. 195.

32. Turner, *Greek Papyri*, pp. 87-88 gives some prices for copying in Egypt in the early third century AD, including 20 and 28 drachma for 10,000 lines. W.J. Martin, *The Dead Sea Scroll of Isaiah* (London: Westminster Chapel, 1954), p. 20, supposed scribes would be paid less and estimated three denarii for the scroll. G.L. Schmeling, *Chariton* (New York: Twayre Publishers, 1974), p. 32, suggested a centurion in the late first century could afford to buy several books a month.

33. R.J. Starr, 'The Circulation of Literary Texts in the Roman World', *The Classical Quarterly* 37 (1987), pp. 213-23. See also L.C.A. Alexander, 'Ancient Book Production and the Circulation of the Gospels', in Bauckham (ed.), *The Gospels for All Christians*, pp. 71-111 ('The Circulation of Texts in the Greco-Roman World', pp. 86-104).

probably only made to order. T. C. Skeat calculated the cost of the Chester Beatty codex of the Gospels and Acts ($\mathfrak{P}^{45}$), from the mid-third century, the earliest extant. The price of the papyrus, 224 pages, would have been about 20 drachmae, the copying about 24, making a total of 44 drachmae or thereabouts.[34]

Reading in Daily Life

The Roman authorities expected to be able to communicate through writing on imperial monuments, by displaying the Senate's decrees in Rome and by despatching written orders and decisions to provincial governors for them to convey to their subjects. A typical example is the letter the emperor Claudius sent in AD 41, as a response to envoys from Alexandria, dealing in part with the status of the Jewish community there. It was read before the people and then, since the whole populace was not present to hear it, it was 'displayed publicly for individual reading'.[35] The attention given to official proclamations is illustrated by a rabbinic commentary on the book of Deuteronomy. Reflecting circumstances in the second century, it remarks on 'These commandments that I give you today are to be upon your hearts' (Deut. 6.6) that the divine commands 'should not be like some antiquated edict to which no one pays any attention, but like a new edict which everyone runs to read'. The Hebrew text simply borrows from Greek the word applied to an imperial of official 'edict', *diatagma*.[36] The attitude remains common!

Placards were another form of public notice. They were used to announce policy and judicial decisions, not only in major towns but in the villages, too. In some cases they were 'written in large clear letters so that those to whom the matter was of concern could readily grasp the sign's message'.[37] Wooden boards coated with whitewash were carried in front of condemned men going to execution, giving the reason for the

34. Skeat, 'A Codicological Analysis of the Chester Beatty Papyrus Codex', pp. 41, 42.

35. H.I. Bell, *Jews and Christians in Egypt* (London: British Museum, 1924), I, 1-9.

36. R. Hammer, *Sifre: A Tanaaitic Commentary on the Book of Deuteronomy* (New Haven: Yale University Press, 1986), p. 62 §33, reference from M. Goodman, *State and Society in Roman Galilee* (Totowa, NJ: Rowman & Allanheld, 1983), p. 141.

37. A.E. Hanson, 'Ancient Illiteracy', in Humphrey (ed.), *Literacy in the Roman World*, pp. 159-98, see pp. 179-80.

punishment (like the notice on the cross of Jesus) and in processions going to offer sacrifices to announce the donor's piety, or, sometimes, loyalty to the ruler for whose sake the offering was made. As the parades passed, people in the streets would learn their purposes from the placards, the illiterate, aware the writing could tell them something, asking the literate for the sense.[38]

The wider demand for writing in the Graeco-Roman world is exhibited in the masses of legal deeds from Egypt and the smaller number from Palestine (see Chapter 4, pp. 91-94, 115). Owning documents, while not conferring literacy, implies knowledge of writing and its value and the expectation of access to a reader when need arose. The hundreds of personal letters on papyrus recovered in Egypt also indicate the presence of readers, with husbands and sons away from home writing to wives and mothers and obviously expecting them to have access to the contents of the letters.[39] A proportion of the Greek literary texts from Egypt was copied and read by the clerks, sometimes economically using the backs of rolls of old accounts or administrative records, scrap paper which the commercial booksellers would have despised. (Here is evidence for the wider circle of readers that is lacking from Roman circles, but, which, it can safely be inferred, existed there, too.) Again, we may assume a comparable situation in Palestine whence businessmen and merchants travelled far and wide and pilgrims gathered from the four corners of the earth. The letters and notes found at Masada and in the Bar Kochba caves attest the same expectation that the addressees could read or easily find readers. Reading documents and letters demanded more effort than reading literary texts because the handwriting was more cursive, not penned with the clarity expected for books that several pairs of eyes might scan over the years. Material in Chapter 4 implies quite a lot of people could read to some extent. The wine jars from Herod's cellars at Masada suggest his butler knew enough Latin to distinguish one vintage from another and the kitchen staff could tell which jar contained salt fish paste and which honey— they might not have kept their heads for long if they served the king with the wrong dish! The legends on coins were pointless unless some users could read them, they were intended as propaganda, and the small

---

38. Such help may be needed in modern, 'literate', societies, too, as when British academics paraded in Westminster with placards reading 'Rectify the anomaly', which was meaningless to the passer-by!

39. Turner, *Greek Papyri*, p. 130.

size of the writing on the Hasmonaean coins in particular demanded some ability for comprehension. Weights, too, were not engraved with their values and the name of the authenticating officer for the satisfaction of modern scholars alone. Curiously, relatively few seals of the Hellenistic and Roman periods carried their owners' names.

The scanty information that can be collected leads to a more positive appraisal than some have offered; we conclude only the most isolated hamlets in Herodian Palestine may have lacked anyone who could read.

Who Wrote?

Scribes were the professional writers in ancient societies, holding a virtual monopoly on the craft in the early cultures of Egypt and Mesopotamia where mastery of the complex systems called for long study. They held the same position in the Levant, but the rise of the simple alphabet and its spread during the Iron Age opened the door to writing for anyone who was determined to learn and the results are evident in ancient Israel.[40] Nevertheless, scribes continued to do most of the writing and that was still the case in the first century. By then the term 'scribe' had attracted a special nuance in Jewish circles. The major task was copying the Scriptures and so becoming closely acquainted with them. Already in the later books of the Old Testament 'scribe' embraced the interpreter of records, in particular of the Law, and that became its special connotation. By New Testament times most scribes still earned their living through clerical tasks, in administrative offices or on the street. The letters and legal deeds from the 'Bar Kochba Caves', which are often signed by the scribe, illustrate their work. Beside them, probably partly identical with them, were scribes who were the academics of the day, experts in explaining the Torah and its meaning for their contemporaries, the first generations of the rabbis.[41] Their preoccupation with the sacred text drew them into minutiae of

40. A.R. Millard, 'The Knowledge of Writing in Iron Age Palestine', *TynBul* 46 (1995), pp. 207-17.

41. See J. Jeremias, *Jerusalem in the Time of Jesus* (trans. F.H. Cave and C.H. Cave; London: SCM Press, 1969), pp. 233-45; M. Goodman, 'Texts, Scribes and Power in Roman Judaea', in A.K. Bowman and G. Woolf (eds.), *Literacy and Power in the Ancient World* (Cambridge: Cambridge University Press, 1994), pp. 99-108 (102-108); C. Schams, *Jewish Scribes in the Second Temple Period* (JSOTSup, 291; Sheffield: Sheffield Academic Press, 1998).

individual words and spellings in the belief that every small difference revealed a facet of God's will, a belief taken to extremes in revisions of the Septuagint translation to reflect the Hebrew as exactly as possible, despite the grammar of Greek, a belief already evident in one Greek manuscript of the first century.[42] Amongst those experts, some would have copied the Scriptures, as Rabbi Meir did (see p. 163), a task held in great respect, ensuring every detail was correct. Lengthy regulations controlling that copying are appended to the Talmud (*Massekheth Sopherim*). Although their present formulation is mediaeval, they have been elaborated from conventions which the Dead Sea Scrolls disclose were in force in the first century BC, designed to aid accuracy in preserving the text and to maintain uniformity as it was presented for public reading. Examples are the spaces to be left between words, the paragraph divisions, unusual ways of writing certain words which were not to be altered, even where they appeared to be wrong, and inconsistent spellings which were not to be harmonized—the ancients were not so concerned about uniformity in that matter as nineteenth- and twentieth-century European societies and teachers have been.[43]

The market for synagogue rolls was continuous, for worn or damaged rolls had to be discarded, reverently buried or secreted in unfrequented places to decay by natural processes because deliberately destroying a text containing the name of God was considered a form of blasphemy. Equally constant was the demand for tiny leather sheets bearing texts from the Law to put in phylacteries (*t^ephillîn*) and on door posts (*m^ezuzâ*). Examples of both types of text recovered from the Qumran caves are written in minute characters, each letter about one millimetre high. One phylactery leaf bearing 26 lines of text measures 2.7 cm in height and 4.4 cm in width (1.06 × 1.73 in). The leather capsules to hold the four leaves of a phylactery worn on the head were also small, one is 20 mm long and 13 mm wide (0.79 × 0.51 in). The small size of these phylacteries contrasts with those in use today and gives force to Jesus' condemnation of the Pharisees who 'go about wearing broad

42. See D. Barthélemy, *Les devanciers d'Aquila* (VTSup, 10; Leiden: E.J. Brill, 1963) and Tov, *The Greek Minor Prophets Scroll*.

43. J. Barr, *The Variable Spellings of the Hebrew Bible* (The Schweich Lectures 1986; Oxford: Oxford University Press for the British Academy, 1989); A.R. Millard, 'Variable Spelling in Hebrew and Other Ancient Texts', *JTS* NS 42 (1991), pp. 106-15.

phylacteries', parading their piety (Mt. 23.5).[44] We may suppose certain scribes specialized in this minuscule writing, perhaps those suffering from myopia, as was the case in mediaeval times.

Everyday life generated a variety of bureaucratic documents. The Jewish kings, the Herodian dynasty and the Roman governors all exacted taxes from the people and they had to be assessed and collected. There were central records, inevitably of considerable volume, and local records and records kept by individual tax-collectors. As they worked on a franchise system, the records would have to be kept carefully and for some time. In Jericho, where he collected tolls on goods crossing the frontier between Roman-ruled Judaea and Transjordanian Peraea, belonging to Herod Antipas, the tax-collector Zacchaeus promised to repay four times any sum he had taken wrongfully, a promise which implies he had accounts he could check (Lk. 19.1-10). The Roman land tax needed surveyors to measure fields and estimate yields and clerks to record the taxes due, so even the most remote peasant farmers would know that the black marks on papyrus rolls or the scratches on waxed tablets spelled out their fate. Other registers would be composed as people paid their poll-tax (Lk. 2.1, 2). From Egypt there survive registers on papyrus which list men aged 14 and over due to pay tax in various villages during the first century, some with amounts paid month by month. There is also a large number of census returns noting details of each member of a household. These records had their counterparts in the different sections of Herodian Palestine, I surmise, allowing for local variations, for 'much of what we find of governmental practice in Egypt was reflected elsewhere in the Roman empire'.[45] The administrations of the Roman governors, the Herodian kings, the Temple and the self-governing cities of the Decapolis and the coast employed teams of secretaries to draw up their documents and distil their data. Letters in the books of Maccabees and the letter of Claudius Lysias, the garrison commander in Jerusalem, to Felix in Acts 23.25-35, exemplify another task of official scribes, taking messages from

44. Y. Yadin, *Tefillin from Qumran* (Jerusalem: Israel Exploration Society, 1970); J.T. Milik, 'Tefillin, Mezuzot et Targums (4Q128-4Q157)' in de Vaux, and Milik, *Qumrân Grotte 4 II (Archéologie et 4Q128-4Q157)*, pp. 33-90 (33-79); A. Millard, *Discoveries from the Time of Jesus* (Oxford: Lion Publishing, 1990), pp. 36-37 (= *Discoveries from Bible Times* (Oxford: Lion Publishing, 1997), pp. 196-97).

45. Hopkins, 'Conquest by Book', pp. 148-49.

dictation. Formal proceedings of city councils were regularly minuted, as some papyri from Egypt prove, and one of the second-century deeds in the Babatha archive presents extracts from the minutes of the Petra city council, as we have already noticed (Chapter 4, p. 115). Legal processes involved records of the claims and accusations. Two papyrus documents from Egypt offer reports on what was apparently the same affair from the different sides. One is a copy of a petition made, apparently, in AD 63, by a mixed group of dissatisfied legionaries who met the Prefect of Egypt while travelling and presented their case to him. He told them to submit details in writing and he would inform the local commanders so that they should be treated properly. Accordingly, each soldier wrote his appeal and they presented them to him individually. A few days later, the Prefect was seated in the tribunal. He made his decision, an official minute was written and two copies of it are extant. They make it clear that the case concerned men recently discharged or about to be discharged and the rights they expected. The prefect enjoined them to go off on their own business, each group—legionaries, auxiliaries, rowers—following its own procedure. He stated the distinction between each group, promised to give the question his attention, and affirmed that he had written to the local commanders that each man receive his due. The slight discrepancies between the papers do not prevent the conclusion that both deal with the same matter, the first being an aide-mémoire for the plaintiffs, the second the official record. That there are two copies of the latter indicates there were several parties interested in the ruling; the petitioners may each have taken home a copy of the record of their submission and of the Prefect's ruling.[46] In Jewish society, rabbinic authorities ruled that there should be two scribes at any legal hearing, one taking down the evidence of one side and one of the other (*m. Sanh.* 4.3; cf. *b. Sanh.* 17b), although there can be no certainty that this was in force in the first century.

46. The papyri are P. Fuad I Univ. 21+ P. Oslo inv. 1451 and P. Yale inv. 1528, edited together by S. Daris, *Documenti per la storia dell'esercito romano in Egito* (Pubblicazioni dell'Università Cattolica del Sacro Cuore; Contributi, ser. 3, Scienze storiche, 9; Milan: Societa Editrice Vita e Pensiero, 1964), nos. 101-10; cf. E.M. Smallwood, *Documents Illustrating the Principates of Gaius, Claudius and Nero* (Cambridge: Cambridge University Press, 1967), no. 297a, b (first and third texts only). Note the discussion by A. Segré, 'PYale Inv.1528 and PFuad 21', *JRS* 30 (1940), pp. 153-54. I am indebted to E.A. Judge for liberally making available to me these references and his unpublished study of these records.

Writing was essential in military circles, too. A roll of receipts for hay paid to 86 auxiliary cavalry soldiers stationed in Egypt in AD 179 appears to display the individual handwritings of almost one third of them.[47] The tattered Latin papyri left by the Roman garrison at Masada hint at the range of paperwork emanating from the military commissariat. They include a list of a soldier's expenses, an account of small quantities of bandages and oil and some letters. There are also some ostraca bearing single names which may have served as tickets; they were written by several hands. It is fair to suppose the various centurions appearing in the Gospels, whether members of the Roman army or of Herod Antipas's forces, would have had clerks accessible when they needed them for administering their troops and for communicating with superior officers. The readiness to write for all manner of reasons in a military garrison is illustrated by the hundreds of messages written on wooden slats found at Vindolanda on Hadrian's Wall. The range of people there who could write is astonishing. While many of the documents were written by secretaries, in addition to the officers 'there is strong evidence for literacy among centurions, decurions and *principales* and some evidence for its presence at lower levels', although not to the extent of 'mass literacy'.[48] We recall the lines of Vergil found at Masada and other Roman camps (see Chapter 4, pp. 130-31) and the report of the Parthians mocking the Romans after the defeat of Crassus at Carrhae (Harran) in 53 BC when they found a book of love stories in the pack of one captured officer.[49]

Archives

The documents resulting from these activities might be kept in private houses and palaces or in public record offices, as in Rome (see Preface). At the start of the Great Revolt, Josephus reports, the rebels put to the torch an archive building near the Temple in Jerusalem, 'eager to destroy the moneylenders' bonds and to prevent the recovery of debts' (*War* 2.427). A sculpture in Rome, portraying a deliberate destruction of ledgers at the time of a tax reform in AD 118, portrays a procession

47. This example is given by Hopkins, 'Conquest by Book', p. 138.
48. See A.K. Bowman, 'The Roman Imperial Army: Letters and Literacy on the Northern Frontier', in Bowman and Woolf (eds.), *Literacy and Power*, pp. 109-25, especially 112 and 119-25.
49. Plutarch, *Crassus* 32.

of men carrying large wooden tablets to be burnt, illustrating a more orderly version of what Josephus reports.[50] Jerusalem was not the only centre for archives in the land; both Josephus and the Mishnah know of a record office at Sepphoris, the original administrative capital of Galilee (*Life* 38; *m. Qid.* 4.5), and it is justifiable to deduce there were others.[51] Archive-keeping was an ancient practice, revealed in detail for this period in Egypt, where villages, as well as towns, had their own offices.[52] Officials kept copies of contracts, leases, loans and other deeds on long rolls of papyrus and made summaries or abstracts of them. Typical, well-preserved, examples were recovered from Tebtunis,

Figure 36. *Wooden tablets containing old records being taken for burning after a tax reform. The Anaglypha Traiani in Rome, early second century* AD. *(Photograph Scala, Florence.)*

50. The Plutei (or Anaglypha) Traiani, see E. Nash, *Pictorial Dictionary of Ancient Rome* (2 vols.; London: Thames and Hudson, rev. edn, 1968), II, p. 177, fig. 905; U. Ruudiger, 'Die Anaglypha Hadriani', *Antike Plastik* 12 (1973), pp. 161-74.

51. See H.M. Cotton in Cotton and Yardeni, *Aramaic, Hebrew and Greek Documentary Texts*, pp. 153-54, for the early second century AD.

52. See E. Posner, *Archives in the Ancient World* (Cambridge, MA: Harvard University Press, 1972), where some of the following references are given.

written in the first century. For example, one ledger holds abstracts of
113 contracts of cash loans made in the years 45–47 and there are
others from different places.[53] In the archives there were also preserved
reports of legal cases, with the speeches of the parties, and, again, the
individual documents were copied or pasted into comprehensive rolls.[54]
Any who wished could go to the offices to have copies made of the
deeds, the cases and the judgments given, and a number of these survive.[55] Egypt was not peculiar in this practice. Dura-Europos on the
Euphrates has yielded similar records, pieces of leather rolls from the
last two centuries BC and the first two AD, containing copies of deeds
including one about a repayment of a loan and another about a mort-
gage.[56] At Dura the excavators unearthed a group of shops by the
market-place which had been remodelled as a repository. The walls
were lined with pigeon-holes, each with numbers carefully scratched on
the plaster giving a sequence of dates between c. 129 BC and AD 198,
implying that documents were filed by years in the compartments.[57]
Public registration of private transactions inevitably made them harder
to dispute or ignore, so destroying them would be a major goal for
indebted peasants and artisans in a rebellion. There is no handbook for
ancient archivists to explain how they worked, but occasionally monumental copies of official documents include the 'shelf-marks' of the
Roman Senate's decrees, giving a hint about the organization of the
originals in Rome.[58] Josephus incorporates such a reference when

53. A.E.R. Boak, *Papyri from Tebtunis*, I (2 vols.; University of Michigan
Studies, Humanistic Series, 28; Michigan Papyri, 2; Ann Arbor, MI: University of
Michigan Press, 1933); E.M. Husselman, A.E.R. Boak and W.F. Edgerton, *Papyri
from Tebtunis*, II (2 vols.; University of Michigan Studies, Humanistic Series, 29;
Michigan Papyri, 5; Ann Arbor, MI: University of Michigan Press, 1944).

54. Grenfell and Hunt, *The Oxyrhynchus Papyri*, I, pp. 62-74, nos. 33, 34.

55. See Grenfell and Hunt, *The Oxyrhynchus Papyri*, I, pp. 79-81, no. 37, for a
first century example of a lawsuit; see further R.A. Coles, *Reports of Proceedings
in Papyri* (Papyrologia Brussellensia, 4; Brussels: Fondation Egyptologique Reine
Elisabeth, 1966).

56. Welles, Fink and Gilliam, *The Excavations at Dura-Europos*, pp. 84-98.

57. M.I. Rostovtzeff, A.R. Bellinger, F.E. Brown and C.B. Welles, *The Excavations at Dura-Europos: Preliminary Report on the Ninth Season of Work, 1935–
1936, Part* 1 (New Haven: Yale University Press, 1944), pp. 28-32, 169-76.

58. R.K. Sherk, *Roman Documents from the Greek East: senatus consulta and
epistulae to the Age of Augustus* (Baltimore, MD: The Johns Hopkins University

quoting a senatorial decision: 'Decree of the Senate copied from the Treasury from the public tablets of the quaestors Quintus Rutilius and Quintus Cornelius, quaestors of the city, second tablet, first column' (*Ant.* 14.221). He boasted about registers of priestly genealogies held in Jerusalem, where checks could be made to ensure a priest's daughter married a man within the right category, Jews from the Diaspora sending for the information (*Apion* 1.31-36).[59] He himself proudly proclaims his priestly descent, verified, he declares in one passage, 'as recorded in the public registers' which were doubtless arranged in some accessible way (*Life* 6).[60]

Shorthand?

Letters, proceedings in councils and debates in law courts all required clerks able to write fast and accurately, raising the question of the use of shorthand. Various types of abbreviated or speedy writing arose in Greece during the classical period, some mentioned by ancient authors, some extant on stone. These include simpler signs than the ordinary letters and a system of syllabic signs. True shorthand, with signs for syllables, endings, frequent terms and so forth, has not been found in Greek before the second century AD. There is an older system for Latin, reputedly invented in the first century BC by Cicero's secretary Tiro, for taking down speeches. It was first put into practice, according to ancient authors, when Cato the Younger spoke in the Senate in 63 BC. Tiro's 'Notes' became the shorthand writing of the Roman Empire, although they are only known from mediaeval manuscripts. The Vindolanda tablets include specimens of what the editors take to be of a form of shorthand.[61] Whether there was an earlier Greek system which Tiro adapted, or Greek scribes took over his invention is debated. The most extensive study of the topic concluded there was no true Greek shorthand until

Press, 1969), p. 8; cf. J.M. Reynolds, *Aphrodisias and Rome* (London: Society for the Promotion of Roman Studies, 1982), pp. 65-66.

59. See M. Stern, 'Aspects of Jewish Society: The Priesthood and Other Classes', in S. Safrai (ed.), *The Jewish People in the First Century* (2 vols; CRINT; Assen: Van Gorcum, 1974) I.2, pp. 561-630 (582-84); Schürer, *History of the Jewish People*, II, p. 242.

60. Against the scepticism of Schürer, *History of the Jewish People*, I, pp. 43-46 see Rajak, *Josephus*, pp. 14-17.

61. Bowman and Thomas, *The Vindolanda Writing Tablets*, II, pp. 71-72.

the second century AD when it was borrowed from the Latin.[62] An investigation of the work of secretaries has argued to the contrary, although apparently in ignorance of the earlier inquiry.[63] In the author's opinion, the extant evidence favours the former view, so there would not be shorthand writers in Herodian Palestine.

Local Scribes and Writers

Outside official circles, commerce, legal matters and family affairs all called for secretarial skills, providing a livelihood for a multitude of scribes in Palestine, in the same way as is so amply illustrated in Egypt. Scribes who copied the Scriptures presumably also wrote legal deeds and other documents of daily life, although there would certainly have been many scribes who wrote the latter but not the former, as we have observed. There are references to private letters in various sources from 1 Maccabees onwards, the Babylonian Talmud (*Sanh.* 11b) recalling how Rabbi Gamaliel II, about AD 100, dictated them to an amanuensis (cf. Paul's use of Tertius, Rom. 16.22). Actual examples on papyrus survive in Palestine from the early second century, and there are short notes in Hebrew and Greek from Masada (see above, Chapter 4, pp. 115-16, 123). The Bar Kochba caves have also yielded legal deeds in Greek and Aramaic, which, in addition to the scribe's signature, carry names of witnesses, often parties to the deeds, many not simply in a list written by the scribe but as the signatures of the men themselves or their representatives. In one case the scribe was the husband of the woman involved in the deed and signed on her behalf, she, it is said, 'borrowed the writing'.[64] For the Greek documents, their editor stated

62. H. Boge, *Griechische Tachygraphie und Tironische Noten: Ein Handbuch der antiken und mittelalterlichen Schnellschrift* (Berlin: Akademie Verlag, 1973).

63. E.R. Richards, *The Secretary in the Letters of Paul* (WUNT, 2. Reihe, 42; Tübingen: J.C.B. Mohr, 1991), pp. 26-43. Richards adduces a document from a cave in Wadi Murabba'at which its editor, P. Benoit, identified as an example of Greek shorthand, but the manuscript is in such bad condition and the text so uncertain that it seems unwise to rest any argument upon it. The text is Benoit, Milik and de Vaux, *Les Grottes de Murabba'ât*, pp. 275-79, no. 164. Note the earlier assertion of R.H. Gundry, *The Use of the Old Testament in St. Matthew's Gospel* (NovTSup, 18; Leiden: E.J. Brill, 1967), p. 182, 'shorthand was used...certainly by Jesus' time', following E.J. Goodspeed, *Matthew, Apostle and Evangelist* (Philadelphia: J.C. Winston, 1959).

64. Cotton and Yardeni, *Aramaic, Hebrew and Greek Documentary Texts*, p. 65, no. 13.

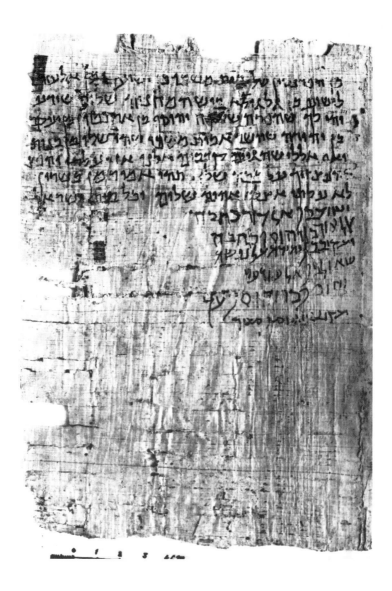

Figure 37. *'Beth Maskhu' deed with signatures of witnesses. P. Benoit, J.T. Milik and R. de Vaux,* Les Grottes de Murabba'ât, *Pl. xlv. (Photograph by courtesy of the Israel Antiquities Authority.)*

'The quality of writing in these subscriptions differ [*sic*].' One man's 'hand may be described as that of a practised, experienced writer' and in fact he wrote other documents. Two other witnesses wrote in a similar able way, but the hands of three others 'may be described as unpractised and clumsy'.[65] While the majority of these deeds date from the beginning of the second century, they continue a type current earlier. The deed dated in Nero's second year (see Chapter 4, p. 92) bears the name of the scribe with the preserved names of two witnesses and a fragmentary Aramaic deed written in a 'late Herodian' hand has the names of five,[66] showing some witnesses would sign their own names in the same way in the first century. That level of ability, if no more, is attested by the inscribed ossuaries (see Chapter 4, pp. 96-99, 113-14, 123). Mostly the names were added at the time of reburial, they were not included in the original decoration, and were often scratched very roughly, presumably inside the tomb. Unless a scribe accompanied each reburial party, someone in the family was evidently capable of writing the names. Putting names on the ossuaries anticipated, of course, later entrants to the tombs being concerned to identify the relatives whose remains were in them. The majority of ossuaries are uninscribed, it is true, although a few with partly abraded notices scribbled in charcoal may indicate there were many more bearing words or names that have vanished. Even so, the number of inscribed ones and the varieties and roughness of many epitaphs weigh in favour of nonprofessional writers.

Writing at a slightly higher level was an integral part of life, according to the Gospels. In the Parable of the Shrewd Manager, the manager instructs his master's debtor, 'Take your bill, sit down quickly and write' half the amount (Lk. 16.6, 7). The priest Zechariah, unable to speak, 'asked for a writing tablet and wrote' (Lk. 1.63) and Jesus himself wrote on the ground (Jn 8.6, although this need not mean writing words). The presence of a few pieces of labelled wine jars in Herod's storehouse at Masada points to a larger quantity of documents which

65. Lewis and Greenfield, *The Documents of the Bar Kokhba Revolt*, p. 136; cf. H.M. Cotton in Cotton and Yardeni, *Aramaic, Hebrew and Greek Documentary Texts*, pp. 144-46. On personal and proxy signatures, see J.C. Greenfield, ' "Because He/She Did Not Know Letters": Remarks on a First Millennium C.E. Legal Expression', *JANESCU* 22 (1993), pp. 39-44.

66 A. Yardeni in Cotton and Yardeni, *Aramaic, Hebrew and Greek Documentary Texts*, pp. 39-51, no. 9

have not survived. The consignments of wine shipped from Italy to Masada were only a small part of the provisions kept there and all of them were but a fraction of the reserves Herod hoarded in his castles throughout the country in case there was a revolt against him. Stocking, checking and renewing these supplies demanded a squad of clerks and supervisors, using, inevitably, roll upon roll of papyrus. Although these establishments were run down after Herod's death, when some of his castles passed into Roman hands, his sons had their own households, no doubt richly provisioned, if on a lesser scale. Their building works inevitably generated fresh files of documents, such as the construction of Herod Philip's city at Caesarea Philippi and Herod Antipas's new capital at Tiberias in Galilee. Chuza, the 'steward' of Herod Antipas (Lk. 8.3) may have had responsibility in the latter task and would have needed more than a secretary or two. The construction of Tiberias would also have increased the amount of work and so of administration in the Galilee area. Beside the scribes employed there, some of the craftsmen might know their letters at least, for stone column drums at Masada and elsewhere were marked by the masons with letters of the alphabet in the square script or in Greek to ensure they were erected in the right order.[67]

Galilee a Backwater?

All of these considerations, together with the material presented in Chapter 4, suggest many non-professionals wrote to some extent, keeping accounts, putting names on pots, ossuaries and other possessions, perhaps writing for their own information memoranda and notes and even copying books in Aramaic or Hebrew or Greek, as we know others did in Egypt at the same time and at Dura Europos a century or two later. However, a distribution map of the inscriptions and documents listed in Chapter 4 would show the majority of them coming from Jerusalem and Judaea. Galilee, where Jesus gave much of his teaching, has yielded very little. At first sight this lack might seem to support those who treat the region as a backwater, an area of self-sufficient country villages where reading and writing would be rare. The fact often overlooked is the paucity of Herodian period material from anywhere in Galilee, especially around the sea itself. Excavations have been made at a number of sites, but the finds mostly belong to later centuries. In several cases, the later remains are extensive and hamper

67. See Ch. 4, pp. 116, 125.

access to earlier levels which their foundations may have destroyed or disrupted. Yet there are various discoveries which do show that basic features of the culture were no different from those in Judaea. Ritual baths which have been identified at Gamla and Sepphoris are like those in Jerusalem and at Qumran. The distinctive stone vessels, thought to have been widely used in Jewish households because they did not have to be destroyed if they contracted ritual impurity, as did terracotta vessels, are found throughout the country. The excavations in Jerusalem brought them to prominence, but they occur at northern sites such as Gamla, Jotapata and Sepphoris, and an apparent factory site for cutting them has been located at Khirbet Reina, north-east of Nazareth.[68] Enough first-century remains have been recovered from Sepphoris, Bethsaida and Gamla to begin to reveal the local lifestyle. Sepphoris was a hellenized city, adorned by Antipas, revealing traces of its splendour as well as of less opulent lifestyles.[69] The other two sites display more of the ordinary person's life. Excavations at Bethsaida since 1988 have cleared a big house of the Hellenistic-Roman period and small parts of other buildings, with a large quantity of pottery. There is promise of more as the place was deserted after the Roman attack.[70] Gamla has proved very informative as there, also, there was no occupation after the Roman attack in AD 67. Ruins of stone-built houses contained coarse and fine ware pottery, metal tools, mill-stones and other equipment for the variety of local industries of a basically self-sufficient community. Some of the pottery was probably made elsewhere, as were the glass vessels found smashed to smithereens. Miscellaneous bronze brooches, stone and glass beads and trinkets are other goods travelling merchants might hawk from town to town. Engraved seal-stones indicate the need of some citizens to secure and mark containers or bundles and, perhaps, to seal documents, while a hoard containing 27 silver shekels (tetradrachms), 20 minted at Tyre and seven issued by Nero, 17

68. J.M. Cahill, 'The Chalk Assemblages of the Persian/Hellenistic and Early Roman Periods', in A. de Groot and D.T. Ariel (eds.), *Excavations at the City of David 1978–85* (Qedem, 33; Jerusalem: Institute of Archaeology, Hebrew University, 1992), pp. 190-274; Z. Gal, 'A Stone Vessel Manufacturing Site in the Lower Galilee', *'Atiqot* 20 (1991), pp. 25*-26*, 179-80.

69. E.M. Meyers, C.L. Meyers and K.G. Hoglund, 'Sepphoris 1994', *IEJ* 45 (1995), pp. 68-70; 'Sepphoris (Sippori), 1996', *IEJ* 47 (1997), pp. 264-68.

70. R. Arav and R.A. Freund, *Bethsaida: A City by the North Shore of the Sea of Galilee* (Kirksville, MO: Thomas Jefferson University Press, 1995).

other shekels of Tyre and seven half shekels demonstrate there were inhabitants with a little wealth. (A shekel was the equivalent of four denarii or drachmae, one denarius being a man's daily wage according to Mt. 20.2; see p. 165.) As might be expected, the preponderance of the coins are the small bronze ones issued by the Hasmonean kings, 63 per cent of the 6,200 found, but the second largest group, 941 (15 per cent) comprises coins from the self-governing cities of the Levant, Sidon, Accho and above all, again, Tyre. These coins from far and near are signs of trade and travel, of contacts beyond the fields of Gamla. In addition, the excavators added unexpectedly to Jewish numismatic history by discovering a few bronze coins struck from roughly engraved dies. On the obverse is a cup with the legend in Hebrew 'For the freedom', and on the reverse the words 'of holy Jerusalem', imitating the well-known silver shekels of the First Revolt. If these coins were minted in Gamla, as the excavator believed, they are further evidence for the value placed upon writing.[71] The foreign coins may have arrived directly from their mints in some cases, brought by travellers passing through the region, for the main route from Egypt to Damascus ran along the north-west shore of the Sea of Galilee, while local tracks followed both sides of the Sea and another from Bashan passed through Bethsaida by the northern edge on its way to Accho.[72] With these paths, the construction work at Tiberias under Antipas and a major business in salting fish located at Magdala (Taricheae), there was little likelihood of one place being isolated from another, or of parochial attitudes developing in ignorance of the wider world. The material remains, therefore, contradict the assertion that 'even the simplest technology, such as writing, was unavailable' in the culture of Herodian Palestine and that 'the possibility that' specialists in writing 'accompanied Jesus through the country side is rather remote'.[73] The evidence indicates the presence of some people, not professional scribes, who could use writing in their

71. Gutman, *Gamla*; D. Syon, 'The Coins from Gamala—Interim Report', *Israel Numismatic Journal* 12 (1992–93), pp. 34-55.

72. The roads are clearly attested for the period of Roman rule and surely followed older routes, Z. Ilan, 'Eastern Galilee, Survey of Roman Roads', *Excavations and Surveys in Israel 1989/1990*, 9 (1991), pp. 14-16; J.F. Strange, 'First Century Galilee from Archaeology', in D.R. Edwards and C.T. McCollough (eds.), *Archaeology and the Galilee: Texts and Contexts in the Graeco-Roman and Byzantine Periods* (Atlanta: Scholars Press, 1997), pp. 39-41.

73. S.J. Patterson, 'Reply to Letters', *Bible Review* 10.1 (1994), p. 10.

daily business throughout Palestine, even in rural regions, able to make notes of a preacher's words if they wished.

Who Wrote Books?

To write lists, accounts, legal deeds, letters, notes, reports or minutes of meetings did not require the same abilities or motivation as writing a book; those were the daily tasks of the professional scribes and jobs that others might do occasionally, books could be composed by people from all walks of life.

Publishers' advances were unknown in the first centuries BC and AD. Authors either lived on the patronage of wealthy men, or on private means, or on their income from employment in government service, in teaching or other work. Once a book was written and copied there was no way an author could take royalties from future copies, for anyone might make them wherever an example of the book was to be found. Vergil, the greatest Roman poet, enjoyed the support of Maecenas and then of the emperor Augustus. After AD 70 it was imperial provision also that enabled the Jewish author Josephus to write in security in Rome. Not all were so fortunate in their patrons. The poet Martial (c. AD 40–104) spent years in poverty after his friends were involved in an ineffective conspiracy against Nero, eventually receiving sufficient help to become independent. His fellow poet Juvenal lived for some time on a very meagre handout. Inherited riches permitted Columella to draw on experience farming his large estates in Italy to compose a comprehensive guide to the best practices in agriculture. Perhaps the majority of Greek and Latin writers of this period were educated men from well-to-do families who were employed in official positions. Gallus, a poetry-writing friend of Vergil, became the first Roman governor of Egypt and there a piece of papyrus found in 1978 preserves the only known copy of any of his verses, two lines alone being quoted by later authors.[74] Pliny the Elder was a soldier, a lawyer and at some time a governor; the historian Tacitus was a military commander, an official and an orator. The orator Quintilian made his living from teaching his skill, the emperor Vespasian paying his salary. Earlier, the poet Horace had to obtain a job as a record-keeper before his poems drew him into the orbit of Maecenas's generosity. In a different class was Phaedrus, a

74. R.D. Anderson, P.J. Parsons and R.G.M. Nisbet, 'Elegiacs by Gallus from Qasr Ibrîm', *JRS* 69 (1979), pp. 125-55.

Latin Aesop. He was the well-educated son of slaves who became a freedman in Augustus's household. Another poet, Titus Calpurnius Siculus, active in Nero's reign, may also have been a freedman.

Each of these authors had a compulsion to write. For those who had patrons it was a necessity; for the wealthy and leisured it was sometimes felt as a responsibility, sometimes it was a diversion. Each had something to communicate and no doubt complex reasons for doing so which are not necessarily evident to-day. Petronius in the mid-first century wrote the *Satyricon*, with its famous account of Trimalchio's dinner, to entertain and, almost certainly, to mock the excesses of his time, while a contemporary politician, Seneca the Younger, advocated a type of Stoicism in his books and plays. Presenting an account of past events was often a way to state a case for change, or to praise past heroes. On one hand were biographers such as Suetonius, who tried to portray personalities in his *Lives of the Caesars*, whereas Tacitus set out to demonstrate the faults of the autocracy in his *Annals*. His *Life of Agricola* portrays his father-in-law as an ideal Roman, making an explicit contrast to the emperor Domitian. On the other hand, Velleius Paterculus, who had served in Germany and the Balkans with Tiberius, tried to create his *History of Rome* to enhance his commander's reputation. Experts wanted to share their knowledge, to advise and to educate. Columella the agriculturalist (see above) and Quinitilian, the orator, wrote for those reasons, as did Frontinus, who wrote about the art of warfare and about water supplies, Celsus, whose books covered many topics, most notably medicine, and Dioscurides, an army doctor, who described the preparation of drugs of all sorts. Beside these, there were authors whose works are lost and some whose works survive but whose names are lost, among the latter being authors of novels or romances, of religious tracts and of magic spells (cf. Acts 19.19).[75]

Propagandistic purposes lay behind the works of Josephus, attempting to make the Jewish Revolt seem comprehensible to a Roman audience, even if unacceptable, and to make Jewish history and religion intelligible. Attacks on his own conduct provoked him to write his biography. The slightly older Alexandrian Jewish writer Philo defended

---

75. See Grant, *Greek and Latin Authors*; P.E. Easterling and B.M.W. Knox (eds.), *The Cambridge History of Classical Literature. I. Greek Literature* (Cambridge: Cambridge University Press, 1985); E.J. Kenney and W.V. Clause (eds.), *The Cambridge History of Classical Literature. II. Latin Literature* (Cambridge: Cambridge University Press, 1982).

his people against popular and imperial attack in some books and tried to interpret the Hebrew Bible in Greek terms in others. The Letters of St Paul fall into this category as they were intended to persuade their addressees to follow his interpretation of the teachings of Jesus. A similar purpose can be seen as the reason for composing the Gospels.[76] In Jewish circles where Aramaic or Hebrew were written there were authors, too, almost all anonymous. The works that survive are the products of religious writers, pious men who penned hymns or composed prophecies and apocalyptic visions, disclosing, if not deliberately propagating, particular doctrines they espoused (see Chapter 4, pp. 90, 91). Who those people were we cannot discover. Priests and lawyers may well have been among them; there is no reason why pious scribes and able laymen should not have contributed also. The Dead Sea Scrolls illustrate how a group of people, whatever their particular affiliation, could engage in a range of composition that covers most genres of literature current in its day.

In Rome it was customary during the first century for an author to give readings of drafts of the work he was preparing to circles of friends, or even to the public. He would note the reaction of his audiences, their comments and criticisms after each reading in order to make improvements as he revised the text for publication, which was essentially making the composition available for reading to wider audiences.[77] The practice is an obvious one—authors still submit their work to friends and colleagues for their opinions—which may have been common.

The impulse to write, therefore, had a multitude of roots, from a desire to amuse to a need for money to a zeal to share a conviction arising from a tradition of literary composition. It was an impulse which was not restricted to the leisured or the wealthy classes, nor to the capital cities, although a large proportion of surviving books did come from those people and those places.

76. See Bauckham, 'For Whom Were the Gospels Written?', pp. 9-48.

77. See E.J. Kenney, 'Authors and Public', in Kenney and Clause (eds.), *Cambridge History of Classical Literature*, II, pp. 10-15; F.G. Downing, 'Word-Processing in the Ancient World: The Social Production and Performance of Q', *JSNT* 64 (1996), pp. 29-48.

Chapter 7

ORAL TRADITION OR WRITTEN REPORTS?

Writing was readily accessible to the inhabitants of Herodian Palestine, as the previous chapters have shown, and used for a variety of purposes. Although there was not a high rate of literacy, there were people who read and wrote; the society was not an illiterate one as was, for example, pre-Roman Britain. There is a strong opinion, however, that a Jewish teacher would not expect his words to be put into writing but passed on by word of mouth and so, it is alleged, that is what happened with the teachings and deeds of Jesus; little or nothing was written until the generation that had witnessed his life had died out and the Romans had taken Jerusalem in AD 70. The grounds for this view need to be investigated.

The Oral Tradition School and its Successors

For most of the twentieth century the dominant theories about the origins of the Gospels have argued, or assumed, that oral traditions lie behind the earliest written texts. According to one standard text-book, 'It is incontrovertible that in the earliest period there was only an oral record of the narrative and sayings of Jesus'. Another authority stated, 'There was a gap of several decades between the public ministry of Jesus and the writing down of his words by the authors of the Gospels. During this time what was known about Jesus was handed on orally.' The Jesus Seminar, attempting to discover 'the real Jesus' by using these criteria, and others, has similarly accepted a phase of oral tradition before any written accounts were produced, but reduced it to two decades, asserting that the followers of Jesus 'were technically illiterate'.[1] His followers spread stories about the deeds of their master and

1.   Kümmel, *Introduction to the New Testament*, pp. 55, 56; E. Lohse, *The Formation of the New Testament* (trans. M.E. Boring; Nashville, TN: Abingdon,

especially reports of his teachings by word of mouth. Only after the fall of Jerusalem were those accounts collected and put into writing as the Four Gospels.

The basic theories about oral tradition in the Bible stem from the work of Hermann Gunkel (1862–1932) who began by taking analogies from Teutonic and early Greek practices as the pattern for delineating the growth of biblical literature. Working on Genesis, he isolated a series of individual Hebrew stories or legends which had little detail of characters or circumstances, only the essentials, with brief speeches, which might be obscure or riddle-like. Often they could be reduced to a single sentence or two, usually in poetry. Such stories were open to expansion as hearers demanded to know more than they were told.[2] After Gunkel, K.L. Schmidt applied this approach to the Gospels, delineating the small segments which at first existed independently in oral form.[3] Martin Dibelius carried this method forward in his dissertation, *Die Formgeschichte des Evangeliums*, published in 1919,[4] and the volume by Rudolph Bultmann, *Die Geschichte der synoptischen Tradition*, published in 1921,[5] laid the foundation for Form Criticism, the analysis of the Gospel narratives by literary genre. They all worked with the assumption that the Gospels are not literature in the sense Western cultures understand it, but rather compilations of small, independent units akin to popular, folk-lore stories, which circulated orally. Their aim was to distinguish between the work of the Evangelists who wrote the Gospels, the pieces of information they wove together and the kernels of that information which might reach back to the time of Jesus himself. Following Gunkel's lead, they defined various forms in the text. First there are sayings, classed as wisdom, prophetic and apocalyptic, parables, legal sayings and rules for the community of Jesus' followers. Often a brief framework sets a saying in a particular situation

1981), p. 106; R.W. Funk and R.W. Hoover, *The Five Gospels: What did Jesus really Say?* (New York: Macmillan, 1993), pp. 18, 26, 27.

2.   H. Gunkel, *The Legends of Genesis: The Biblical Saga and History* (trans. W.H. Carruth, 1901, repr., with Introduction by W.F. Albright; New York: Schocken Books, 1964).

3.   K.L. Schmidt, *Der Rahmen der Geschichte Jesu* (Berlin: Trowitzsch, 1919).

4.   2nd edn, 1933; *From Tradition to Gospel* (trans. B.L. Woolf; London: Nicholson & Watson, 1934).

5.   3rd edn, 1958; *The History of the Synoptic Tradition* (trans. J. Marsh; Oxford: Basil Blackwell, 1968).

and sometimes a discussion or dispute serves to highlight the point. Second are the stories of miracles and other events, stories about individuals and about religious activities. At first all these circulated in very short forms without any context or connection between them. The oral traditions were variable, the short sayings could appear in different circumstances, parables could be reapplied for new situations. Now the identification of these various forms was bound to the supposition that they came from the preaching and teaching of the early church. Consequently, they might reflect the situations in which they were used, their life setting (*Sitz im Leben*). The church, therefore, had a major part in creating the Gospel traditions. When problems arose as the church grew and extended far beyond the frontiers of Palestine, appropriate words of Jesus would be quoted and perhaps expanded or adapted as seemed fit. Indeed, there would be little compunction in producing new sayings or stories and associating them with Jesus to cope with a difficulty if no suitable tradition existed. As preaching and teaching proceeded, separate sayings were linked together and the settings elaborated. Form critics claim to be able to peel away those accretions to arrive close to the earliest memories about Jesus by applying several criteria. These are the principal ones: dissimilarity—if a saying or deed of Jesus is different from anything usual in Jewish circles of his time and in the early church, then it may be attributed to him; multiple attestations—there is some ground for confidence in a text that is found in more than one of the Gospels, or more than one of their putative sources ('Q' etc.); Semitic background—strong signs of underlying Aramaic language and poetic style or first century Palestinian background may also point to the origin of a passage in the earliest days of Christianity; finally, the coherence of one passage with others sharing the same subject may indicate an accurate reminiscence.

The application of form criticism to the Gospels led, at its most extreme, to the verdict that 'the message of Jesus as given to us by the Synoptists is, for the most part, not authentic but was minted by the faith of the primitive Christian community',[6] with the number of sayings thought to be traceable to Jesus put at no more than 40. Recently, the Jesus Seminar, working in America since 1985, has concluded less than 20 per cent of the sayings placed on Jesus' lips in the Gospels could have originated with him.

6.   E. Käsemann, *Essays on New Testament Themes* (London: SCM Press, 1968), p. 15.

Teaching and Learning in Rabbinic Style

In the 1950s, the Swedish scholars H. Riesenfeld and B. Gerhardsson drew attention to an aspect of the life-setting of oral tradition in the Gospel records which had been largely disregarded. Pointing out that Jesus and most of his followers were Jews, they emphasized the way tradition was handed down in Jewish circles by word of mouth and the high degree of accuracy that could be expected in the oral transmission of a Jewish teacher's words. Jesus, like a rabbi, would expect his disciples to learn his teachings by heart and would deliver them in ways that could be memorized easily. Then, as the early Christians came to regard them as holy, they would preserve them in fixed forms, without alteration.[7] Those forms are still visible in passages where an Aramaic poetic pattern is traced behind the Greek text, Riesenfeld citing Mt. 7.24-27 as an example.[8] This was a positive advance inasmuch as it grew from knowledge of early Jewish practice reaching back to the first century.

The Gospels clearly portray Jesus as a wandering teacher without a permanent base or school. Only once did he write, and then in a highly impermanent way (Jn 8.6-8[9]). He gave all his teaching orally (see the numerous occurrences of 'he said, he spoke' in any concordance) and he could assume many of his hearers knew the Bible well from their schooling and from regular synagogue readings (see Chapter 6, pp. 157-58). He built upon that as he preached, using common techniques of exposition, expecting his audience to understand his reasoning, even if they did not understand his mission (see, e.g., Mk 10.1-12; Lk. 20.27-29). Like the teachers of his day, he started from the current situation, in particular from the way the Law was explained and applied in daily life and the ways he saw people behaving around him.

7.   H. Riesenfeld, *The Gospel Tradition and its Beginnings* (London: Mowbray, 1957); B. Gerhardsson, *Memory: Tradition and Transmission in Early Christianity* (Acta Seminarii Neotestamentici Upsaliensis, 22; Lund: C.W.K. Gleerup, 1964).

8.   Riesenfeld, *The Gospel Tradition*, pp. 24-25.

9.   Although the manuscript evidence for this episode varies, it is generally considered to be a genuine report from the first century, see B.M. Metzger, *Textual Commentary on the Greek New Testament* (London: United Bible Societies, 2nd edn, 1994) *ad loc.*

The Oral Torah

The whole of Jewish teaching was based upon the written Torah and the chain of its interpreters traced from Moses through Ezra to the leading exponents of the Herodian period, Hillel and Shammai. This interpretation was the Oral Law. The Torah formed the book *par excellence* and, even where it was unintelligible, no other book could be set on a par with it. The authorities in Palestine permitted a free translation into Aramaic (a targum) to follow synagogue readings from the Hebrew rolls and give the sense of the text, adducing the pattern of Ezra's assembly (Neh. 8.8; see Chapter 4, p. 86). The rendering was made verse by verse, extempore or from memory; unlike the one reading the Hebrew, the interpreter was allowed neither to read his words, nor to look at the Scripture text. Thus there should be no confusion of the fixed, sacred original with a current or transient understanding. This attitude applied to the Law of Moses (the Torah) above all the other books of Scripture. Yet people had long recognized the need to explain the Law more extensively. By the time of the Hasmonean kings, society had changed in major ways from the days of the Achaemenid Persian rule, let alone the Israelite Monarchy, so new circumstances needed applications adjusted to them, or new laws. Towns which had grown since the writing of the Torah, like Sepphoris, Jotapata and Gamla in the Galilee area had to be included within the scope of the laws (see *m. 'Arak.* 9.6). While Moses was the unequalled authority, for he had conveyed God's commands, the biblical texts took for granted many practical details that had to be spelt out, so rules were agreed, for example, over the methods permitted for slaughtering animals and those which were not allowed (compare Deut. 12.21, 'you may slaughter animals… as I have commanded you,' with *m. Ḥul.* 1.2-4 which specify the methods). Among matters not covered in the Torah yet demanding regulation was the important question of what made one's hands ritually unclean (*m. Yadaim*). Discussion of some of the laws of Moses extended them far beyond their apparent sense. That is very obvious in the case of the prohibition, 'Do not cook a kid in its mother's milk' which appears thrice in the Torah, once thought to be rejecting a Canaanite custom (Exod. 23.19; 34.26; Deut. 14.21).[10] In order to avoid

10. The assertion that it is mentioned in a text of the thirteenth century BC from Ugarit, proposed by H.L. Ginsberg in 1935 ('Notes on "The Birth of the Gracious

the possibility of breaking that rule, the Oral Law declared no meat should be cooked in milk, meat and milk or cheese should not come into contact; fish and fowl were excepted because their mothers have no milk (*m. Ḥul.* 8). Those developments form one basis for the continuing food laws of observant Jews (*kosher* food). Much of the Oral Law probably came into being with the rise of the group that became known as the Pharisees in the second century BC.

The agreed practices were formulated as regulations. Where there was uncertainty or dispute, the rulings respected teachers gave were handed on in their names by their pupils, sometimes altered and adapted, or coupled with alternative views. This stream of opinions grew into a torrent flowing through Herodian times and on into the second century AD. After the Fall of Jerusalem and the loss of the Temple, the altered situation in Palestine forced great changes on the religious community and left much to be remembered in the hope of a restoration (such as details of the Temple buildings and rituals). There was a variety of devices for formulating and collating the teachings so that they could be memorized more readily—for example, by catchwords, by numbers, by pattern—and the majority of them were condensed into one or a few sentences, for the same reason. The emphasis lay upon correct transmission of the contents rather than the exact words, in fact, the terse formulations removed most traces of individuality.[11]

Leading teachers made efforts to collect and arrange the mass of memorized opinions; we hear of set arrangements of traditional material being prepared earlier in the second century, in the days of the rabbis Meir and Akiba, culminating in the work of Rabbi Judah the

---

and Beautiful Gods"', *JRAS* [1935], pp. 45-72) and often repeated, was undermined by A. Herdner's re-reading (*Corpus des tablettes en cunéiformes alphabétiques découvertes à Ras-Shamra-Ugarit de 1929 à 1939* [Institut français d'archéologie de Beyrouth, Bibliothèque archéologique et historique, 79; Paris: Geuthner, 1963], p. 98) and doubted for some time (e.g. P.C. Craigie, 'Deuteronomy and Ugaritic Studies', *TynBul* 28 [1977], pp. 155-69, especially 156-59) has fallen in the face of fresh collation of the cuneiform tablet, see R. Ratner and B. Zuckerman, 'A Kid in Milk?: New Photographs of KTU 1.23, Line 14', *HUCA* 57 (1986), pp. 15-60.

11. See J.M. Baumgarten, 'Form Criticism and the Oral Law', *JSJ* 1 (1974), pp. 34-40, especially 36, with references; P.S. Alexander, 'Orality in Pharisaic-Rabbinic Judaism at the Turn of the Era', in H. Wansborough (ed.), *Jesus and the Oral Gospel Tradition* (JSNTSup, 64; Sheffield: Sheffield Academic Press, 1991), pp. 159-84.

Prince, about AD 200. His achievement is the Mishnah.[12] This large compilation groups the sayings under topical headings (e.g. Tithes, Heave Offerings, the Sabbatical Year, Marriage Settlements). In due course that work attracted discussion, explanation and commentary, producing the Jerusalem Talmud (about AD 400) and the Babylonian Talmud (about AD 500). The process of study, elucidation and application of the Torah and the accumulation of interpretations continues to this day (see Chapter 8, p. 219). The earliest written texts of parts of the Mishnah that survive belong to the end of the first millennium. They were found in the Cairo Genizah, a synagogue room in which unwanted books and documents were stored from the ninth century until they were brought to Europe in the 1890s, providing an immense source of information about mediaeval Jewish society, letters and thought.[13] The same source provided pieces of talmudic texts, but an extraordinary witness to a section of the Palestinian Talmud exists in a mosaic inscription of 29 lines laid at the synagogue of Rehov near Beth-Shan about 600. The text details the requirements of tithes and the sabbatical year Jews living in the Holy Land were expected to follow. Part of the same text was found painted on a plastered column. That has indications that the whole composition was originally a letter sent to advise the community about the matters mentioned.[14]

Although there is room for some uncertainty, it seems possible that Rabbi Judah's compilation was a written book. Nevertheless, the Talmud always assumes there are scholars who know the Mishnah by heart and does not quote it as a written source.[15] Before his action, the Oral Law was, officially, unwritten. The Babylonian Talmud sets out the rule 'You are not to pass on sayings (received) in writing by word of mouth; you are not to pass on sayings (received) by word of mouth in writing' (*Giṭ.* 60b). Writing was banned not only for the Oral Law but for almost everything with religious content, so the rabbis opposed the writing of

12. The standard English translation is H. Danby, *The Mishnah* (London: Oxford University Press, 1933).

13. S.C. Reif, *A Guide to the Taylor-Schechter Genizah Collection* (Cambridge: Cambridge University Library, 1973).

14. See J. Naveh, *On Stone and Mosaic: The Aramaic and Hebrew Inscriptions from Ancient Synagogues* (Jerusalem: Israel Exploration Society, 1978), pp. 79-85 [in Hebrew]; F. Vitto, 'Rehob' in Stern (ed.), *New Encyclopedia*, pp. 1272-74 .

15. Gerhardsson, *Memory*, pp. 159-60.

prayers for communal use, also.[16] The transition from oral to written took place between the seventh and ninth centuries, only occasionally earlier, according to S.C. Reif, and the 'current scholarly consensus' accepts there was 'a distinct preference not to commit [prayers and blessings] to an authoritative written text' earlier than that period.[17]

The Swedish scholars' focus on Jewish teaching practices and in particular the transmission of the Oral Law to elucidate the methods of Jesus and the earliest history of the Gospel material drew criticism because of the date of the Mishnah.[18] It came into being as we have it a century or more after the Gospel period and also after the catastrophes of the Fall of Jerusalem and the failure of the Bar Kochba Revolt (AD 132–35) had indelibly marked and transformed the practices of Judaism; therefore its evidence cannot be regarded as satisfactorily reflecting first-century customs without caution. Moreover, the Mishnah codifies the teachings of the party that survived the Fall of Jerusalem, the descendants of the Pharisees, while other parties may not have worked in the same ways and certainly disagreed with the Pharisees on many questions. Indeed, the basic attitudes it portrays in this matter had probably not changed greatly through those years as the Dead Sea Scrolls reveal. The similarities with the practice of Greek teachers from Socrates onwards also support that.

Oral Teaching in Greek Circles

The parade statement for the key role of oral teaching in the classical world is taken from one of the last of Plato's dialogues, *Phaedrus*. Plato (c. 427–347 BC), presenting a discussion between Socrates and Phaedrus, had a mythical Egyptian king confronted with the first writing say: '…this invention will produce forgetfulness in those who learn to use it, because they will not practice their memory' and 'it would be an elixir

16. *b. Šab.*13.4, cited by S. Safrai, 'Oral Tora', in S. Safrai (ed.), *The Literature of the Sages* (CRINT, II. 3a; Assen: Van Gorcum, 1987), pp. 35-119 (45-49).

17. S.C. Reif, *Judaism and Hebrew Prayer* (Cambridge: University Press, 1993), p. 124; cf. his 'Codicological Aspects of Jewish Liturgical History', *BJRL* 75 (1993), pp. 117-31 (118-21).

18. See the criticisms by M. Smith, 'A Comparison of Early Christian and Early Rabbinic Tradition', *JBL* 82 (1963), pp. 169-76, and G. Widengren, 'Tradition and Literature in Early Judaism and in the Early Church', *Numen* 10 (1963), pp. 42-83, with B. Gerhardsson's response, *Tradition and Transmission in Early Christianity* (ConNT, 20; Lund: C.W.K. Gleerup, 1964).

of reminding'. Written words, Plato observed, are immutable and available to all,[19] whereas, as he stated in his Seventh Letter, 'every serious man in dealing with really serious subjects carefully avoids writing, lest thereby he may possibly cast them as a prey to the envy and stupidity of the public'.[20] Plato reverenced the highest and first truths of Nature and would not expose what he perceived of them to the world in writing. Accordingly, he announced, 'there will never be any treatise of mine dealing therewith'.[21]

Those comments have to be read in the light of their context. When he wrote the Seventh Letter, Plato was angry that his former student, Dionysius of Syracuse, had published under his own name the lessons he had learnt from the philosopher. More importantly, he was arguing that books hinder the inquiring mind, for they may impart information or remind the reader of what he has already heard, but they cannot engage in dialogue. In that respect they can never be a substitute for 'the word which is written with intelligence in the mind of the hearer, of which the written word may justly be called the image…the living and breathing word of one who knows'. Writing had value only as an *aide mémoire*: one 'will write, when he writes, to treasure up reminders (ὑπομνήματά) for himself when he comes to the forgetfulness of old age, and for others who follow the same path…'[22]

Common experience shows hearing a speaker or teacher at first hand is more effective than reading the words in books, for intonation, pauses and gestures are part of the message which cannot be carried in writing without distracting from the theme. The speaker's presence has its own impact. Members of a class, a congregation or an audience can relay what they have experienced, often with appropriate vocal or physical emphases, again in a multi-dimensional 'speech', more impressive than ink on paper can ever be. More readily remembered still are the words and ideas that spring from the student in response to a teacher's expositions and questions, the dialogue or 'dialectic' that was the hallmark of Plato's Academy. That was the 'living voice' which was pri-

19. Plato, *Phaedrus* §§274, 275.

20. Plato, *Epistles*.

21. Plato, *Epistles*. That determination is repeated in the Second Letter, probably a later concoction, addressed to Dionysius of Sicily who is commanded to burn the letter after receiving it, and to listen to Plato's ideas conveyed by one of his pupils. Plato, *Epistles* 2.314C.

22. Plato, *Phaedrus* §§267A, D.

mary for some teachers. Quintilian, the Roman teacher of rhetoric living in the first century AD wrote of those who 'have the advantage not merely of reading' someone's book, 'but of having heard most of his views from his own lips', then noted the value of reading as well as listening.[23] Following Plato's observation that reading does not confer skill,[24] the physician Galen in the second century AD scorned those who relied on books for identifying plants. Only an experienced instructor could demonstrate how to tell the difference between one herb and another for preparing medicines, and other experts reckoned practical experience was the only way to learn their subjects. 'Reading from a book is not the same as...learning from the living voice.'[25] Further, Galen required his books, even on philosophy, to be read with a teacher, for many of them are versions of his lectures. Thus the attitude Plato displayed in the fourth century BC is seen to continue in the second century AD. While the problem is comprehensible, for we recognize the difference between reading a speech by, for example, Sir Winston Churchill, and hearing the author declaim it, in a society so conditioned by writing as ours, a clearer comparison may be made with music. Inventions of the twentieth century have made it possible to preserve records of composers playing or conducting their own compositions, so we can hear how they wanted them to be played. In contrast, the works of a Beethoven or a Brahms, a Bach or a Handel can be subject to a variety of interpretations because the written scores cannot convey every nuance of the composers' concepts, they are as immutable and as limited as the written word.

Oral Tradition in the Early Church

Naturally, the influence of Greek academic tradition appears in writings of early Christians who had been educated in that way. Most relevant to the present study is the boast of one of the earliest Christian writers of the post-Apostolic age, Papias, who died in 130. His books are lost and

23. Quintilian, *Inst. Orat.* 5. 7.7; 10.1.16-19.
24. *Phaedrus* §268C.
25. L.C.A. Alexander, 'The Living Voice: Scepticism towards the Written Word in Early Christian and in Graeco-Roman Texts', in D.J A. Clines, S.E. Fowl and S.E. Porter (eds.), *The Bible in Three Dimensions: Essays in Celebration of Forty Years of Biblical Studies in the University of Sheffield* (JSOTSup, 87; Sheffield: Sheffield Academic Press, 1990), pp. 221-47.

we rely on the church historian Eusebius for quotations from them, including this one: 'I did not suppose that things from the books would aid me so much as the things from the living and continuing voice.' It stands in an introductory section where he explains that he took care to teach only things he was sure were true, attentively seeking the recollections of people who had learnt from the lips of the original disciples.[26] Not long afterwards, Clement of Alexandria (c. 150–215), the Christian scholar who taught Origen, produced several important studies. His *Stromateis* begins with what has recently been characterized as 'an elaborate justification for the use of writing' in which Clement 'apparently feels the need to apologize for producing a book at all': 'Now this treatise is not a carefully-wrought piece of writing for display, but just my notes stored up for old age, a "remedy for forgetfulness", nothing but a rough image, a shadow of those clear and living words which I was thought worthy to hear, and of those blessed and truly worthy men.'[27] His words 'a remedy for forgetfulness' are a deliberate allusion to Plato's comments in *Phaedrus* reported above, used to defend his action in writing a sort of Christian philosophy.[28] At the same time, he had no hesitation in writing other books on Christian behaviour (*Paedagogus* and *Protrepticus*) and the words quoted may be read as an expression of modesty on his part. Again, the reports of those who heard from first-hand witnesses are held in the highest esteem; 'the role of the living teacher was crucial', the written text was secondary, 'in that it may only be studied with the aid of a teacher and stands ready at any time to be corrected, updated or revised'.[29]

The Acceptance of Oral Tradition

With the evidence for the role of oral tradition in the ancient world so clear, the majority of scholars accept such statements as 'All our knowledge of him [Jesus] is drawn from the deposit of a tradition which was transmitted for several decades by word of mouth.'[30] They then assume

---

26. For Papias's work, see A.D. Baum, 'Papias als Kommentator evangelischer Aussprüche Jesu', *NovT* 38 (1996), pp. 257-76.

27. Alexander, 'The Living Voice', p. 221.

28. Alexander, 'The Living Voice', p. 242.

29. Alexander, 'The Living Voice', p. 244.

30. F.W. Beare, *The Earliest Records of Jesus* (Oxford: Basil Blackwell, 1962), p. 16.

a fluidity in the tradition which allowed the early church to mould what it received and augment it, as we have seen. This attitude can reach an extreme which appears to rule out any other suggestions. Any teacher may act as the following sentence supposes: 'Oral tradition is fluid. Jesus no doubt altered his aphorisms and parables from time to time, from occasion to occasion, adapting them each time to his audience.'[31] In a reworked form published two years later—the reworking observable because both versions are extant—it raises serious questions:

> We can imagine Jesus speaking the same aphorism or parable on different occasions. We can further imagine that his followers would find themselves repeating these sayings in contexts of their own, not in Jesus' precise words, but in their own words as they recalled the essence of what he had said. Various leaders in the Jesus movement would then have started to develop their own independent streams of tradition, and these streams would eventually culminate in written gospels.[32]

Together the rabbinic and Greek educational styles and the remarks of early Christian writers make a case strongly in favour of the theory that the Christian Church preserved the teachings of Jesus principally in oral form through the first three to five decades of its life. Persuasive as the case has been for the majority of New Testament scholars, objections can be raised and arguments adduced which weaken it, while the discoveries about writing in Palestine and publication of more texts from the Dead Sea Scrolls suggest that it can no longer stand unchallenged. In his examination of the history of the Gospel traditions, Martin Dibelius wrote, 'one requires a constructive method which attempts to include the conditions and activities of life of the first Christian Churches'.[33] For Dibelius the 'constructive method' was largely devised from the very texts he was studying, with the form-critical presuppositions about oral literature outlined above (p. 186). After eight decades, to meet Dibelius's requirement, currently accessible evidence has to be brought into play, both from literary and from material sources.

31. R.W. Funk, R.W. Hoover and M.H. Smith, *The Gospel of Mark: Red Letter Edition* (Sonoma, CA: Polebridge Press, 1991), p. 3.

32. Funk and Hoover, *The Five Gospels*, p. 29.

33. Dibelius, *From Tradition to Gospel*, p. 10.

Criticisms of Form Criticism

While it is clearly right to try to discover the circumstances in which the episodes in the Gospels arose, the contexts the Form Critics have envisaged had a deeper foundation in supposition than in actual situations of the first century and, furthermore, their methods of defining the oral tradition were not drawn from the world of the ancient Near East. They have also attracted considerable opposition on the grounds that they are contrary to logic and reality.[34] Without entering the debate about the criteria of Form Criticism, there are some comments to be made which are relevant to the present study.

Hermann Gunkel's basic vision of very brief oral sayings does not conform to the attested examples of oral tradition in non-literate societies. Extremely long compositions existed and were passed on, compositions which followed certain patterns, yet could diverge at will, and which might interweave various forms of narrative with differing contents (Homer's epics are examples). At no point in the first century should we suppose oral tradition was incapable of handling anything longer than one- or two-line sayings or very short stories, or that a teacher would deliver a lesson peculiar to him on only one occasion.

Often the Gospel texts are treated as if they arose in an entirely illiterate society. A distinction is set up between the educated élite, with those who used writing for business purposes in the major urban centres, and the rural, peasant population who would be ignorant of it. As we have seen, that is an unlikely picture, writing would have been known about everywhere (Chapter 6). Consequently, there were usually people present who could have written something they heard, whether for their own reference or to inform others. The waxed writing-tablets

---

34. See for example, C.L. Blomberg, *The Historical Reliability of the Gospels* (Leicester: IVP, 1987); a clear general discussion is given by G.N. Stanton, *Gospel Truth? New Light on Jesus and the Gospels* (London: Harper-Collins, 1995), pp. 49-62. On the attribution to Jesus of rulings or 'prophetic words' created to deal with problems that arose in the post-Easter church, F.F. Bruce pertinently observed how the absence of any Gospel texts about one of the major questions that troubled the early Christians, whether Gentile converts should be circumcised or not, could imply that inventing authoritative sayings of Jesus was not a normal practice, see 'Are the New Testament Documents still Reliable?', in K. Kantzer (ed.), *Evangelical Roots: A Tribute to Wilbur Smith* (Nashville, TN: Thomas Nelson, 1978), pp. 49-61 (54).

provided a simple, handy method. That means the spoken words might be fixed quickly and in the form given. That also means there need be no great dichotomy between the spoken and the written. Exaggerated emphasis has been placed upon the change made to oral compositions by writing them; change there may be, but there need not be, especially if a report is being prepared. Greek papyri from Egypt and one of the documents of Babatha (Chapter 4, p. 115) preserve minutes of town council meetings and tribunals with the statements of the parties while letters may preserve immediate observations and reports (see Chapter 6). There are form critical questions about these documents and their stylistic features, yet they can be analysed and dissected, as are the Gospels, without any possibility of treating them as compositions put together long after the events or tailored to suit other situations. Oral form does not preclude written tradition; from the moment of utterance, words could be preserved in writing.

Another hypothesis involved in some form critical studies relates to the reason for writing the Gospels. The events of the First Jewish Revolt are seen as creating a crisis situation for the early Church. The eyewitnesses to Jesus' life were disappearing and might soon all be dead, so their memories should be harvested and preserved. The same hypothesis has been applied to Old Testament books, especially the prophetical ones: they came into being as a result of political crises when uncertainty and the threat of attack set the scribes writing what had hitherto been held in mens' minds.[35] Dated manuscripts from Assyria and Babylonia prove this to be untrue. In those societies literary works were committed to writing or copied at all times, without waiting for sudden stresses, and there is no reason to suppose any other behaviour in Palestine in either the Old Testament period or the New.[36] In the most obvious case, the First Jewish Revolt, which lasted several years, there is no hint of Jewish scribes feverishly attempting to record their traditions before everyone who remembered them should be killed. It was only after the Revolt was over that they tried to recollect

35. Safrai, 'Oral Tora', p. 47; K. Koch, *The Growth of the Biblical Tradition* (trans. S.M. Cupitt; London: A. & C. Black, 1969), p. 86.

36. See my essays 'The Last Tablets of Ugarit', in M. Yon, M. Sznycer and P. Bordreuil (eds.), *Le pays d'Ougarit autour de 1200 av. J.-C.* (Ras Shamra-Ougarit XI; Paris: Editions Recherche sur les Civilisations, 1995), pp. 119-24 and 'Observations from the Eponym Lists', in S. Parpola and R.M. Whiting (eds.), *Assyria 1995* (Helsinki: Neo-Assyrian Text Corpus Project, 1997), pp. 207-15.

their knowledge, at the Council of Jamnia. Nothing in the history of Greek and Roman literature or the distribution of literary texts among the papyri from Egypt supports the idea, either. If someone wanted to write, he would write when it was convenient for him to write. The evangelistic mission of the early Church gave birth to congregations all around the eastern Mediterranean, and further to the west and to the east, which the chief witnesses of Jesus' life themselves could not expect to instruct in detail about him and which might only receive fragmentary oral reports at third or fourth hand (compare the need to instruct the partially informed Apollos at Ephesus, Acts 18.24-28), so there would be good reason to prepare written texts for circulation among the churches. That may be echoed in the tradition that Matthew wrote first in Aramaic. It was known to Irenaeus in the latter part of the second century and elaborated by Eusebius, 'Matthew, who preached earlier to Hebrews, when he was about to go to others, put his gospel into writing in his native language to make up for the loss of his presence'.[37]

The Use of Writing in Greek Education

In the face of the strong emphasis on oral tradition in both rabbinic and Greek sources, the place of written tradition deserves attention. After all, even Plato's certainty about the superior value of the 'living voice' is known to-day only because it was put into writing by his followers. To Plato writing had value for all sorts of recording. Contrary to the pronouncement of E.A. Havelock, Plato was not 'very close to total non-literacy';[38] writing had been in use for laws, historiography, poetry and plays for at least a century before his time, books could be found in private possession and written notices seen in public places, fine vases had the names of characters depicted written beside them, while the practice of ostracism brought a function of writing to the attention of every citizen. In the sixth century, it can be said, 'literacy was widespread among many sectors of the Athenian population', and, although the writer continued 'Attic literacy was inextricably bound up

---

37. Irenaeus, *Adv. haer.* 3.1.1-2: F. Sagnard, *Irénee de Lyon: Contre les hérésies* (Paris: Cerf, 1952), p. 96; Eusebius, *Hist. Eccles.* 3.24.5.

38. E.A. Havelock, *Origins of Western Literacy* (Toronto: Ontario Institute for Studies in Education, 1976), p. 7.

with the oral, narrative and visual culture of the time',[39] it is clear books were being written and read. Throughout the fifth century BC vase painters in Athens and other places depicted people reading rolls, sometimes including sufficient words for ancient and modern admirers to identify a specific work.[40] In fact, Plato did not denigrate writing. He argued that it was not a satisfactory vehicle for training philosophers because it prevented a meeting of minds—and in that the other philosophers followed him—the book cannot answer back, it is fixed, reliance upon it may lead to superficial knowledge as the reader does not stop to think for himself. One commentator remarked,

> The *Phaedrus*, then, devaluates writing merely in contrast with speaking, conversing, or teaching. It says nothing about the impossibility of expressing in words the last truths of Nature; nor does it condemn writing, as does the [seventh] epistle, on the basis of its usefulness or uselessness for the few or the many. Moreover…it considers that books, though they do not deserve to be treated with 'great' seriousness, are nevertheless of serious import…[41]

At the same time, Plato named several rhetoricians in other towns who were known to him through their writings, discouraging the use of writing in such exercises lest they become merely literary exercises, but recognizing the value of writing for laws and even poetry.[42] It is noteworthy that he portrayed Socrates as reading a book of the philosopher Anaxagoras which he had bought, in order, it is safe to assume, to learn what the author thought. Actually he bought it for a very low price, either an indication of the low value set upon the author, or of a small book, or of how cheap books were—perhaps this was a secondhand copy.[43] Writing a few years later, Xenophon, also a pupil of Socrates,

39. J. Whitley, 'Cretan Laws and Cretan Literacy', *AJA* 101 (1997), pp. 675-61 (644).

40. E.G. Turner, *Athenian Books in the Fifth and Fourth Centuries B.C.* (London: H.K. Lewis, 1951), pp. 8-10, 13-23; for the vase paintings see J.G. Beazley, 'Hymn to Hermes', *AJA* 52 (1948), pp. 336-40; H.R. Immerwahr, 'Book Rolls on Attic Vases', in C. Henderson (ed.), *Classical Mediaeval and Renaissance Studies in Honor of Berthold Louis Ullman* (2 vols.; Rome: Edizioni di Storia e Letteratura, 1964), I, pp. 17-48 and the illustrations collected in F.A.G. Beck, *Album of Greek Education* (Sydney: Cheron Press, 1975).

41. L. Edelstein, *Plato's Seventh Letter* (Philosophia Antiqua, 14; Leiden: E.J. Brill, 1966), p. 82.

42. *Phaedrus* §§266-67, 271C, 278D, E.

43. Turner, *Athenian Books*, p. 21.

portrays him as reading 'the treasures of the ancient wise men which they have left written in books'. He would study them with his friends and they would extract whatever they thought valuable.[44] It was possible for a young scholar to collect a small library of books in Socrates' day, according to Xenophon, for Euthydemus had books of the best poets and philosophers, although Xenophon relates Socrates' disparagement of the young man, who acquired his collection of works and 'supposed himself a prodigy of wisdom' by virtue of his ownership.[45] Plato's own works were written out by his students, one of whom took copies to Sicily for sale, without the author's consent, according to a later report.[46] A little over 30 years after Plato's death, inquirers were allowed to read those of his books which were not in general circulation in the Academy in Athens, on payment of a fee.[47] The next most renowned philosopher, Aristotle (c. 384–322 BC), a pupil of Plato, certainly had no hesitation about books. Plato had protested 'against the tendency encouraged by books to depend on others and consequently to cease to think oneself... Yet science and historical scholarship are not possible on this basis, as Aristotle saw, and his method was therefore opposed to that of his predecessor'.[48] He had his own library[49] and himself wrote lectures which he circulated among his inner circle of students as a basis for discussion, revising them frequently. Those lectures were copied by others and preserved, a development of which Aristotle could hardly have been unaware. At one point in his *Rhetoric*, he discusses an uncertainty caused by the absence of punctuation—something almost unknown in ancient Greek texts—in another man's work, originally composed a century and a half earlier and deposited in a temple.[50] Aristotle's own library and the texts of his own works passed to his two successors as head of the Lyceum in Athens and then were moved and

44. Xenophon, *Memorabilia* 1.6.14, reference from Kenyon, *Books and Readers in Greece and Rome*, pp. 21, 22, who estimated the extent of the library as 'a few score scrolls'.

45. Xenophon, *Memorabilia* 4.2.1.

46. Cited by B.A. Van Groningen, 'ΕΚΔΟΣΙΣ', *Mnemosyne* 16 (1963), pp. 1-17 (10).

47. Diogenes Laertius, *Lives of Eminent Philosophers* 3.67.

48. Turner, *Greek Papyri*, p. 107.

49. Strabo, *Geography* 13.1.54; reference from Kenyon, *Books and Readers*, p. 25.

50. Aristotle, *Rhetoric* 1407b; reference from Turner, *Athenian Books*, pp. 13, 17.

lost to sight for some time, badly hindering the study of philosophy in Greek schools for two centuries until the rolls were recovered and copies of them were made in the first century BC.[51] Whatever the reservations some great thinkers expressed about committing their teachings to fixed form in writing as they represented an ideal, the process proved unavoidable, for students took notes of their teachers' words. Plato himself recorded one instance in his *Theaetetus*. In a dialogue between Eucleides and Terpsion, Eucleides tells how Theaetetus related to him a conversation he had held with Socrates. Eucleides said, 'I made notes at the time as soon as I reached home', later, writing down at leisure what he recalled, then he asked Socrates about the things he could not remember and made corrections accordingly. Having told how it came about, Eucleides proceeded to show the book to Terpsion.[52] From such notes the disciples of Plato compiled the books of his wisdom that have reached us. (In the twentieth century a major example of the same thing is the posthumous publication of Ferdinand de Saussure's *Cours de linguistique générale* in 1916 on the basis of his students' notes.) Even Plato's 'unwritten teachings' given to his intimates can be reconstructed to a certain extent from various summaries and reports, although he himself may have considered those teachings unsuitable for wider circulation, and apparently protected them from written dissemination, because he was not yet entirely satisfied with them.[53] Ideal as learning through dialogue and contemplation might be to Plato, reality was recognized, neither in his day nor before was there an embargo on writing and circulating a teacher's words in Greece, nor was there later, not even in the Graeco-Roman world of the first century AD. As noted already, the only library preserved from this time contained almost solely philosophical essays (Chapter 1, p. 21). Quintilian, whose comments on the value of reading as well as hearing we have already seen, complained

> two books on the art of rhetoric are at present circulating under my
> name, although never published by me or composed for such a purpose.
> One is a two days' lecture which was taken down by the boys who were

51. The fate of the manuscripts is reported by Strabo, *Geography* 13.1.54; summarized by Roberts, *Buried Books in Antiquity*, pp. 6-10.

52. Plato, *Theaetetus* §143; cf. G. Kennedy, 'Classical and Christian Source Criticism', in W.O. Walker, (ed.), *The Relationship among the Gospels* (San Antonio, TX: Trinity University Press, 1978), pp. 125-55 (131).

53. M.D. Richard, *L'enseignement orale de Platon* (Paris: Cerf, 1986).

my audience. The other consists of such notes as my good pupils succeeded in taking down from a course of lectures on a somewhat more
extensive scale.[54]

When Galen wrote in the second century, he certainly asserted the
superiority of the 'living voice', yet at the same time he made copies of
his writings for beginners, pupils and friends. Although he claimed he
had no desire to make them generally available for his contemporaries
or for future generations, he was aware that copies had been made and
circulated in spite of his wishes.[55] He further claimed that neither
doctors nor philosophers paid attention to their colleagues' writings,
something which was certainly not true of Socrates, as the episode of
his purchase of another philosopher's book, mentioned above, proves.

Teachers naturally preferred to instruct their pupils themselves, to
maintain the personal meeting which could stimulate and fertilize the
student's mind, creating dialogue or placing the master's hand upon the
learner's, but they were also aware of the value of written texts and
built no barrier against them. Where time or distance prevented a meeting, the book was the substitute. Even then, an interpreter might be necessary to ensure correct understanding, an interpreter who was im-
mersed in the matter of a particular work, for technical books, in particular, were not composed on the 'do it yourself' principle.[56] While the
teachers' preference is understandable, it did not prevent their teachings
being circulated in writing, with owners and copyists making money
from them. Whatever the theory, there was clearly no practical bar to
writing a teacher's words in the Greek world. A classical scholar, discussing the history of the Gospels in the light of Greek and Roman
custom, concluded, 'the existence of notes on the preaching of the
Apostles would not have surprised a first-century Roman interested in
Christianity, and the request for such a record by a Christian group
would have been predictable'.[57]

54. *Inst. Orat.* I, proem. 7.
55. Galen, *De Ordine Librorum* 19.49, cited by Van Groningen, 'ΕΚΔΟΣΙΣ',
p. 2. See the recent discussion by Alexander, 'Ancient Book Production', pp. 94-97.
56. See Alexander, 'The Living Voice'; compare H. Karpp, 'Viva Vox', in A.
Stuiber and A. Hermann (eds.), *Mullus: Festschrift T. Klauser* (JAC Ergänzungsband, 1; Münster: Aschendorffsche Verlagsbuchhandlung, 1964), pp. 190-98.
57. Kennedy, 'Classical and Christian Source Criticism', p. 131.

The Use of Writing in Jewish Circles

The place of the Torah and other sacred scriptures set the book at the heart of Jewish society. No human ideas should be allowed to vie with God's Word or be mistaken for it. The written text stood as a control; it was read publicly in synagogue services and could be consulted whenever necessary; the fact that most scholars had committed it to memory did not reduce its final authority, for they had learnt it from the written text, not from oral tradition, even if they sat in groups repeating what the teacher read. The presence of the text itself at the heart of Judaism and in its regular services should not be underestimated. It is a feature which weighs against characterizations of Herodian Palestine as an 'oral world'.[58] The prohibition on reading a targum as the Scriptures were read in the synagogue did not mean no written targums existed. Early in the first century when someone brought a written targum of Job to Gamaliel the Elder in the Temple he ordered it to be hidden away so that it could not be used; his reasons are not explained (see above, Chapter 4, p. 89).[59]

Although the Oral Law was not to be written as a formal book, there are several references to pupils noting their teachers' sayings, to notebook collections and to 'secret scrolls'. Gerhardsson wrote:

> We hear that teachers and pupils have writing tablets and notebooks or 'scrolls of secrets' at their disposal, or that a teacher or a pupil makes notes in a haggadah book. We even find the resourceful pupil making notes on the college wall! There is clear witness to the character and purpose of such notes: it is evidently a matter of private notes intended to facilitate learning and continued memorization, practice and future repetition. Books served as 'reminder books'.

According to Gerhardsson, they were unofficial, 'illegitimate in principle and therefore formally suppressed'.[60] Yet the illegitimacy of such memoranda was not recognized by the rabbinic authority S. Lieberman, writing at almost the same time as Gerhardsson:

> Now the Jewish disciples of Jesus, in accordance with the general rabbinic practice, wrote the sayings of their master, pronounced not in form

---

58. See Alexander, 'Orality in Pharisaic-Rabbinic Judaism at the Turn of the Era'.

59. *b. Šab.*115a.

60. Gerhardsson, *Memory and Manuscript*, pp. 160-61.

of a book to be published, but as notes in their *pinakes*, codices, or in their note-books (or in private small rolls). They did this because otherwise they would have transgressed the law.[61]

In a later study, Gerhardsson also allowed that the same practice may have existed at an early stage in church history,

> regular acts of transmitting texts occurred in early Christianity…either in written form or by impressing the text on the memory. If in written form, it must have involved unofficial notes, 'secret scrolls' as the rabbis called them, or 'memoranda' as the Greek teachers referred to them, but not complete books.[62]

Within 'orthodox' or 'rabbinic' circles, therefore, the possibility of unofficial written records of religious teaching was recognized and allowed. While the understanding was, apparently, that they were for personal use only, they had no formal status and were not to be treated as authoritative or read in public, there may have been many more of these private copies than has been envisaged. For the Sadducees only written regulations were valid, according to Josephus.[63]

Until 1947 there were no first hand records from Jewish sources in Herodian Palestine, Josephus having written in Greek for Gentile audiences. The Dead Sea Scrolls and other texts from the Judaean desert, described in Chapter 4, have revolutionized the scene. Their additions to knowledge of languages, books and writing in Herodian Palestine have been outlined already. They contribute to the present discussion as examples of Jewish religious writings contemporary with the life of Jesus. The writers and owners of the Scrolls shared the same respect for the Torah and the other Scriptures as the Pharisees and they read many of the 'apocryphal' and other books which circulated among wider Jewish audiences (see above, Chapter 4). Where they parted company with the main stream Jewish scholastics was in creating and possessing in writing just the types of text which the later rabbis maintained should not be set down permanently. As we have seen, they had written targums which expanded and explained the biblical texts and they had paraphrases or rewritings of biblical texts, all intended to clarify the

---

61. Lieberman, *Hellenism in Jewish Palestine*, p. 203.

62. B. Gerhardsson, *The Origins of the Gospel Traditions* (London: SCM Press, 1979), p. 68; cf also his remark, 'private notes were probably made rather early', p. 76.

63. *Ant.* 13.297.

meaning of the ancient books. In this respect, they were anticipating the development of written targums and explanatory texts (*midrash*) in rabbinic Judaism. However, they far exceeded those later writings. They wrote, or possessed, hymns echoing the biblical Psalms which are unexceptional and the *Thanksgiving Hymns* which relate more directly to the sect. In some of those the speaker is a persecuted teacher who trusts God and is saved, in others the speaker is a member of God's elect who praises him for his privileges, present and future. That other pious Jews were writing hymns in the first century BC can be seen from the *Psalms of Solomon*, only surviving in Greek, but originally composed in Hebrew after Pompey entered Jerusalem and the Temple in 63 BC. The surprise of the Scrolls lies in the way they combine biblical Psalms in the same rolls with others, at least one attributed to David, not all the others the creations of the sect. Does this mean all these compositions were considered 'canonical'? The question continues to divide scholars, some taking these rolls as equivalents of modern hymn books which contain Psalms and metrical versions of Psalms beside the verses of Martin Luther, Charles Wesley and John Henry Newman, others, assuming that the canon of the Hebrew Bible had not yet been fixed, suppose all the poems had equal authority. A different composition is 'The Songs of the Sabbath Sacrifice', a series of 13 'songs', one for the first Sabbath of each month. Nine copies were recovered from the Qumran caves and a tenth at Masada, showing either that a member of the Qumran group took refuge at Masada or that these songs had wider use. Very damaged rolls contain prayers and liturgies written for services, contrary to rabbinic regulations. And the owners of the Scrolls were not alone in that, for fragments of a Hebrew prayer said after meals, written on parchment, lay in a street near the synagogue at Dura Europos, destroyed in AD 256, a prayer evidently committed to writing in what might be thought a time when rabbinic opinion enjoyed some strength (see above, pp. 191-92).[64]

With the *Temple Scroll* comes an even greater surprise, for this, the longest of the Scrolls, presents itself as a book of laws given by God to his people. It is given in the first person in the same style as parts of the Torah and in very similar language, drawn from biblical texts, patching some together, elaborating or altering them. Most space is devoted to

64. Welles, Fink and Gilliam, *The Excavations at Dura-Europos*, pp. 74-75; cf. p. 192 above and n. 17.

Figure 38. *Wooden writing tablet with remains of wax, found in Roman levels in Cologne. (Domgrabung 69-421. Photograph by courtesy of the Römische-Germanisches Museum, Cologne.)*

the structure of an enormous new temple, a temple which would have covered an area four times as large as Herod's Temple and involved filling in the Kidron valley. The description of the temple and its services is parallel to the biblical directions for the erection of the Tabernacle. Detailed commands about festivals, purity and many other aspects of life follow, repeating biblical laws and inventing new ones. These rules are very strict, in keeping with other regulations of the sect, and may be formulated deliberately to oppose other interpretations. The place this book held in the Qumran community is not known: Was it a sixth book of the Torah, on a par with the established five ? Only two copies have survived, in contrast to the 11 copies of the *Rule of the Community*, suggesting it was not of first importance (but the accidents of survival may mislead us).

In discussing the question of 'canonicity' among the Dead Sea Scrolls, there is one point of difference in treatment between the *Temple Scroll* and other 'sectarian' writings and the 'canonical' works that may mark a conscious distinction, that is, the presence of commentaries (*peshārîm*) on the biblical books alone. There are pesharim on Isaiah, Hosea, Micah, Nahum, Habakkuk, Zephaniah, Malachi and some Psalms, but none have been identified for any of the extra-biblical works, neither for the apocrypha and pseudepigrapha which survived in Jewish and Christian circles, nor for the sectarian writings. Accident of preservation and discovery might be the reason for this absence, or, alternatively, the meaning of the Community's own writings may have been clear to its members, who knew its history, whereas the older, inherited texts were obscure and, at first sight, irrelevant.

For our purpose, the significance of the *Temple Scroll* is its presence as written law in a Jewish setting in Palestine at a period when, according to rabbinic principles, Judaism would have dismissed even the thought of a book that could so easily be confused with the Torah itself.

Oral Tradition in the First Century Church

The Gospels clearly envisage oral teaching on the part of Jesus' disciples and report the spread of news about him by word of mouth in his lifetime (Mk 6.14; 7.1; 10.1; Mt. 28.19, 20). The disciples and evangelists told their story over and over again from their first hand knowledge wherever they went, a process which continued as long as there were any eye-witnesses alive, into the lifetime of Papias (see pp. 194-95). Some who received the information disseminated it in turn, as did Paul who 'received' and passed on to his friends information about Jesus, notably regarding the Last Supper (1 Cor. 11.23). In this case, however, Paul also shared the tradition in writing and there is no reason to suppose he was the first to do so. He also mentions, in what may be one of his earliest epistles, how he passed on his teachings to the Christians in Thessalonica both orally and by letter (2 Thess. 2.15). Whenever records about Jesus were written, in his lifetime, after the first Easter, after the Fall of Jerusalem, the memories would continue and, in turn, be reproduced as they were shared, although they would eventually die out. The poverty of that oral tradition in salvaging anything extra to the canonical Gospels is notable:

> Throughout the second century there were some who carefully treasured up whatever floating scraps of primitive tradition (sayings ascribed to Jesus and the like) had been preserved in Christian memory, but by the last quarter of the century the stream had dried up. Even in the first quarter of the century it had been reduced to a trickle, to judge by what Papias bishop of Hierapolis, was able to collect in his declared prefer-

ence for the testimony of a 'living and abiding voice' over what he could find in a book.[65]

The words of Papias, however, should not be taken to mean he held the written Gospels to be secondary to the memories he heard. Rather, he was concerned to ascertain the apostolic origin of oral reports, to seek the best sources among living witnesses to set beside the Gospels.[66] By his day, shortly after the end of the first century, the written text had gained primacy among the majority; Christianity had become fully a religion of the book.

65. F.F. Bruce, 'Thoughts from my Study: Apostolic Tradition', *Calling* 12.3 (1970), pp. 10-13 (13); cf. *idem*, *Tradition Old and New* (Exeter: Paternoster Press, 1970), p. 111.

66. See A.F. Walls, 'Papias and Oral Tradition', *VC* 21 (1967), pp. 137-40; A.D. Baum, 'Papias, der Vorzug der *Viva Vox* und die Evangelienschriften', *NTS* 44 (1998), pp. 144-51; see also p. 195 n. 26.

Chapter 8

WRITING AND THE GOSPELS

The surviving examples of writing from Herodian Palestine and the available literary references show that writing in Greek, Aramaic and Hebrew was widespread and could be found at all levels of society. Writing was used to label jars, send messages, keep accounts and legal deeds and to preserve and propagate teaching and literature. Although the villages and hillsides of Galilee were the scene for much of Jesus' teaching, it is a mistake to insist this was an uncouth, isolated rural setting where people 'displayed only tenuous connections with literate culture'.[1] Galilee was the site of first Sepphoris and then Tiberias as local capitals and straddled a major route into Syria; Bethsaida was a frontier crossing with appropriate officials. Quite apart from the use of Scripture in the regular services, the Gospels themselves assume a familiarity with writing in daily life (see below, p. 223). That was the environment in which Jesus worked. The amount of information demands a fresh look at the question, 'Could those who heard Jesus preaching have written down what they heard?' The previous chapters demonstrate a wide use of writing in Herodian Palestine, so that no one can object on technical grounds to the proposition that some among Jesus' followers might have written his words in a world where note-taking was unexceptional. In this respect, the assumption many have made about the Jewish milieu, expressed by C.H. Roberts, the papyrologist, also needs further attention: 'Prohibition on recording or publishing oral Law' was 'an attitude that powerfully influenced the early Church'.[2] Here the opposite opinion of S. Lieberman, a leading Jewish

---

1. Kelber, *The Oral and the Written Gospel*, p. 21; notice the response by J. Halverson, 'Oral and Written Gospel: A Critique of Werner Kelber', *NTS* 40 (1994), pp. 180-95.
2. Roberts, 'Books in the Graeco-Roman World', p. 49.

authority on the early rabbinic period, is worth citing: following his study of the evidence for writing among the early rabbis, he concluded, 'In line with the foregoing, we would naturally expect the *logia* of Jesus to be originally copied in codices' (cf. Chapter 7, pp. 204-205).[3] Finally, we ask, 'In the light of attitudes to writing a teacher's words in the ancient world, might people who heard Jesus preaching have written down what they heard?'

Writing among the Early Christians

Well before the Fall of Jerusalem the early Christians were familiar with written texts, through the letters the Apostles wrote to the churches in Antioch, Syria and Pisidia (Acts 15) and especially Paul's correspondence beginning shortly before AD 50. Paul refers to information he had received about Jesus' teaching, but he nowhere hints that he had read any accounts of it and everyone assumes he had it by word of mouth from the early disciples whom he met, notably when he spent time with Peter and James (Gal. 1.18, 19). How far back in Christian history did the use of writing for 'religious' purposes stretch? If Paul wrote letters less than 20 years after the Crucifixion, giving advice and expecting his audience to know its basis, were others already circulating memoirs about their Teacher? If the Apostolic Council could send the letter of Acts 15, then there enters the possibility that the 'apostles and elders' in Jerusalem could have circulated reports of Jesus' words and deeds.

Whereas Paul had his training with a leading rabbi in Jerusalem, Gamaliel I (Acts 22.3; cf. 23.6; 26.5), perhaps with some earlier exposure to Hellenistic education in Tarsus, and there were some other figures from the Jewish establishment in the early Church, the majority of the members were probably not closely attached to any mainstream academic circle (cf. 1 Cor. 1.26). There would thus be no ideological obstacle to their compiling records of the life of Jesus as there might have been in orthodox Jewish circles, as described in Chapter 7. Recent discoveries and discussion have led to a recognition of greater variety of practices in first century Judaism than anyone previously suspected.

3.   Lieberman, *Hellenism in Jewish Palestine*, p. 203.

A Leader's Teachings in the Dead Sea Scrolls

The writings of the sect that owned the Dead Sea Scrolls are particularly significant here. We have already seen how those people accepted what may be considered an addition to the Torah in the *Temple Scroll* and they had their own regulations in the *Rule of the Community*, which is written in an impersonal style. Beside that they had another rule book, the *Damascus Document.* This first came to modern knowledge when pages copied in the tenth and twelfth centuries and later discarded in the *geniza* of an old synagogue in Cairo were brought to Cambridge with thousands of other mediaeval Jewish papers at the end of the nineteenth century (see Chapter 7, p. 191).[4] The pages, parts of two copies of the writing, present an exhortation to people to join the faithful remnant of Israel who are covenanted to follow the laws of God as revealed through a 'Teacher of Righteousness', or 'Righteous Teacher' whom God had sent. It is called the *Damascus Document* because Damascus is named as the place of exile where the covenant was made. Some scholars suppose Damascus to be a code name for Babylon, others for Qumran; Damascus itself need not be excluded. The group identified itself as 'the sons of Zadok'—hence the work has sometimes been titled the 'Zadokite Document'—after the high priestly family which held office until the Maccabees took power. Many strict laws are spelt out for the conduct of the congregation of this exclusive Israel, both in the religious and in the mundane spheres of life. For example, 'No-one shall help an animal to give birth on the Sabbath day. If it should fall into a cistern or a pit, he shall not lift it out on the Sabbath day' (11.12, 13; contrast Lk. 14.5). The author sets himself as an interpreter of God's laws, occasionally using the first person : 'Listen to me, all who are entering the covenant, and I shall explain to you the paths of the wicked' (2.2, 3); 'Listen to me, my sons, and I shall explain to you so that you can understand the works of God…' (2.14). With the discovery of the Dead Sea Scrolls, these pages can be better understood, for there are pieces of duplicate copies among the Scrolls, some giving additional material, indicating that the Geniza pages lack the beginning of the text, although the Scrolls only supply disjoint phrases for that

---

4.   S. Schechter, *Documents of Jewish Sectaries.* I. *Fragments of a Zadokite Work* (Cambridge: Cambridge University Press, 1910); M. Broshi (ed.), *The Damascus Document Reconsidered* (Jerusalem: Israel Exploration Society, 1992).

part. Where the mediaeval text begins, 'Now listen all those who know justice...', one Scroll fragment has a first person pronoun, 'Now then, listen to me, all you who know justice...' The facts that there were at least 10 copies in the Qumran caves and that there are many points in common between other Scrolls and the Damascus Document, demonstrate that it was taken as one of the basic texts for the sect, whether it originated within it, or not.[5]

In this foundational address, the feature to be noted is the presence of first person speech in three passages. Although identical with the style of Hebrew wisdom literature, as in Proverbs and Ben Sira, in that aspect, 'Listen, my son!', this book is not a book of wisdom, but of law, with its historical introduction comparable to the opening of Deuteronomy. The unidentified speaker assumes an authoritative role, addressing a congregation obviously expected to receive his words with respect.

The Unique Document MMT

That speaker's position is more strikingly exemplified in another of the Dead Sea Scrolls. In 1984 publicity was first given to a text reconstructed from fragments which its editors named *Miqṣat Ma'aśeh Ha-Torah*, abbreviated as *MMT*. Ten years later Elisha Qimron and John Strugnell published their official edition of the text with extensive notes and commentaries.[6] They identified parts of six manuscripts of the work (4Q394-399), five on leather like the majority of the Scrolls and one on papyrus, written in a slightly more cursive script than the others (4Q398). No copy is complete; by combining all the fragments the editors produced 130 lines, which they estimated to be about two-thirds of the original composition; the opening is missing. As reconstructed, a form of calendar comes first (denoted A by the editors), tabulating the occurrences of Sabbath days on the basis of the 364-day solar year favoured by the Community. The calendar is only present in one manuscript, so it is widely considered it may not have stood in all,[7] indeed,

---

5. See J. Baumgarten and J.T. Milik, *Qumran Cave 4: XIII: The Damascus Document (4Q266-273)* (DJD, 18; Oxford: Clarendon Press, 1997).

6. *Qumran Cave 4.V. Miqṣat Ma'aśeh Ha-Torah* (DJD, 10; Oxford: Clarendon Press, 1994).

7. See J. VanderKam, 'The Calendar, 4Q327 and 4Q394', in M. Bernstein,

one copy has a margin wide enough to imply that it started with the following section (4Q395). That section, the central part (B), opens with the phrase 'These are some of our rules', introducing a number of regulations about ritual purity in various situations, especially concerning Jerusalem and the Temple. For example,

> Dogs should not be brought into the holy camp because they might eat some of the bones from the t[emple while] the flesh (of sacrifices) is still on them. For Jerusalem is the holy camp and it is the holy place which He has chosen out of all the tribes of Israel, since Jerusalem is the chief of Israel's camps (B 58-62).

The work closes with an assertion of the authors' purity and righteousness and an exhortation to follow their injunctions, so gaining God's favour and avoiding his curses, 'for your good and Israel's' (C) .

The contents of this scroll relate to some of the Community's basic tenets, very strict teachings that followed the literal sense of the Law, distinguishing it from the mainstream of early Judaism, teachings that are found in other books, notably the *Temple Scroll*. The rulings on several cases are set down to contradict positions which a different party, also unidentified, held, positions which were later defended by rabbinic teachers, as reported in the Mishnah and the Talmud. A handful of samples exhibit the situation clearly. One incomplete clause appears to condemn the acceptance of sacrifices offered by foreigners (B 8, 9), something the Jerusalem authorities were ready to do, although not with total agreement. In the arcane matter of the ashes of the red heifer put in water for purification rites (Numbers 19), *MMT* pronounces the participants in the burning of the animal impure until after sunset, even though they had taken a ritual bath (B 13-17, following Num. 19.8). The cleansed leper, also, only attained purity after sunset on the prescribed day (B 71, 72; cf. Lev. 22.7). The Mishnah tells how the rabbis actively maintained there was no need to wait until sunset in either case, deliberately opposing the position held by people like the speaker in *MMT*, which they attributed to 'the Zadokites' (*m. Par.* 3.7). The most peculiar of all *MMT*'s precepts, to modern eyes, deals with liquid pouring from one container into another (B 55-58). Obviously, clean liquid transferred into a ritually unclean vessel becomes impure; amazingly, here the ruling asserts that 'the streams of liquid do not separate

J. García Martínez and J. Kampen (eds.), *Legal Texts and Issues* (Leiden: E.J. Brill, 1997), pp. 179-94.

the unclean from the clean, because the liquid of the streams and of the receptacle are alike, a single liquid'. That is to say, the impurity of the receptacle travels up the stream of liquid to render its source impure. This is a concept the Mishnah, again, attributes to 'the Zadokites' (*m. Yad.* 4.7). It is so extraordinary that a well-informed nineteenth century scholar wrote, 'it can only have been intended as mockery, for the Sadducees would surely not agree...that the "stream" should be declared unclean when poured from a clean vessel to an unclean'.[8] *MMT* proves this was a serious issue before AD 70!

Figure 39.   *MMT papyrus fragment 4Q398. E. Qimron and J. Strugnell,* Qumran Cave 4.V, *pl. viii, upper. (Photograph by courtesy of the Israel Antiquities Authority.)*

The rabbinic association of rulings like some of those in *MMT* with 'the Zadokites' adds to information already deduced from other Scrolls concerning the origin of the Community. Since it saw no need to write its own history, scholars today have to reconstruct that from hints, allusions and rare references in the texts. The *Damascus Document*, we have already noted, points to an association with the priestly house of Zadok ousted from its place in the second century BC. Now as the *Temple Scroll* and especially *MMT* contain rulings in line with those

---

8.   Schürer, *A History of the Jewish People in the Age of Jesus Christ*, II.2, p. 36 n. 96; the comment is retained in the revised English version, Schürer, II (1979), p. 410 n. 31.

later termed Zadokite by the Mishnah, this association gains some strength. The origin of the Community may be associated with dissension among the priestly parties at the time of the rise of the Hasmonaeans. Unable to accept the more lenient interpretation of the Torah that became the characteristic of the Pharisees, accommodating it to changed circumstances, one group separated itself from the majority and developed into the exclusive sect to which the Community belonged. (The Dead Sea Scrolls and the Qumran settlement should not be viewed as the only books and home of members of the Community; it is highly likely there were individual members who lived in towns and villages in Palestine and further afield and, if Qumran is in any way typical, they could have had their own collections of books. Should the identity of these people with the Essenes be accepted, then the testimony of Josephus and Philo about their distribution across Palestine in that way can be drawn in.)

While the *Damascus Document* stands apart from the other Scrolls in twice using the first person singular (see above, p. 212), *MMT* singles itself out even more. It is written in the form of an address from one party to another, with attention to a third, opposing group. At first the editors called it a letter, notwithstanding the lack of the opening which might give the names of an addressee and a sender and any greetings, according to the normal pattern.[9] The closing exhortations of the scroll (C) could suit a letter as well as other types of document. Alas, no Hebrew epistles exist from the time, only brief personal messages survive, such as the Bar Kochba letters, so there is no material for close comparison.

The distance between the Scrolls, pre-eminently *MMT*, and the behaviour of the rabbis seen in the rulings quoted extends further to the fact of the document itself. It exemplifies exactly what was normally outlawed, the writing of rulings in a book (see above, Chapter 7, pp. 189-92, 204), and it goes beyond the laws for the Temple and the Holy City in the *Temple Scroll* and the regulations for the Community in the *Rule* and the *Damascus Document* and in its personal style. Divine oration characterizes the first of those works, anonymity the second and a mainly impersonal form the third (but see above, p. 212), but *MMT* is an address from 'us' to 'you' with reference to 'them'. The expression 'we reckon' or 'in our opinion' (*ʾanaḥnû ḥōšebîm*) occurs four times,

---

9.   D. Pardee, *Handbook of Ancient Hebrew Letters* (Chico, CA: Scholars Press, 1982).

'we say' (*^{a}naḥnû 'ōm^{e}rîm*) three times, 'we give' (*^{a}naḥnû noṯ^{e}nîm*), 'we recognize' (*^{a}naḥnû makkîrîm*), 'we have written' (*^{a}naḥnû kāṯaḇnû*) once each. There is no perceptible nuance dictating the use of 'we reckon' rather than 'we say' and the editors rendered both by 'in our opinion'. Whether that was the voice of a group or of an individual is debatable. The contrast with the 'I' of the *Damascus Document* might favour the former, although consistency should not be a high expectation of these texts; on the other hand, the role of the Teacher of Righteousness in the Community's history could suggest it is an individual's voice. A small group associated with or led by him seems the most satisfactory solution.[10] If that is accepted, or authorship sought elsewhere, the observation is still valid that the voice is not identified with a single person, the authority is a communal one.

Nevertheless, *MMT* is giving opinions on disputed matters without claiming any external support, simply resting on and interpreting Scripture. There is no appeal to earlier teachers by name or to a chain of tradition as in many rabbinic texts. The audience is expected to recognize the voice they hear as one they should heed. Yet the document is not a series of edicts like the other works mentioned, it is more an attempt to demonstrate the superiority of its authors' teaching. That becomes clear in the final section: 'We have written to you some of the works of the Law which we think are good for you and your people, for we have s[ee]n you have wisdom and knowledge of the Law' (C 26-28). Those addressed are neither firmly opposed to the writers, nor, perhaps, wholly on their side. In the body of the text, the audience is a group, addressed in the plural, 'you know' (*'attem yōḏ^{e}'îm*, B80), while the conclusion has the singular 'you'. Shifts of person occur in biblical and other ancient Near Eastern texts, where they have no significance, and that may be happening here. However, the presence of many biblical citations in the conclusion, which are couched in the second person singular, could have affected the form of expression.

In common with many of the other Scrolls, *MMT* rests on the Torah. It is not a targum, explaining the text verse by verse, nor a commentary uncovering its application for the present, different, age; rather, it falls into the category of law or regulations for conduct (*halachâ*). While it is based on Scripture, its authors assume knowledge of the sacred text, quoting it regularly, alluding to it or paraphrasing it. Specific reference

---

10. See Strugnell's discussion, *Qumran Cave 4.V*, pp. 116-21.

Figure 40. *Jar labelled 'balsam' in Aramaic, first century* BC. *Height 50.5 cm. (Israel Museum 68.34.214; photograph by courtesy of the Israel Museum.)*

is made to it by the term, 'it is written' (*kāṯûḇ*), occurring 13 times, twice in the form 'as it is written' (*šekāṯûḇ*, *miššekāṯûḇ*, C21, B76); the latter are only linguistically different from 'as it is written' (*ka'ᵃšer kāṯûḇ*) in the Hebrew Bible itself and in other Scrolls.[11] Here it shares

---

11. See G. Brooke, 'Luke–Acts and the Qumran Scrolls: The Case of MMT', in C.M. Tuckett (ed.), *Luke's Literary Achievement* (JSNTSup, 116; Sheffield: Sheffield Academic Press, 1995), pp. 72-90 (89); *idem*, 'The Explicit Presentation of Scripture in 4QMMT', in Bernstein, García Martínez and Kampen (eds.), *Legal Texts and Issues*, pp. 67-88 (70-71).

its procedure with the New Testament writers, revealing the Hebrew equivalents of Greek terms used in biblical citations there.[12]

The Nature of MMT

Gamaliel and successive religious leaders in Jerusalem during the first and second centuries sent instructions to Jewish communities within the Holy Land and beyond, in Babylonia and Media, following the pattern of Mordecai (Est. 9.20-32) and seen later in 2 Macc. 1.1-10. The few examples preserved in later compositions are brief directives, without discussion or scriptural support for their requirements. They are very different from *MMT*, but they show that letters were sent from one community to another.[13] Although no Hebrew text from the Herodian period is known comparable with *MMT*, the editors noted similarities in form between it and some of the New Testament epistles, for most of those are a special type of letter, not a personal message but exhortations and advice sent to groups of people, the churches in Corinth, Rome, Colossae, and so on. Comparison with Paul's letter to the Corinthians where the apostle controverts some people's ideas about personal conduct in the church at Corinth, setting his authority against those who wanted to go their own way, is apposite. Both writers introduce a topic with a similar expression in Hebrew and in Greek, translated 'now concerning' (*wᵉ'ap 'al* in *MMT*, περὶ δὲ τῶν in Paul). The relevance of *MMT* for one aspect of New Testament study will occupy us shortly, but at this juncture reference to a later genre of Hebrew literature may help in understanding the document itself.

The same phrase that introduces topics in *MMT* was also used in early mediaeval times by leading rabbis who answered inquiries about the application of the Law to unusual situations it did not appear to cover, the 'Responses' which senior rabbis continue to issue today.

Once the Mishnah had become the basic source for application of the Torah in daily life, questions arose about situations that were not foreseen there, because, like the Torah itself, the Mishnah was a code that had its own cultural context. Indeed, there is a report of a letter sent to

---

12. J.A. Fitzmyer, 'The Use of Explicit Old Testament Quotations in Qumran Literature and in the New Testament', *NTS* 7 (1960–61), pp. 297-333, reprinted in Fitzmyer, *Essays on the Semitic Background of the New Testament*, pp. 3-58.

13. For the texts see S.D. Sperling, 'Fragments of Tannaitic Letters Preserved in Rabbinic Literature', in Pardee (ed.), *Handbook of Ancient Hebrew Letters*, pp.183-96; Beyer, *Die aramäischen Texte*, p. 359.

Rabbi Judah, who was the compiler of the Mishnah, by his pupil Rab (Abba Arika), who took the Mishnah to the Jews in Babylonia, asking advice on a legal matter, and of Rabbi Judah's reply.[14] That was early in the third century. The Talmud mentions several exchanges of letters in the fourth and fifth centuries between various teachers in Palestine and the highly regarded rabbis of Babylonia. Questions about observing and applying the Law in various circumstances were submitted for a considered answer. The practice can be observed growing enormously from the fifth century onwards, when the letters streamed to Babylonia. In the initial period the heads of the academies in Babylonia faced a problem: Should they send their answers, involving the Oral Law, in written replies? Would that not break the ban on writing the Oral Law? Yet the expansion of the body of legal rulings was reaching a stage where it was too large to memorize. The solution was to distinguish the new interpretations and allow them to be written, whereas the existing tradition handed down orally could not itself be written. At its earliest point, however, a modern writer stated, 'The major novelty lay in the committing of halakhic subjects to writing, the prohibition against committing to writing words transmitted orally (*b. Giṭ.* 60b) still being in force at the time'.[15]

The Responses became a regular literary practice by the eighth century, cast in the form: 'X to Y… Peace be upon you…we are ever seeking your welfare… As for your questions, we have decided…' An instructive example is the framework of a response the leading teacher in Babylonia, Sherira Gaon, sent in 986: 'As for your questions…the rabbis taught us…furthermore … Our view is as follows… As for your question…[factual statement]…for we see [citation from the Babylonian Talmud]…', ending with a blessing.[16]

In any society which has a set code of laws the need for fresh interpretation and application for new situations is bound to arise. The Romans in the first and other centuries had their system of *iuris consulti*

14. *b. Ket.* 69a; *y. Giṭ.* 5.3.

15. I.M. Ta-Shma, 'Responsa', *EncJud*, XIV, cols. 83-88 (84).

16. See J.Z. Lauterbach, 'She'elot u-Teshubot', *JewEnc*, XI, pp. 240-50; Ta Shma, 'Responsa', col. 83; S.B. Freehof, *The Response Literature* and *A Treasury of Responsa* (New York: Jewish Publication Society, 1955, 1962; reprinted in one volume, New York: Ktav, 1973), examples from I, p. 104, II, pp. 6-11; L. Ginzberg, *Geonica*. I. *The Geonim and their Halakic Writings*; II, *Geniza Studies* (New York: Jewish Theological Seminary, 1909; repr. New York: Hermon Press, 1968).

whereby lawyers could obtain informed guidance from experienced men when dealing with new or awkward cases.[17] Without its first paragraphs, we cannot know if *MMT* bore an address, but the body of the text, with its 'now concerning,' its 'these are some of our regulations', 'in our opinion' and 'you know', its scriptural citations and allusions and its final warnings and blessing, belongs to the same context. *MMT* can well be read as responses by a leader or by leading figures in the Qumran Community to inquiries from the followers or to known problems they faced. In this way this peculiar document may be defined as a precursor by a few centuries of the mediaeval and later rabbinic 'Response' literature. The similarities with Paul's Letters, mentioned already, suggests this may be the sole survivor of an earlier generation of 'Responses' written outside 'normal' Judaism.

MMT and Gospel Records
However, a further comparison can be made with first-century material which is more arresting for this study. This is not with the letters of St Paul but with the Gospel reports of Jesus' teaching. The Sermon on the Mount has the most obvious cases, where Matthew records Jesus saying, 'You have heard that it was said to the people long ago... But I tell you...' (Mt. 5.21, cf. 27-28, 31-32, 33-34, 38-39, 43-44).[18] That was the position clearly presented for all his teaching, whether reformulating the Law, as in Matthew 5, or contradicting traditions which had been created with the aim of protecting people from breaking it, but had become onerous, as explained in Mark 7. His stance provoked the observation, 'unlike the scribes, he taught with a note of authority' (Mk 1.22, REB). He also drew the comment 'the common people heard him gladly' (Mk 12.37). Jesus was evidently not a teacher in the normal rabbinic pattern; he did not live and teach in one place, he had his circle of disciples but, in addition, there was a larger group of followers and

---

17. See the summary in P.S. Alexander, 'Quid Athenis et Hierosolymis? Rabbinic Midrash and Hermeneutics in the Graeco-Roman World', in P.R. Davies and R.T. White (eds.), *A Tribute to Geza Vermes* (JSOTSup, 100; Sheffield: Sheffield Academic Press, 1990), pp. 101-24 (109-10).

18. M. Weinfeld noted the similarity in a discussion when *MMT* was first made public, in A. Biran (ed.), *Biblical Archaeology Today* (Jerusalem: Israel Exploration Society, 1985), p. 430; for further comment see J. Kampen, 'The Sectarian Form of the Antitheses within the Social World of the Matthaean Community', *Discoveries in the Judean Desert* 1 (1994), pp. 338-63 (343-57).

crowds who, it is reported, flocked to hear him speak. He was an expounder of Scripture, applying it to current situations, like the Pharisees and the author(s) of *MMT*, but his teaching was not centred upon details of the Law and its application, as their teachings were, his words concerned wider and deeper aspects of behaviour before God and before man: he came 'to fulfil the Law' (Mt. 5.17).

If the teaching of Jesus stands on a different plane from the customary practice of the rabbis, may not the means his followers used to preserve and disseminate it also follow a different path? It is noteworthy that his disciples did not disband after his death, or join another teacher or become independent, as disciples of the rabbis did, but kept their cohesive group and enlarged it.[19] Could some who heard him speaking and saw him helping the weak have written down his words and noted what they saw? Those from Jewish circles would have been used to regular readings from authoritative texts in the synagogues and so could readily have taken to reading whatever came to hand about the one they reckoned 'greater than Moses' whom they followed.

The previous chapters have shown the ubiquity of writing in first-century Palestine, the variety of writing materials and scripts, and the range of circumstances in which people wrote. The last chapter made a case against the heavy emphasis placed upon oral tradition, the basis from which most New Testament scholars working in the twentieth century have begun their attempts to trace the history of the formation of the Gospels. The contemporary documents from Qumran just cited are evidence for more diversity within Jewish circles than previously suspected. When those texts were first written is unknown; none of the literary manuscripts among the Dead Sea Scrolls carries a date and there is no way to identify any of them as an autograph or an author's approved copy. However, we may quote S. Talmon's conclusion concerning the *Damascus Document*, 'If these speeches can indeed be ascribed to the Teacher [of Righteousness], we may assume with much confidence that they were submitted to writing almost simultaneously with their oral delivery, or after a minimal lapse of time.' He went further, taking account of the careful attention to manuscripts at Qumran, to state, 'and in view of the Teacher's singular standing in the community and the momentous weight which the members attached to his message, it stands to reason that his pronouncements were collected and

19. P. Alexander made this point, 'Orality in Pharisaic-Rabbinic Judaism', p. 163.

written down in his lifetime'. Talmon had also surmised that the text of *MMT* had derived from a waxed tablet (*pinax*),[20] as Lieberman had earlier suggested the sayings of Jesus had been (see above, Chapter 7, pp. 204-205).

Writing and the Gospels

The Gospels themselves attest the ready availability of writing materials: when Zechariah requested a small tablet to write his son's name, it was easily to hand (Lk. 1.63), and the Shrewd Manager in the parable tells the debtors to rewrite their accounts forthwith (Lk. 16.6, 7 see p. 178). Jesus' followers and audiences included people of various occupations who would use writing, tax collectors (Levi, Zacchaeus are named), centurions, who, if not writing themselves, would have had secretaries, and we have cited cases of soldiers of lower rank writing letters. Joanna, wife of a high official of Herod Antipas (Lk. 8.1-3) and no doubt other unnamed courtiers and officials of both native and Roman government would have been used to writing, in addition to scribes, Pharisees and members of the Sanhedrin. To imagine any of these people going out with papyrus roll, pen and ink to take down the words of a travelling preacher would be absurd. To imagine some of them opening note-books they carried for their day-to-day business, perhaps hung at the belt, and jotting down a few of the striking sayings they had heard, or writing a summary of what they had experienced while it was fresh in the memory is quite feasible.[21] (The possibility of shorthand records of Jesus words was aired and rejected by Ernest Renan in 1888 and has been repeated since,[22] but cannot be entertained in the light of current knowledge, see Chapter 6, pp. 175-76.) The case being made is for written notes of individual sayings, or a collection of some, and reports of remarkable events. This is not to say the Evangelists began to compose the Gospels in Jesus' lifetime, but that some, possibly much, of their source material was preserved in writing from

20. S. Talmon, 'Oral Tradition and Written Transmission, or the Heard and the Seen Word in Judaism of the Second Temple Period', in Wansborough (ed.), *Jesus and the Oral Gospel Tradition*, pp. 121-58 (158, 148).

21. The hypothesis that Matthew made notes which underlay his Gospel is upheld by Gundry, *The Use of the Old Testament in St. Matthew's Gospel*, pp. 182-83.

22. E. Renan, *La vie de Jésus* (Paris: Calmann Lévy, 19th edn, 1888), pp. xcii-xciii, quoted by Boge, *Griechische Tachygraphie und Tironische Noten*, pp. 96-97.

that period, especially accounts of the distinctive teachings and actions of Jesus.

An analogy may be drawn from papyri surviving in Egypt from the first century AD. We have seen how official records were open to consultation through the citation of minutes of a meeting of the Petra city council in one of the papers of Babatha (see above, Chapter 4, p. 115) and how veteran soldiers might have their own copies (Chapter 6, p. 171). Another group of texts which drew upon similar sources is the collection of papyri known as Acts of the Alexandrian Martyrs.[23] The Greek citizens of Alexandria were often at loggerheads with the large Jewish population in the first century—there was a major pogrom in 38—and both parties sent envoys to present their cases to the emperors. Other ambassadors went to plead for the restoration of the city council which Augustus had abolished. The latter texts reveal a strength of anti-Roman feeling which led some Alexandrians to oppose the emperors so determinedly that they were executed. Perhaps related to these Acts are other papyri which concern the same matters, but which are clerical rather than literary products, in one case apparently with a note of the file reference in the archives from which it was copied. The incomplete reports of appearances to plead before the emperors and their agents in the Acts of the Alexandrian Martyrs seem to be basically historical, drawing from official reports like those other papyri, rewritten within a partly fictional framework and with an apparent propagandist purpose. They were composed close in time to the events they describe and some may have been pamphlets passed from hand to hand as a sort of newssheet. Their production ceased when the council was restored at the end of the second century. Commenting on one concerning events of AD 18–19 written soon after the occasion, a leading papyrologist wondered whether the repeated presence of the phrase 'the crowd called out' in it and in the Gospel accounts of the trial of Jesus might be 'good evidence for the circulation shortly after the event of private narratives of the trial of Jesus'.[24]

23. H.A. Musurillo, *The Acts of the Pagan Martyrs* (Oxford: Clarendon Press, 1954). For other papyri, see E.G. Turner in E. Lobel and E.G. Turner (eds.), *Oxyrhynchus Papyri*, XXV (London: Egypt Exploration Society, 1959), pp. 102-12 (no. 2435) and P.J. Parsons, *Oxyrhynchus Papyri*, XLII (London: Egypt Exploration Society, 1974), pp. 69-76 (nos. 3020, 3021).

24. See Turner, *Greek Manuscripts of the Ancient World*, no. 57 (P. Oxy 25.2435) and *idem, Greek Papyri*, p. 151.

A Scene in a Galilean Village

Based on the information here collected, let us imagine how the process might have begun. We are entering a first century village on the shore of Lake Galilee, like Capernaum. In the market-place people are buying and selling, bartering freshly caught fish for bottles of newly pressed olive oil, selling small birds for a few copper coins. Among the coins are shiny new ones, the writing on them is in Greek. One or two people read out the legends, 'Of Herod Antipas, year 34 [=AD 30], Tiberias'; they have been minted for local use in the king's new city on the west side of the Lake. Two men come down a street, discussing a small piece of land one is selling to the other. They reach the market-place and go to the scribe who sits in a shaded corner. They tell him what they have agreed, so he takes a sheet of papyrus and sets out the terms in Aramaic, following the approved legal formulae, while the two men call some bystanders over. The scribe reads out the deed he has written and asks if it is correct. When the two parties have assented, he signs it and asks them to sign it as well. The seller cannot sign, so the scribe writes his name for him, adding a note to that effect. After the buyer has taken the pen and slowly written his own name, he invites two of the on-lookers to be witnesses. The first adds his name in Aramaic quite easily, the second writes his in Greek, he has come from the coast to visit relatives. The scribe folds up the papyrus for the buyer and seller to seal it, the money is paid, the buyer takes the document and all depart. Now another man is walking from stall to stall, met by glum faces and muted greetings. He is a tax-collector, checking that no one in the village has evaded their payment. His multi-leaved tablets have all their names and dues listed on them. As one pays off his last instalment for the year, the flat end of the stylus erases his debit from the wax and marks him as paid up. There is a smile of relief on one face!

Near the market is a fine synagogue which a well-meaning and sympathetic centurion has had built for the people. Inside the doorway a teacher sits with half a dozen boys around him chanting phrase by phrase as he reads from a biblical scroll, the boys reading as he names them in turn. Further inside is another teacher asking and answering questions with a class of older youths. One or two of them make notes of his replies on small writing tablets. The hum of study is suddenly interrupted by a group of youngsters bursting in: 'The teacher from Nazareth is coming!' they announce. Lessons are forgotten as everyone hurries to the hill slope beyond the houses where a crowd is gathering.

There are those who have heard this man before and are keen to hear him again and there are those who have only heard about him. The first busily repeat to the others some of the surprising stories he has told and amazing feats he has performed. A small huddle of teachers beckons to their colleagues to join them. They are not happy at the rumours they have heard and settle down to listen critically. As Jesus speaks, they begin to mutter. 'You have heard it was said...,' he says, 'but I say to you...' Who is this man who dares to teach as if he is equal with Moses? One of the teachers makes some notes on his wax tablet. Afterwards he and his friends will send a letter to Jerusalem to inform the priests precisely what Jesus is saying and how he is challenging their status as interpreters of the Law. Not all of them are so annoyed and one goes home to sit down and write out neatly on a scroll what he has heard. 'My son should know about this when he grows up,' he thinks.

Figure 41. *Sculpture of tax collectors sitting at their table with coins and tablets, tax-paying farmers with hooded cloaks stand behind. From a Roman tomb at Nijmegen, third century AD. (Photograph courtesy of the Rheinisches Landesmuseum, Trier.)*

When the preaching is over, Jesus and his followers move on to the next village. They are met by some of the elders with a plea for him to come to heal the centurion's valued sick slave. Then another message from the officer follows, suggesting Jesus can order the healing without visiting the house, and soon a third message arrives to say the slave is well. The centurion, astounded and delighted, tells everyone. He calls his secretary and dictates a letter to his brother, who is a centurion far away in Gaul, relating all the day's amazing events, adding a greeting at the end in his own hand.

Written Sources for the Gospels

There is no objective means to define written sources within the present Gospel texts, although literary criticism controlled by knowledge of ancient practices may be able to make some attempts. The classic theory assumes that Matthew and Luke are based upon Mark and another collection of material, 'Q'. It is generally agreed that Q was a written text; the reports of John the Baptist's words, in particular, point to that through the '99% verbal correspondence between Matthew and Luke'.[25] Alternatives proposed from time to time, for example that Mark is an abridgement of Matthew and Luke, or that Luke drew upon Matthew as well as Mark, have never attracted a wide following.[26]

If written sources are allowed to stand behind the Gospels, then there is also the possibility that some of them were copied and circulating when the idea of assembling a connected account of Jesus' life was realized. There is no good reason why Mark may not be seen as a work based upon written sources as well as oral ones. My contention would envisage numerous random notes and reports, often about the same words and events, some preserved by individuals, some perhaps collected by interested believers. As the church grew and spread to regions beyond the physical reach of the apostolic community, so there would be greater demands for first-hand accounts of the Master's life and teachings, stimulating compositions resulting in the Gospels (see above, Chapter 7). The episodes peculiar to one Gospel or another, such as Matthew's account of Jesus paying the Temple Tax (Mt. 17.24-27), or the report of Jesus' saying about seed growing in secret unique to Mark (4.26-29) might be attributed to those earlier records. Luke mentions earlier accounts and announces his researches in his Prologue (1.1-4), so he could have obtained the picture of the friend seeking help at midnight and its lesson (11.5-13), with the famous parables of the Prodigal Son and the Good Samaritan, found only in his Gospel, from older written reports. Once material about Jesus was put into writing, it

25. G.D. Fee, 'A Text-Critical Look at the Synoptic Problem', *NovT* 22 (1980), pp. 12-28 (23). A helpful summary of the standard hypothesis about Gospel sources can be found in Stanton, *A Gospel for a New People*.

26. Lately two sources, or 'notebooks', have been posited from which Matthew, Mark and Luke selected their material, the second notebook being a revision of the first: B.E. Wilson, 'The Two Notebook Hypothesis: An Explanation of Seven Synoptic Problems', *ExpTim* 108 (1997), pp. 265-68.

might be more difficult to change or modify the words attributed to him and, as has often been observed, the basically identical content of the pictures the four Gospels present demonstrates the strength of the common tradition. That is not to say the words written down were necessarily written down exactly as spoken, nor that mistakes might not be made. The rhetorician Quintilian expressed his irritation because 'speeches which circulate as mine have little in them that actually fell from my lips, having been corrupted by the carelessness of the shorthand-writers who took them down with a view to making money out of them',[27] but there the writers had no deep concern for the contents, an attitude which would have diverged widely from that of anyone taking down the words of Jesus. Ancient historians portrayed their heroes and villains according to their own purposes and tastes and may have invented or tailored the speeches put into their mouths to suit their aims,[28] yet in some instances they agree sufficiently or contain enough distinctive elements for modern historians to be sure about the original content of speeches and activities of characters. The Gospels do not belong to the same genre and so should not be judged as if they do. They report the words and deeds of one who was so radical and impressive that, after his death, hundreds, thousands of people adopted his teachings, took his name, spread his message peacefully and were prepared to die rather than renounce their loyalty to him. With the life of such a figure to describe, we may doubt the Evangelists would have engaged in the invention or major alteration of received traditions—the rapid spread of the church and the evident lack of central control would have made that difficult on a large scale—and without a range of unique teachings accompanied by impressive acts centred upon an authoritative figure we may doubt the Christian church would have grown as it did.

The ubiquity of writing in Herodian Palestine and its use in the affairs of daily life, religious and secular, was no less than the use of writing in other parts of the eastern Mediterranean at that time, indeed, the Jewish religious tradition may have given it wider currency. The material evidence and related arguments set out in these chapters indicate far more weight than has been allowed should be given to the

---

27. *Inst. Orat.* 7.2. 24; see Alexander, 'Ancient Book Production', pp. 94-95.
28. See Kennedy, 'Classical and Christian Source Criticism'.

role of writing in preserving information about Jesus of Nazareth from his lifetime onwards and so in forming the Gospel tradition.

Figure 42. *Bronze coin of Herod Antipas, bearing his name and the date (AD 28–29) on the obverse and the name of his capital, Tiberias, on the reverse. (Photograph by courtesy of the Heberden Coin Room, Ashmolean Museum, Oxford.)*

BIBLIOGRAPHY

Greek and Latin works are cited from the Loeb Classical Library editions.

Abd-Allâh, Y., and I. Gajda, *Yémen, au pays de la reine de Saba* (Paris: Flammarion, 1997).

Abel, F.M., 'Chronique: Tombeau et ossuaires juifs récemment découverts', *RB* 10 (1913), pp. 262-77.

—'Topographie des campagnes machabéennes', *RB* 35 (1926), pp. 510-33.

Ackroyd, P.R., and C.F. Evans (eds.), *Cambridge History of the Bible*, I (Cambridge: Cambridge University Press, 1970).

Adam-Rayewitz, D., M. Aviam and D.R. Edwards, 'Yodafat 1992', *IEJ* 45 (1995), pp. 191-97.

Adams, J.N., 'The Language of the Vindolanda Writing Tablets: An Interim Report', *JRS* 85 (1995), pp. 86-134.

Aland, K., 'Noch einmal: der ROTAS/SATOR-Rebus', in Baarda *et al.* (eds.), *Text and Testimony*, pp. 9-23.

Aland, K., and B. Aland, *The Text of the New Testament* (trans. E.F. Rhodes; Grand Rapids, MI: Eerdmans, 1987).

Alexander, L.C.A., 'Ancient Book Production and the Circulation of the Gospels', in Bauckham (ed.), *The Gospels for All Christians*, pp. 71-111.

—*The Preface to Luke's Gospel* (SNTSMS, 78; Cambridge: Cambridge University Press, 1993).

—'The Living Voice: Scepticism towards the Written Word in Early Christian and in Graeco-Roman Texts', in Clines, Fowl and Porter (eds.), *The Bible in Three Dimensions*, pp. 221-47.

Alexander, P.S., 'Orality in Pharisaic-Rabbinic Judaism at the Turn of the Eras', in Wansborough (ed.), *Jesus and the Oral Gospel Tradition*, pp. 159-84.

—'Quid Athenis et Hierosolymis? Rabbinic Midrash and Hermeneutics in the Graeco-Roman World', in Davies and White (eds.), *A Tribute to Geza Vermes*, pp. 101-24.

Allegro, M., *Qumran Cave 4 I (4Q158-4Q186)* (DJD, 5; Oxford: Clarendon Press, 1968).

Aly, Z., and L. Koenen, *Three Rolls of the Early Septuagint: Genesis and Deuteronomy* (Bonn: Habelt, 1980).

Anderson, R.D., P.J. Parsons and R.G.M. Nisbet, 'Elegiacs by Gallus from Qasr Ibrîm', *JRS* 69 (1979), pp. 125-55.

Applebaum, S., A. Oppenheimer, U. Rappaport and M. Stern (eds.), *Jerusalem in the Second Temple Period: Abraham Schalit Memorial Volume* (Jerusalem: Yad Izhak ben-Zvi, 1980).

Arav, R., and R.A. Freund, *Bethsaida: A City by the North Shore of the Sea of Galilee* (Kirksville, MO: Thomas Jefferson University Press, 1995).

Ariel, D.T., *Excavations at the City of David 1978–1985 Directed by Yigal Shiloh*. II. *Imported Stamped Amphora Handles, Coins, Worked Bone and Ivory, Glass* (Qedem, 30; Jerusalem: Hebrew University, 1990).

Atkinson, D., 'The Origin and Date of the "Sator" Word-Square', *JEH* 2 (1951), pp. 1-18.

Atkinson, K., 'On Further Defining the First-Century CE Synagogue: Fact or Fiction?', *NTS* 43 (1997), pp. 491-502.

Aune, D. (ed.), *The Gospel of Matthew in Current Study: Essays in Honor of William Thompson S.J.* (Grand Rapids: Eerdmans, 2000).

Avi-Yonah, M., *Abbreviations in Greek Inscriptions (The Near East, 200 BC–AD 1000)* (*Quarterly of the Department of Antiquities of Palestine*, Supplement 9, 1940).

Avi-Yonah, M., and A. Kloner, 'Mareshah (Marisa)', in E. Stern (ed.), *New Encyclopedia*, III, pp. 948-57.

Avigad, N., 'Aramaic Inscriptions in the Tomb of Jason', *IEJ* 17 (1967), pp. 101-11.

—*Discovering Jerusalem* (Nashville, TN: Thomas Nelson, 1983).

—*Hebrew Bullae from the Time of Jeremiah: Remnants of a Burnt Archive* (Jerusalem: Israel Exploration Society, 1988).

—'A Bulla of King Jonathan', *IEJ* 25 (1975), pp. 245-46.

—'A Bulla of Jonathan the High Priest', *IEJ* 25 (1975), pp. 8-12.

Avni, G., and Z. Greenhut, *The Akeldama Tombs* (Jerusalem: Israel Antiquities Authority, 1996).

Baarda, T. *et al.*, (eds.), *Text and Testimony: Essays on New Testament and Apocryphal Literature in Honour of A.F.J. Klijn* (Kampen: Kok, 1988).

Babcock, W. (ed.), *Paul and the Legacies of Paul* (Dallas, TX: Southern Methodist University Press, 1990).

Bagnall, R.S., *Reading Papyri, Writing Ancient History* (London: Routledge, 1995).

Baillet, M., J.T. Milik and R. de Vaux, *Les 'Petites Grottes' de Qumran* (DJD, 3; Oxford: Clarendon Press, 1962).

Baines, J., and C.J. Eyre, 'Four Notes on Literacy', *Göttinger Miszellen* 61 (1983), pp. 65-96.

Baines, J., 'Literacy and Ancient Egyptian Society', *Man* 18 (1983), pp. 572-99.

Barr, J., 'Hebrew, Aramaic and Greek in the Hellenistic Age', in W.D. Davies and L. Finkelstein (eds.), *The Cambridge History of Judaism* (2 vols.; Cambridge: University Press, 1989), II, pp. 79-114.

—''Abba isn't "Daddy"'', *JTS* NS 39 (1988), pp. 28-47.

—*The Variable Spellings of the Hebrew Bible* (The Schweich Lectures, 1986; Oxford: Oxford University Press for the British Academy, 1989).

Barthélemy, D., *Les devanciers d'Aquila* (VTSup, 10; Leiden: E.J. Brill, 1963).

Bass, G.F. *et al.*, 'The Bronze Age Shipwreck at Ulu Bürün: 1986 Campaign', *AJA* 93 (1989), pp. 1-29.

Bauckham, R., 'For Whom Were the Gospels Written?', in Bauckham (ed.), *The Gospels for All Christians*, pp. 9-48.

Bauckham, R., (ed.), *The Gospels for All Christians: Rethinking the Gospel Audiences* (Grand Rapids, MI: Eerdmans; Edinburgh: T. & T. Clark, 1998).

—*Palestinian Setting: The Book of Acts in its First Century Setting*, IV (5 vols; Grand Rapids, MI: Eerdmans; Carlisle: Paternoster Press, 1995).

Baum, A.D., 'Papias als Kommentator evangelischer Aussprüche Jesu', *NovT* 38 (1996), pp. 257-76.

—'Papias, der Vorzug der *Viva Vox* und die Evangelienschriften', *NTS* 44 (1998), pp. 144-51.

Baumgarten, J.M., 'Form Criticism and the Oral Law', *JSJ* 1 (1974), pp. 34-40.

Baumgarten, J.M., and J.T. Milik, *Qumran Cave 4: XIII The Damascus Document (4Q266-273)* (DJD, 18; Oxford: Clarendon Press, 1997).

Beare, F.W., *The Earliest Records of Jesus* (Oxford: Basil Blackwell, 1962).

Beazley, J.G., 'Hymn to Hermes', *AJA* 52 (1948), pp. 336-40.

Beck, F.A.G., *Album of Greek Education* (Sydney: Cheron Press, 1975).

Bell, H.I., *Jews and Christians in Egypt* (London: The British Museum, 1924).

Bell, H.I., and T.C. Skeat, *Fragments of an Unknown Gospel and other Early Christian Papyri* (London: The British Museum, 1935).

Ben-Ḥayyim, Z. (ed.), *The Historical Dictionary of the Hebrew Language: Materials for the Dictionary, Series 1 200 BCE–300 CE* (Jerusalem: Academy for the Hebrew Language, 1988) (on microfiche).

Benoit, P., J.T. Milik and R. de Vaux, *Les Grottes de Muraba'ât* (DJD, 2; Oxford: Clarendon Press, 1962).

Berges, D., 'Die Tonsiegel aus dem Karthagischen Tempelarchiv', *Mitteilungen des deutschen archäologischen Instituts, Römische Abteilung* 100 (1993), pp. 249-68.

Bernard, P., and C. Rapin, 'Un parchemin gréco-bactrien d'une collection privée', *CRAIBL* (1994), pp. 261-94.

Bernstein, M., J. García Martínez and J. Kampen (eds.), *Legal Texts and Issues* (Leiden: E.J. Brill, 1997).

Best, E., and R.McL. Wilson (eds.), *Text and Interpretation: Studies in Honour of M. Black* (Cambridge: Cambridge University Press, 1979).

Beyer, K., *The Aramaic Language* (trans. J.F. Healey; Göttingen: Vandenhoeck & Ruprecht, 1986).

—*Die aramäischen Texte vom Toten Meer* (Göttingen: Vandenhoeck & Ruprecht, 1984).

—*Die aramäischen Texte vom Toten Meer, Ergänzungsband* (Göttingen: Vandenhoeck & Ruprecht, 1994).

Bierbrier, M. (ed.), *Papyrus: Structure and Usage* (British Museum Occasional Paper, 60; London: Department of Egyptian Antiquities, British Museum, 1986).

Bingen, J. *et al.*, *Mons Claudianus: Ostraca Graeca et Latina I (O.Claud. 1 à 190)* (Cairo: Institut français d'archéologie orientale, 1992).

Biran, A., *Biblical Dan* (Jerusalem: Israel Exploration Society, 1994).

Biran, A. (ed.), *Biblical Archaeology Today* (Jerusalem: Israel Exploration Society, 1985).

Black, M., *An Aramaic Approach to the Gospels and Acts* (London: Oxford University Press, 3rd edn, 1967).

Blanchard, A. (ed.), *Les débuts du codex* (Bibliologia, 9; Brepols: Turnhout, 1989).

Blass, F., A. Debrunner and F. Rohrkopf, *Grammatik des neutestamentlichen Griechisch* (Göttingen: Vandenhoeck and Ruprecht, 14th edn, 1975).

Blomberg, C.L., *The Historical Reliability of the Gospels* (Leicester: IVP, 1987).

Boak, A.E.R., *Papyri from Tebtunis*, I (2 vols.; University of Michigan Studies, Humanistic Series 28; Michigan Papyri, 2; Ann Arbor, MI: University of Michigan Press, 1933).

Boardman, J., 'An Inscribed Sherd from Al Mina', *Oxford Journal of Archaeology* 1 (1982), pp. 365-67.

Boge, H., *Griechische Tachygraphie und Tironische Noten: Ein Handbuch der antiken und mittelalterlichen Schnellschrift* (Berlin: Akademie Verlag, 1973).

Boismard, M.-E., 'A propos de 7Q5 et Mc 6, 52-53', *RB* 102 (1995), pp. 585-88.

Boter, G., *The Textual Tradition of Plato's Republic* (Leiden: E.J. Brill, 1989).

Boussac, M.-F., 'Sceaux déliens', *Revue archéologique* (1988), pp. 307-38.

Boussac, M.-F., and A. Invernizzi (eds.), *Archives et sceaux du monde hellénistique: Archivi e sigilli nel mondo ellenistico, Torino, Villa Gualino, 13–16 gennaio 1993* (Bulletin de Correspondance Hellénique, Sup, 29; Athens: Ecole française d'Athenes, 1996).

Bowker, J., *The Targums and Rabbinic Literature* (Cambridge: Cambridge University Press, 1969).

Bowman, A.K., *Egypt after the Pharaohs, 332 BC–AD 642* (London: British Museum, 1986).

—*Life and Letters on the Roman Frontier: Vindolanda and its People* (London: British Museum, 1994).

—'The Roman Imperial Army: Letters and Literacy on the Northern Frontier', in Bowman and Woolf (eds.), *Literacy and Power*, pp. 109-25.

Bowman, A.K., and J.D. Thomas, *Vindolanda: The Latin Writing Tablets* (Britannia Monograph Series, 4; Gloucester: Alan Sutton, 1983).

—*The Vindolanda Writing-tablets: Tabulae Vindolandenses*, II (London: British Museum Press, 1994).

Bowman, A.K., and G. Woolf (eds.), *Literacy and Power in the Ancient World* (Cambridge: Cambridge University Press, 1994).

Bowman, A.K. *et al.*, *The Oxyrhynchus Papyri*, L (London: Egypt Exploration Society, 1983).

Brooke, G., 'Luke–Acts and the Qumran Scrolls: The Case of MMT', in Tuckett (ed.), *Luke's Literary Achievement*, pp. 72-90.

—'The Explicit Presentation of Scripture in 4QMMT', in Bernstein, García Martínez and Kampen (eds.), *Legal Texts and Issues*, pp. 67-88.

Broshi, M. (ed.), *The Damascus Document Reconsidered* (Jerusalem: Israel Exploration Society, 1992).

Bruce, F.F., 'Are the New Testament Documents still Reliable?', in Kantzer (ed.), *Evangelical Roots*, pp. 49-61.

—'Languages (Latin)', *ABD*, IV, pp. 222-22.

—'Thoughts from my Study: Apostolic Tradition', *Calling* 12.3 (1970), pp. 10-13.

—*Tradition Old and New* (Exeter: Paternoster Press, 1970).

Budge, Sir E.A. Wallis, *By Nile and Tigris* (2 vols.; London: John Murray, 1920).

Bultmann, R., *The History of the Synoptic Tradition* (trans. J. Marsh; Oxford: Basil Blackwell, 1968).

Burney, C.F., *The Aramaic Origin of the Fourth Gospel* (Oxford: Clarendon Press, 1922).

—*The Poetry of our Lord* (Oxford: Clarendon Press, 1925).

Butler, A.J., *The Arab Conquest of Egypt* (rev. P.M. Fraser; Oxford: Clarendon Press, 2nd edn, 1978).

Cahill, J.M., 'The Chalk Assemblages of the Persian/Hellenistic and Early Roman Periods', in de Groot and Ariel (eds.), *Excavations at the City of David 1978–85*, pp. 190-274.

Cameron, R., 'Thomas, Gospel of', *ABD*, VI, pp. 535-40.

Caminos, R.A., 'Some Comments on the Reuse of Papyrus', in Bierbrier (ed.), *Papyrus: Structure and Usage*, pp. 43-61.

Canfora, L., *The Vanished Library: A Wonder of the Ancient World* (trans. M. Ryle; Berkeley: University of California Press, 1989)

Cantineau, J., *Le nabatéen* (2 vols.; Paris: Leroux, 1932).

Capasso, M., *Manuale di papirologia ercolanese* (Lecce: Galatina, 1991).

Caquot, A., and M. Philonenko (eds.), *Hommages à A. Dupont-Sommer* (Paris: Adrien-Maisonneuve, 1971).

Caquot, A., J.-M. de Tarragon and J.L. Cunchillos, *Textes Ougaritiques*, II (2 vols.; Paris: Cerf, 1989).

Carmignac, J., *La naissance des évangiles synoptiques* (Paris: O.E.I.L., 1984) .

Cavallo, G., 'Libro e pubblico alla fine del mondo antico', in *idem* (ed.), *Libri, editori e pubblico nel mondo antico*, pp. 81-132.

Cavallo, G. (ed.), *Libri, editori e pubblico nel mondo antico: Guida storica e critica* (Bari: Laterza, 1975).

Chapa, J., review of *Rekindling the Word: In Search of Gospel Truth* (Leominster: Grace-wing, 1995), by C.P. Thiede, in *JTS* NS 4-8 (1997), pp. 221-27.

Charlesworth, J.H., 'The Manuscripts of St Catherine's Monastery', *BA* 43 (1980), pp. 26-34.

Clarysse, W., and K. Vandorpe, *Zenon, un homme d'affaires grecs à l'ombre des pyramides* (Louvain: Presses Universitaires, 1995).

Clines, D.J.A., S.E. Fowl and S.E. Porter (eds.), *The Bible in Three Dimensions: Essays in Celebration of Forty Years of Biblical Studies in the University of Sheffield* (JSOTSup, 87; Sheffield: Sheffield Academic Press, 1990).

Cockle, W.E.H., 'Writing and Reading Exercises', in Bingen *et al.*, *Mons Claudianus*, pp. 179-90 .

Coles, R.A., *Reports of Proceedings in Papyri* (Papyrologia Brussellensia, 4; Brussels: Fondation Egyptologique Reine Elisabeth, 1966).

Colin, G., *Hypérides: Discours* (Paris: Les Belles Lettres, 1946).

Collard, C., *Euripides* (Oxford: Clarendon Press for the Classical Association, 1981).

Collard, C., M.J. Cropp and K.H. Lee, *Euripides: Selected Fragments. Plays*, I (War-minster: Aris and Phillips, 1995).

Comfort, P.W., 'Exploring the Common Identification of Three New Testament Manu-scripts: $\mathfrak{P}^4$, $\mathfrak{P}^{64}$ and $\mathfrak{P}^{67}$', *TynBul* 46 (1995), pp. 43-54.

Comfort, P.W., and D.P. Barrett, *The Complete Text of the Earliest New Testament Manuscripts* (Grand Rapids: Baker Book House, 1999).

Cotton, H.M., 'The Archive of Salome Komiase, Daughter of Levi: Another Archive from the "Cave of Letters"', *ZPE* 105 (1995), pp. 171-208.

Cotton, H.M., and A. Yardeni, *Aramaic, Hebrew and Greek Documentary Texts from Nahal Hever and Other Sites* (DJD, 27; Oxford: Clarendon Press, 1997).

Cotton, H.M., and J. Geiger, *Masada*. II. *The Latin and Greek Documents* (Jerusalem: Israel Exploration Society, 1989).

Cotton, H.M., W.E.H. Cockle and F.G.B. Millar, 'The Papyrology of the Roman Near East: A Survey', *JRS* 85 (1995), pp. 214-35.

Cotton, H.M., O. Lernau and Y. Goren, 'Fish Sauces from Herodian Masada', *Journal of Roman Archaeology* 9 (1996), pp. 123-28.

Coxon, P.W., 'Greek Loan-words and the Alleged Greek Loan Translations in the Book of Daniel', *Transactions of the Glasgow University Oriental Society* 25 (1973–74), pp. 24-40.

Craigie, P.C., 'Deuteronomy and Ugaritic Studies', *TynBul* 28 (1977), pp. 155-69.

Cribbiore, R., *Writing, Teachers and Students in Graeco-Roman Egypt* (Atlanta, GA: Scholars Press, 1996).

Cross, F.M., 'A Report on the Samaria Papyri', in J.A. Emerton (ed.), *Congress Volume: Jerusalem 1986* (VTSup, 40; Leiden: E.J. Brill, 1988), pp. 17-26.

Cross, F.M., and E. Eshel, 'Ostraca from Khirbet Qumrân', *IEJ* 47 (1997), pp. 17-28.

Cuaderlier, P., 'Les tablettes grecques d'Egypte: Inventaire', in Lalou (ed.), *Les tablettes à écrire de l'antiquité à l'époque moderne*, pp. 63-94

Cunchillos, J.L., 'Correspondence', in Caquot, de Tarragon and Cunchillos, *Textes Ougaritiques*, II (Paris: Cerf, 1989).

Curtis, R.L., *Garum and Salsamenta: Production and Commerce in Materia Medica* (Studies in Ancient Medicine, 3; Leiden: E.J. Brill, 1991).

Daitz, S.G., *The Jerusalem Palimpsest of Euripides* (Berlin: W. de Gruyter, 1970).

Dalman, G., *Aramäische Dialektproben* (Leipzig: J.C. Hinrichs, 1927).

—*Grammatik des jüdisch-palästinischen Aramäisch* (Leipzig: J.C. Hinrichs, 2nd edn, 1905 [1894]).

—*The Words of Jesus Considered in the Light of Post-Biblical Jewish Writings and the Aramaic Language* (Edinburgh: T. & T. Clark, 1902).

—*Die Worte Jesu* (Leipzig: J.C. Hinrichs, 2nd edn, 1930 [1898]).

Danby, H., *The Mishnah* (London: Oxford University Press, 1933).

Daris, S., *Il lessico latino nel greco d'Egitto* (Barcelona: Institut de Teologia Fondamental, Seminario de Papirologia, 2nd edn, 1991).

—*Documenti per la storia dell'esercito romano in Egito* (Pubblicazioni dell'Università Cattolica del Sacro Cuore; Contributi, ser. 3; Scienze storiche, 9; Milan: Societa Editrice Vita e Pensiero, 1964).

Davies, P.R., and R.T. White (eds.), *A Tribute to Geza Vermes* (JSOTSup, 100; Sheffield: Sheffield Academic Press, 1990).

Davies, W.D., and L. Finkelstein (eds.), *The Cambridge History of Judaism*, II (Cambridge: Cambridge University Press, 1989).

Deissmann, A., *Light from the Ancient East* (trans. L.R.M. Strachan; London: Hodder & Stoughton, rev. edn, 1927; repr. Grand Rapids, MI: Baker Book House, 1980).

Demsky, A., 'When the Priests Trumpeted the Onset of the Sabbath', *BAR* 12.6 (1986), pp. 50-52.

Dibelius, M., *From Tradition to Gospel* (trans. B.L. Woolf; London: Nicholson & Watson, 1934).

Downing, F.G., 'Word-Processing in the Ancient World: The Social Production and Performance of Q', *JSNT* 64 (1996), pp. 29-48.

Driver, G.R., *Aramaic Documents of the Fifth Century B.C.* (Oxford: Clarendon Press, 1954; reduced and rev. edn, 1965).

Duncan, J.A., 'Excerpted Texts of Deuteronomy at Qumran', *Revue de Qumran* 69 = 18.1 (1997), pp. 43-62.

Easterling, P.E., and B.M.W. Knox (eds.), *The Cambridge History of Classical Literature.* I. *Greek Literature* (Cambridge: Cambridge University Press, 1985).

Edelstein, L., *Plato's Seventh Letter* (Philosophia Antiqua, 14; Leiden: E.J. Brill, 1966).

Edwards, D.R., and C.T. McCollough (eds.), *Archaeology and the Galilee: Texts and Contexts in the Graeco-Roman and Byzantine Periods* (Atlanta: Scholars Press, 1997).

El-Din, M.S. *et al.*, *Sinai: The Site and the History* (New York: New York University Press, 1998).

Elliott, J.K. (ed.), *Studies in New Testament Language and Text: Essays in Honour of George D. Kilpatrick* (NovTSup, 44; Leiden: E.J. Brill, 1976).

—review of *The Jesus Papyrus* (London: Weidenfeld & Nicholson, 1996), by C.P. Thiede and M. d'Ancona, in *NovT* 38 (1996), pp. 393-99.

Ellis, E.E., and E. Grässer (eds.), *Jesus und Paulus: Festschrift für Werner Georg Kümmel zum 70. Geburtstag* (Göttingen: Vandenhoeck & Ruprecht, 1975).

Emerton, J.A., '*Maranatha* and *Ephphatha*', *JTS* NS 18 (1967), pp. 427-31.

Emery, W.B., *Archaic Egypt* (Harmondsworth: Penguin Books, 1961).

Emmel, S., 'Greek Biblical Papyri in the Beinecke Library', *ZPE* 112 (1996) pp. 289-94.

Enste, S., 'Qumran-Fragment 7Q5 ist nicht Markus 6, 52-53', *ZPE* 126 (1999), pp. 189-93.

Eph'al, I., and J. Naveh, *Aramaic Ostraca of the Fourth Century BC from Idumaea* (Jerusalem: Magnes Press, 1996).

Epp, E.J., 'The Codex and Literacy in Early Christianity and at Oxyrhynchus: Issues Raised by Harry Y. Gamble's *Books and Readers in the Early Church*', *CR* 10 (1997), pp. 15-37.

—'New Testament Papyrus Manuscripts and Letter Carrying in Greco-Roman Times', in Pearson (ed.), *The Future of Early Christianity*, pp. 35-56.

—'The New Testament Papyri at Oxyrhynchus in their Social and Intellectual Context', in Petersen, Vos and de Jonge (eds.), *The Sayings of Jesus*, pp. 47-68.

Erlemann, K., 'Papyrus Egerton 2: "Missing Link" zwischen synoptischer und johanneischer Tradition', *NTS* 42 (1996), pp. 12-34.

Eshel, E., and A. Kloner, 'An Aramaic Ostracon of an Edomite Marriage Contract from Maresha, Dated 176 B.C.E.', *IEJ* 46 (1996), pp. 1-22.

Eyre, C.J., A. Leahy and L.M. Leahy (eds.), *The Unbroken Reed: Studies in the Culture and Heritage of Ancient Egypt in Honour of A.F. Shore* (London: The Egypt Exploration Society, 1994).

Farrer, J.A., *Literary Forgeries* (London: Longmans, Green & Co, 1907).

Fee, G.D., 'A Text-Critical Look at the Synoptic Problem', *NovT* 22 (1980), pp. 12-28.

Feisel, D., and J. Gascou, 'Documents d'archives romains inédits du Moyen-Euphrate (IIIe siècle après J.-C.)', *CRAIBL* (1989), pp. 535-61.

Fink, R.D., *Roman Military Records on Papyrus* (Cleveland: Case Western Reserve University Press, 1971).

Fitzmyer, J.A., 'Aramaic Kepha' and Peter's Name in the New Testament', in Best and Wilson (eds.), *Text and Interpretation*, pp. 121-32.

—'The Aramaic Qorbân Inscription from Jebel Hallet et-Tûri and Mk 7:11/ Mt 15:5', *JBL* 78 (1959), pp. 60-65, repr. in *idem, Essays on the Semitic Background of the New Testament*, pp. 93-100.

—*A Wandering Aramean: Collected Aramaic Essays* (Missoula, MT: Scholars Press, 1979).

—'Did Jesus Speak Greek ?', *BAR* 18.5 (1992), pp. 58-63.

—*Essays on the Semitic Background of the New Testament* (London: Geoffrey Chapman, 1971).

—'The Languages of Palestine in the First Century A.D.', reprinted from *CBQ* 32 (1970), pp. 501-31, in *idem, A Wandering Aramean*, pp. 29-56.

—'The Use of Explicit Old Testament Quotations in Qumran Literature and in the New Testament', *NTS* 7 (1960–61), pp. 297-333, repr. in *idem, Essays on the Semitic Background of the New Testament*, pp. 3-58.

—review of *An Aramaic Approach to the Gospels and Acts* (London: Oxford University Press, 3rd edn, 1967), by M. Black, in *CBQ* 30 (1968), pp. 417-28.

Fitzmyer, J.A., and D.J. Harrington, *Palestinian Aramaic Texts* (Biblica et Orientalia, 34; Rome: Biblical Institute Press, 1978).

Foerster, G., *Masada*.V. *Art and Architecture* (Jerusalem: Israel Exploration Society, 1997).

Fraser, P.M., *Cities of Alexander the Great* (Oxford: Clarendon Press, 1996).

—*Ptolemaic Alexandria* (Oxford: Clarendon Press, 1972).

Freedman, D.N., and K.A. Matthews, *The Paleo-Hebrew Leviticus Scroll* (Winona Lake, IN: Eisenbrauns for the American Schools of Oriental Research, 1985).

Freehof, S.B., *The Response Literature* and *A Treasury of Responsa* (New York: Jewish Publication Society, 1955, 1962; reprinted in one volume, New York: Ktav, 1973).

Frere, S.S., and R.S.O. Tomlin, *The Roman Inscriptions of Britain*. II. fasc. 6, *Painting and Graffiti* (Stroud: Alan Sutton, 1994).

—*The Roman Inscriptions of Britain*. II. fasc. 4, *Tools, Decor, Ornaments etc.* (Stroud: Alan Sutton, 1992).

Funk, R.W., and R.W. Hoover, *The Five Gospels: What did Jesus really Say ?* (New York: Macmillan, 1993).

Funk, R.W., R.W. Hoover and M.H. Smith, *The Gospel of Mark: Red Letter Edition* (Sonoma, CA: Polebridge Press, 1991).

Gal, Z., 'A Stone Vessel Manufacturing Site in the Lower Galilee', *'Atiqot* 20 (1991), pp. 25*-26*, 179-80.

Gallo, I., *Greek and Latin Papyrology* (trans. M. Falviere and J.R. March; London: Institute of Classical Studies, 1986).

Gamble, H.Y., *Books and Readers in the Early Church* (New Haven: Yale University Press, 1995).

—'The Pauline Corpus and the Early Christian Book', in Babcock (ed.), *Paul and the Legacies of Paul*, pp. 265-80.

Garbini, G., *History and Ideology in Ancient Israel* (trans. J. Bowden; London: SCM Press, 1988).

García Martinez, F., *The Dead Sea Scrolls Translated: The Qumran Texts in English* (trans. W.G.E. Watson; Leiden: E.J. Brill, 1994).

Gasque, W.W., and R.P. Martin (eds.), *Apostolic History and the Gospel: Biblical and Historical Essays Presented to F.F. Bruce* (Exeter: Paternoster Press, 1970).

Geller, M., Review of Beyer, *Die aramäischen Texte*, in *BSOAS* 51 (1988), pp. 315, 316.

Geraty, L.T., 'The Historical, Linguistic, and Biblical Significance of the Khirbet el-Kôm Ostraca', in C.L. Meyers and M. O'Connor (eds.), *The Word of the Lord Shall Go Forth: Essays in Honor of David Noel Freedman* (Winona Lake, IN: Eisenbrauns, 1983), pp. 545-48.

—'Kôm, Khirbet el-, Ostraca', *ABD*, IV, pp. 99-100.

—'The Khirbet el-Kôm Bilingual Ostracon', *BASOR* 220 (1975), pp. 55-61.

Gerhardsson, B., *Memory: Tradition and Transmission in Early Christianity* (Acta Seminarii Neotestamentici Upsaliensis, 22; Lund: C.W.K. Gleerup, 1964).

—*The Origins of the Gospel Traditions* (London: SCM Press, 1979).

—*Tradition and Transmission in Early Christianity* (ConNT, 20; Lund: C.W.K. Gleerup, 1964).

Gibson, S., and J.E. Taylor, *Beneath the Church of the Holy Sepulchre* (London: Palestine Exploration Fund, 1994).

Gigante, M., *Philodemus in Italy: The Books from Herculaneum* (trans. D. Obbink; Ann Arbor: University of Michigan Press, 1995).

Ginsberg, H.L., 'Notes on "The Birth of the Gracious and Beautiful Gods" ', *JRAS* (1935), pp. 45-72

Ginzberg, L., *Geonica*. I. *The Geonim and their Halakic Writings*; II. *Geniza Studies* (New York: Jewish Theological Seminary, 1909; repr. New York: Hermon Press, 1968).

Giovannini, A., and M. Hirot, 'L'inscription de Nazareth: nouvelle interprétation', *ZPE* 124 (1999), pp. 107-32.

Goodman, M., *State and Society in Roman Galilee* (Totowa, NJ: Rowman & Allanheld, 1983).

—'Texts, Scribes and Power in Roman Judaea', in Bowman and Woolf (eds.), *Literacy and Power in the Ancient World*, pp. 99-108.

Goodspeed, E.J., *Matthew, Apostle and Evangelist* (Philadelphia, Toronto: J.C. Winston, 1959).

Goranson, S., 'Qumran: A Hub of Scribal Activity', *BARev* 20.5 (1994), pp. 36-39.

Grandet, P., *Le Papyrus Harris I (BM 9999)* (Cairo: Institut francais d'Archéologie orientale, 1994).

Grant, M., *Greek and Latin Authors 800 B.C.–A.D. 1000* (New York: H.H. Wilson Co., 1980).

Grayson, A.K., *Assyrian Royal Inscriptions* (2 vols; Wiesbaden: Otto Harrassowitz, 1972–76).

—*Assyrian Rulers of the Early First Millennium B.C. I.* (Royal Inscriptions of Mesopotamia, Assyrian Periods, 2; Toronto: University Press, 1991).

Green, J.B., S. McKnight and I.H. Marshall, (eds.), *Dictionary of Jesus and the Gospels* (Leicester : InterVarsity Press; Downers Grove, IL: InterVarsity Press, 1992).

Greenfield, J.C., ' "Because He/She Did Not Know Letters": Remarks on a First Millennium C.E. Legal Expression', *JANESCU* 22 (1993), pp. 39-44.

—'Languages of Palestine, 200 B.C.E.–200 C.E.', in H.H. Paper (ed.), *Jewish Languages: Theme and Variations* (New York: Ktav, 1978), pp. 143-154.

Greenhut, Z., 'The "Caiaphas" Tomb in North Talpiyot, Jerusalem', *'Atiqot* 21 (1992), pp. 63-71.

Grelot, P., 'Note sur les propositions du Pr Carsten Peter Thiede', *RB* 102 (1995), pp. 589-91.

Grenfell, B.P., and A.S. Hunt, *The Oxyrhynchus Papyri*, I (London: Egypt Exploration Fund, 1898).

—*The Oxyrhynchus Papyri*, VI (London: Egypt Exploration Fund, 1908).

—*The Oxyrhynchus Papyri*, XI (London: Egypt Exploration Fund, 1915).

—*The Oxyrhynchus Papyri*, XIII (London: Egypt Exploration Society, 1919).

Groot, A. de, and D.T. Ariel (eds.), *Excavations at the City of David 1978–85 Directed by Yiagal Shiloh*. III. *Stratigraphical, Environmental and Other Reports* (Qedem, 33; Jerusalem: Institute of Archaeology, Hebrew University, 1992).

Grzybek, E., and M. Sordi, 'L'édit de Nazareth et la politique de Néron à l'égard des chrétiens', *ZPE* 120 (1998), pp. 279-91.

Guarducci, M., 'Dal gioco letterale alla critografio mistice', *ANRW* II 16.2 (Berlin: W. de Gruyter, 1978), pp. 1763-73.

Gundry, R.H., *The Use of the Old Testament in St. Matthew's Gospel* (NovTSup, 18; Leiden: E.J. Brill, 1967).

Gunkel, H., *The Legends of Genesis: The Biblical Saga and History* (trans. W.H. Carruth, 1901; repr., with Introduction by W.F. Albright; New York: Schocken Books, 1964).

Gutman, S., *Gamla: A City in Revolt* (Jerusalem: Ministry of Defence, 1994) [Hebrew].

Haberman, W., 'Zur chronologischen Verteilung der papyrologischen Zeugnisse', *ZPE* 122 (1998), pp. 144-60.

Hachlili, R., 'The Goliath Family Tomb in Jericho: Funerary Inscriptions from a First Century A.D. Jewish Monumental Tomb', *BASOR* 235 (1979), pp. 31-65.

—'A Jerusalem Family Tomb in Jericho', *BASOR* 230 (1978), pp. 45-56.

—'The Origin of the Synagogue: A Re-assessment', *JSJ* 28 (1997), pp. 34-47.

Haelst, J. van, *Catalogue des papyrus littéraires juifs et chrétiens* (Paris: Publications de la Sorbonne, 1976).

—'Les origines du Codex', in Blanchard (ed.), *Les débuts du codex*, pp. 13-35.

Hagedorn, U., D. Hagedorn, L.C. Youtie and H. Youtie, *Das Archiv des Petaus* (*Pap. Colon.* IV) (Cologne: Westdeutscher Verlag, 1969).

Halverson, J., 'Oral and Written Gospel: A Critique of Werner Kelber', *NTS* 40 (1994), pp. 180-95.

Hammer, R., *Sifre: A Tanaaitic Commentary on the Book of Deuteronomy* (New Haven: Yale University Press, 1986).

Handley, E.W., and U. Wartenberg *et al.*, *The Oxyrhynchus Papyri*, LXIV (London: Egypt Exploration Society, 1997).

Hanson, A.E., 'Ancient Illiteracy', in Humphrey (ed.), *Literacy in the Roman World*, pp. 159-98.

Haran, M., 'Codex, *Pinax* and Writing Slat', *Studies in Memory of Abraham Wasserstein*, I, *Scripta Classica Israelica* 15 (1996), pp. 212-22.

Harding, Lankester G., and E. Littmann, *Some Thamudic Inscriptions from the Hashemite Kingdom of Jordan* (Leiden: E.J. Brill, 1952).

Hardy, E.G., *The Monumentum Ancyranum* (Oxford: Clarendon Press, 1923).

Harris, W.V., *Ancient Literacy* (Cambridge, MA: Harvard University Press, 1989).

Haslam, M.W. *et al.*, *The Oxyrhynchus Papyri*, LXV (London: Egypt Exploration Society, 1998).

Havelock, E.A., *Origins of Western Literacy* (Toronto: Ontario Institute for Studies in Education, 1976).

Head, P.M., 'The Date of the Magdalen Papyrus of Matthew (*P.Magd.Gr.*17 = $\mathfrak{P}$64): A Response to C.P. Thiede', *TynBul* 46 (1995), pp. 251-85.

Head, P.M., and M. Warren, 'Re-Inking the Pen: Evidence from P. Oxy 657 ($\mathfrak{P}^{13}$) Concerning Unintentional Scribal Errors', *NTS* 43 (1997), pp. 466-73.

Healey, J.F., *The Nabataean Tomb Inscriptions of Mada'in Salih* (JSS Supplement, 1; Oxford: Oxford University Press, 1993).

Helck, W., E. Otto and W. Westendorff, *Lexikon der Ägyptologie* 1 (Wiesbaden: Otto Harrassowitz, 1972–).

Henderson, C. (ed.), *Classical Mediaeval and Renaissance Studies in Honor of Berthold Louis Ullman* (2 vols.; Rome: Edizioni di Storia e Letteratura, 1964).

Hengel, M., *The 'Hellenization' of Judaea in the First Century after Christ* (trans. J. Bowden; London: SCM Press, 1989).

—*Studies in the Gospel of Mark* (London: SCM Press, 1985).

Herdner, A., *Corpus des tablettes en cunéiformes alphabétiques découvertes à Ras-Shamra-Ugarit de 1929 à 1939* (Institut français d'archéologie de Beyrouth, Bibliothèque archéologique et historique, 79; Paris: Geuthner, 1963)

Hestrin, R. *et al.*, *Inscriptions Reveal: Documents from the Time of the Bible, the Mishna and the Talmud* (Israel Museum Catalogue, 100; Jerusalem: Israel Museum, 2nd edn, 1973).

Hill, P.A.L., 'Review Article', *The Jesus Papyrus* (London: Weidenfeld & Nicholson, 1996), by C.P. Thiede and M. d'Ancona, in *Buried History* 32 (1996), pp. 82-95.

Hopkins, K., 'Conquest by Book', in Humphrey (ed.), *Literacy in the Roman World*, pp. 133-58.

Horbury, W., and D. Noy, *Jewish Inscriptions of Graeco-Roman Egypt* (Cambridge: Cambridge University Press, 1992).

Horbury, W., 'The "Caiaphas" Ossuary and Joseph Caiaphas', *PEQ* 126 (1994), pp. 32-48.

Hordern, J., 'An Erotic Inscription from Marisa, Judaea (I.U. Powell, Collectanea Alexandrina 184)', *ZPE* 126 (1999), pp. 81-82.

Horn, H.G., and C.B. Rüger (eds.), *Die Numider: Reiter und Könige nordlich der Sahara* (Cologne: Rheinland Verlag, 1979).

Horsley, G.H.R., 'Classical Manuscripts in Australia and New Zealand', *Antichthon* 27 (1993), pp. 60-83.

Horsley, R.A., *Archaeology, History and Society in Galilee* (Valley Forge, PA: Trinity Press, 1996).

Houghton, A. *et al.*, (eds.), *Studies in Honor of Leo Mildenberg* (Wetteren: Editions NR, 1984).

Howard, M., 'Technical Description of the Ivory Writing-Boards from Nimrud', *Iraq* 17 (1955), pp. 14-20.

Humphrey, J.H. (ed.), *Literacy in the Roman World* (Journal of Roman Archaeology Supplement Series, 3; Ann Arbor, MI: Journal of Roman Archaeology, 1991).

Hunt, A.S., *The Oxyrhynchus Papyri*, VII (London: Egypt Exploration Fund, 1910).

Hurtado, L.W., 'The Origin of the Nomina Sacra: A Proposal', *JBL* 117 (1998), pp. 655-73.

Husselman, E.M., A.E.R. Boak and W.F. Edgerton, *Papyri from Tebtunis*, II (University of Michigan Studies, Humanistic Series, 29; Michigan Papyri, 5; Ann Arbor, MI: University of Michigan Press, 1944).

Ilan, Z., 'Eastern Galilee, Survey of Roman Roads', *Excavations and Surveys in Israel 1989/1990*, 9 (1991), pp. 14-16.

Immerwahr, H.R., 'Book Rolls on Attic Vases', in Henderson (ed.), *Classical Mediaeval and Renaissance Studies in Honor of Berthold Louis Ullman*, I, pp. 17-48

Invernizzi, A., 'Seleucia sul Tigri: Gli archivi', in *idem, La terra tra i due fiumi* (Turin: Il Quadrante, 1985), pp. 92-93, 124-26, 175-78.

—'Ten Years' Research in the Al-Mada'in Area, Seleucia and Ctesiphon', *Sumer* 32 (1976), pp. 167-75.

Isaac, B., 'A Donation for Herod's Temple in Jerusalem', *IEJ* 33 (1983), pp. 86-92.

—'A Seleucid Inscription from Jamnia-on-the-Sea: Antiochus V Eupator and the Sidonians', *IEJ* 41 (1991), pp. 132-44.

Jastram, N., '4QNum[b]' in Ulrich and Cress (eds.), *Qumran Cave 4: VII*, pp. 205-67.

Jastrow, M., *A Dictionary of the Targumim, Talmud Babli, Yerushalmi and the Midrashic Literature* (2 vols.; New York & Berlin: Choret; London: Shapiro Vallentine, 1926).

Jeffery, A.L., *Local Scripts of Archaic Greece* (Oxford: Clarendon Press, rev. A.W. Johnston, 1990).

Jeremias, J., *Jerusalem in the Time of Jesus* (trans. F.H. Cave and C.H. Cave; London: SCM Press, 1969).

Judge, E.A., and S.R. Pickering, 'Papyrus Documentation of Church and Community in Egypt to the Mid-Fourth Century', *JAC* 20 (1977), pp. 47-71.

Kampen, J., 'The Sectarian Form of the Antitheses within the Social World of the Matthaean Community', *Discoveries in the Judean Desert* 1 (1994), pp. 338-63.

Kane, J.P., 'The Ossuary Inscriptions of Jerusalem', *JSS* 23 (1978), pp. 268-82.

Kantzer, K. (ed.), *Evangelical Roots: A Tribute to Wilbur Smith* (Nashville, TN: Thomas Nelson, 1978)

Karpp, H., 'Viva Vox', in Stuiber and Hermann (eds.), *Mullus: Festschrift T. Klauser* (JAC Ergänzungsband, 1; Münster: Aschendorffsche Verlagsbuchhandlung, 1964), pp. 190-98

Käsemann, E., *Essays on New Testament Themes* (London: SCM Press, 1968).

Kearsley, R.A., 'The Goliath Family at Jericho', in S.R. Llewellyn (ed.), *A Review of the Greek Inscriptions and Papyri Published in 1980–1981* (New Documents Illustrating Early Christianity, 6; Macquarie University, NSW: Ancient History Document Research Centre, 1992), pp. 162-64.

Keenan, J.G., review of *Il lessico latino nel greco d'Egitto* (Barcelona: Institut de Teologia Fondamental, Seminario de Papirologia, 2nd edn, 1991) by S. Daris, in *Bulletin of the American Society of Papyrologists* 29 (1992), pp. 219-20.

Kelber, W., *The Oral and the Written Gospel* (Philadelphia: Fortress Press, 1983).

Kennedy, G., 'Classical and Christian Source Criticism', in Walker (ed.), *The Relationship among the Gospels*, pp. 125-55.

Kenney, E.J., and W.V. Clause (eds.), *The Cambridge History of Classical Literature. II. Latin Literature* (Cambridge: Cambridge University Press, 1982).

—'Authors and Public', in Kenney and Clause (eds.), *Cambridge History of Classical Literature*, II, pp. 10-15.

Kenyon, F.G., *Books and Readers in Ancient Greece and Rome* (Oxford: Clarendon Press, 2nd edn, 1951).

Khairy, N.I., 'Inkwells of the Roman Period from Jordan', *Levant* 12 (1980), pp. 155-62.

Kilgour, R., *Four Ancient Manuscripts in the Bible House Library* (London: British and Foreign Bible Society, 1928).

Killebrew, A., 'Jewish Funerary Customs during the Second Temple Period in the Light of Excavations at the Jericho Necropolis', *PEQ* 115 (1983), pp. 109-32.

Kilpatrick, G.D., 'Dura-Europos: The Parchments and Papyri', *GRBS* 5 (1964), pp. 215-25.

Kinnier Wilson, J.V., *The Nimrud Wine Lists* (London: British School of Archaeology in Iraq, 1972).

Kitchen, K.A., 'From the Brickfields of Egypt', *TynBul* 27 (1976), pp. 137-47.

—'The Aramaic of the Book of Daniel', in Wiseman *et al.*, *Notes on Some Problems in the Book of Daniel*, pp. 31-79.

Klengel-Brandt, E., 'Eine Schreibtafel aus Assur', *Altorientalische Forschungen* 3 (1975), pp. 169-71

Koch, K., *The Growth of the Biblical Tradition* (trans. S.M. Cupitt; London: A. & C. Black, 1969).

Kümmel, W.G., *Introduction to the New Testament* (trans. A.J. Mattill; London: SCM Press, rev. edn, 1975).

Kushnir-Stein, A., 'An Inscribed Lead Weight from Ashdod: A Reconsideration', *ZPE* 105 (1995), pp. 81-84.

Kutscher, E.Y., 'Aramaic', in Seboek (ed.), *Linguistics in South-West Asia and North Africa*, pp. 347-412.

—*A History of the Hebrew Language* (Jerusalem: Magnes Press, 1982).

—'Hebrew Language, Mishnaic', *EncJud*, XVI, cols.1590-1607.

Lalou, E., (ed.), *Les tablettes à écrire de l'antiquité à l'époque moderne* (Turnhout: Brepols, 1992)

Landau, Y.H., 'A Greek Inscription Found near Hefzibah', *IEJ* 16 (1966), pp. 54-70.

Lauterbach, J.Z., 'She'elot u-Teshubot', *JewEnc*, XI, pp. 240-50.

Layton, B., *The Gnostic Scriptures* (London: SCM Press, 1987).

Leaney, A.R.C., 'Greek Manuscripts from the Judaean Desert', in Elliott (ed.), *Studies in New Testament Language and Text*, pp. 285-300.

Lemaire, A., *Nouvelles inscriptions araméennes d'Idumée* (Paris: J. Gabalda, 1996).

Lemaire, J., and E. van Balberghe (eds.), *Calames et cahiers: Mélanges de codicologie et de paléographie offerts à Léon Gilissen* (Brussels: Centre d'etude des manuscrits, 1985).

Lerberghe, K. van, and A. Schoors (eds.), *Immigration and Emigration within the Ancient Near East: Festschrift E. Lipinski* (Orientalia Lovaniensia Analecta, 65; Leuven: Peeters, 1995).

Levick, B., 'Propaganda and the Imperial Coinage', *Antichthon* 16 (1982), pp. 104-16.

Lewis, N., *Papyrus in Classical Antiquity* (Oxford: Clarendon Press, 1974).

Lewis, N., and J.C. Greenfield (eds.), *The Documents from the Bar Kokhba Period in the Cave of Letters*. I. *Greek Papyri* (Jerusalem: Israel Exploration Society, 1989).

Lieberman, S., *Hellenism in Jewish Palestine* (New York: Jewish Theological Seminary, 1962).

—*Tosefta ki-Fšuṭah: A Commentary on the Tosefta* (8 vols.; New York: 1955–73).

Lifschitz, B., 'Notes d'épigraphie palestinienne. I. L'exhortation à la jouissance de la vie dans une inscription tombale juive à Jérusalem', *RB 73* (1966), pp. 248-57.

Lindsey, R.L., *A Hebrew Translation of the Gospel of Mark* (Jerusalem: Dugith Publishers, 2nd edn, 1973 [1969]).

Llewellyn, S.R. (ed.), *A Review of the Greek Inscriptions and Papyri Published in 1980–1981* (New Documents Illustrating Early Christianity, 6; Macquarrie University, NSW: Ancient History Documentary Research Centre, 1992).

—'The Development of the Codex', in *idem* (ed.), *A Review of the Greek Inscriptions and Papyri Published in 1982–1983* (New Documents Illustrating Early Christianity, 7; Macquarrie University, NSW: Ancient History Document Research Centre, 1994), pp. 249-56.

Lobel, E., and E.G. Turner (eds.), *Oxyrhynchus Papyri*, XXV (London: Egypt Exploration Society, 1959).

Lohse, E., *The Formation of the New Testament* (trans. M.E. Boring; Nashville, TN: Abingdon Press, 1981).

Lucas, A., *Ancient Egyptian Materials and Industries* (rev. edn J.R. Harris; London: Edwin Arnold, 4th edn, 1962).

Lucchesi, E., and H.D. Saffrey (eds.), *Mémorial André-Jean Festugière: Antiquité païenne et chrétienne* (Geneva: Cramer, 1984).

Luchner, K., '4443. LXX, Esther E16-9.3', in Haslam *et al.*, *The Oxyrhynchus Papyri* LXV, pp. 4-8.

Macalister, R.A.S., *The Excavation of Gezer 1902–1905 and 1907–1909* (London: Palestine Exploration Fund, 1912).

Macdonald, M.C.A., 'Inscriptions, Safaitic', *ABD*, III, pp. 418-23.

MacKenzie, D.N., 'Avroman Documents', in E. Yarshater (ed.), *Encyclopaedia Iranica*, III (3 vols. so far; London: Routledge & Kegan Paul, 1989), p. 111.

Mallowan, M.E.L., *Nimrud and its Remains* (2 vols.; London: Collins, 1966).

Marichal, R., 'Les tablettes à écrire dans le monde romain', in Lalou (ed.) *Les tablettes à écrire de l'antiquité à l'époque moderne*, pp. 165-85.

Martin, W.J., *The Dead Sea Scroll of Isaiah* (London: Westminster Chapel, 1954).

Mazar, B., 'The Archaeological Excavations near the Temple Mount', in Y. Yadin (ed.), *Jerusalem Revealed* (trans. R. Grafman; Jerusalem: Israel Exploration Society, 1976), pp. 25-40.

—'The Excavations in the Old City of Jerusalem', *Eretz Israel* 9 (1969), pp. 161-76 [Hebrew].

—'The Excavations in the Old City of Jerusalem near the Temple Mount, Preliminary Report of the Second and Third Seasons, 1969–1970', *Eretz Israel* 10 (1971), pp. 1-33 [Hebrew].

—'Herodian Jerusalem in the Light of the Excavations South and Southwest of the Temple Mount', *IEJ* 28 (1978), pp. 230-37.

McCormick, M., 'The Birth of the Codex and the Apostolic Life-Style', *Scriptorium* 39 (1985), pp. 150-58.

McDowell, R.H., *Stamped and Inscribed Objects from Seleucia on the Tigris* (Ann Arbor, MI: University of Michigan Press, 1935).

Merell, J., 'Nouveaux fragments du Papyrus 4', *RB* 47 (1938), pp. 5-22.

Merker, I.L., 'A Greek Tariff Inscription in Jerusalem', *IEJ* 25 (1975), pp. 238-44.

Meshorer, Y., *Ancient Jewish Coinage* (2 vols.; New York: Amphora Books, 1982).

—'The Mints of Ashdod and Ascalon during the Late Persian Period', *Eretz Israel* 20 (1989), pp. 287-91 [Hebrew].

—*Nabataean Coins* (Qedem, 3; Jerusalem: Hebrew University, 1975).

—'One Hundred Ninety Years of Tyrian Shekels', in A. Houghton *et al.*, (eds.), *Studies in Honor of Leo Mildenberg* (Wetteren: Editions NR, 1984), pp. 171-79.

—'A Stone Weight from the Reign of Herod', *IEJ* 20 (1970), pp. 97, 98.

Metzger, B.M., 'Ancient Astrological Geography and Acts 2:9-11', in Gasque and Martin (eds.), *Apostolic History and the Gospel*, pp. 123-33.

—*The Early Versions of the New Testament* (Oxford: Clarendon Press, 1977).

—'The Emperor's New Clothes', *BR* 12.4 (1996), pp. 12, 14.

—*Manuscripts of the Greek Bible* (New York: Oxford University Press, 1981).

—'The Nazareth Inscription Once Again', in Ellis and Grässer (eds.), *Jesus und Paulus*, pp. 221-38.

—*New Testament Studies: Philological, Versional, and Patristic* (Leiden: E.J. Brill, 1980).

—*Textual Commentary on the Greek New Testament* (London: United Bible Societies, 2nd edn, 1994).

Meyers, C.L., and M. O'Connor (eds.), *The Word of the Lord Shall Go Forth: Essays in Honor of David Noel Freedman* (Winona Lake, IN: Eisenbrauns, 1983).

Meyers, E.M., C.L. Meyers and K.G. Hoglund, 'Sepphoris 1994', *IEJ* 45 (1995), pp. 68-70.

—'Sepphoris (Sippori), 1996', *IEJ* 47 (1997), pp. 264-68.

Milik, J.T., 'Le couvercle de Bethphagé', in Caquot and Philonenko (eds.), *Hommages à A. Dupont-Sommer*, pp. 75-94.

—'Tefillin, Mezuzot et Targums (4Q128-4Q157)', in de Vaux and Milik, *Qumrân Grotte 4 II (Archéologie et 4Q128-4Q157)*, pp. 33-90.

Millar, F., *The Roman Near East 31 BC–AD 337* (Cambridge, MA: Harvard University Press, 1993).

Millard, A.R., 'Ancient Abbreviations and the *Nomina Sacra*', in Eyre, Leahy and Leahy (eds.), *The Unbroken Reed*, pp. 221-26.

—*Discoveries from Bible Times* (Oxford: Lion Publishing, 1997).

—*Discoveries from the Time of Jesus* (Oxford: Lion Publishing, 1990).

—'The Knowledge of Writing in Iron Age Palestine', *TynBul* 46 (1995), pp. 207-17.

—'The Last Tablets of Ugarit', in Yon, Sznycer and Bordreuil (eds), *Le pays d'Ougarit autour de 1200 av. J.-C.*, pp. 119-24.

—'Latin in First Century Palestine', in Zevit, Gitin and Sokoloff (eds.), *Solving Riddles and Untying Knots*, pp. 451-58.

—'Observations from the Eponym Lists', in Parpola and Whiting (eds.), *Assyria 1995*, pp. 207-15.

—'The Small Cuboid Incense Burners: A Note on their Age', *Levant* 16 (1984), pp. 172-73.

—'Strangers from Egypt and Greece: The Signs for Numbers in Early Hebrew', in van Lerberghe and Schoors (eds.), *Immigration and Emigration within the Ancient Near East*, pp. 189-94.

—'Variable Spelling in Hebrew and Other Ancient Texts', *JTS* NS 42 (1991), pp. 106-15.

Minnen, P. van, 'Taking Stock: Declarations of Property from the Ptolemaic Period', *Bulletin of the American Society of Papyrologists* 31 (1994), pp. 89-99.

Minns, E.H., 'Parchments of the Parthian Period from Avroman in Kurdistan', *JHS* 35 (1915), pp. 22-65.

Moeller, W.O., *The Mithraic Origins and Meanings of the Rotas-Sator Square* (Leiden: E.J. Brill, 1973).

Morag, S., 'ἐφφαθα (Mark vii.34): Certainly Hebrew not Aramaic?', *JSS* 17 (1972), pp. 198-202.

Moran, W.L., *The Amarna Letters* (Baltimore: The Johns Hopkins University Press, 1982).

Moule, C.F.D., *An Idiom Book of New Testament Greek* (Cambridge: Cambridge University Press, 2nd edn, 1959).

Muraoka, T. (ed.), *Studies in Qumran Aramaic* (Abr Nahrain Sup, 3; Leuven: Peeters, 1992).

Muro, E.A., 'The Greek Fragments of Enoch from Qumran Cave 7', *RevQ* 18.2=70 (1997) pp. 307-12.

Murray, O., *Early Greece* (London: Fontana, 1993).

Musurillo, H.A., *The Acts of the Pagan Martyrs* (Oxford: Clarendon Press, 1954).

Nash, E., *Pictorial Dictionary of Ancient Rome* (2 vols.; London: Thames and Hudson, rev. edn, 1968).

Naveh, J., 'An Aramaic Tomb Inscription Written in Paleo-Hebrew Script', *IEJ* 23 (1973), pp. 82-91.

—'Dated Coins of Alexander Jannaeus', *IEJ* 18 (1968), pp. 20-26.

—*Early History of the Alphabet* (Jerusalem: Magnes Press, 1982).

—'The Inscriptions', in E. Netzer (ed.), *Greater Herodium* (Qedem, 13; Jerusalem: Hebrew University, 1981), p. 71.

—'On Formal and Informal Spelling of Unpronounced Gutturals', *Scripta Classica Israelitica* 15 (1996), pp. 263-67.

—*On Stone and Mosaic: The Aramaic and Hebrew Inscriptions from Ancient Synagogues* (Jerusalem: Israel Exploration Society, 1978) [Hebrew].

—*On Sherd and Papyrus* (Jerusalem: Magnes Press, 1992) [Hebrew].

—'The Ossuary Inscriptions from Giv'at Ha-Mivtar', *IEJ* 20 (1970), pp. 33-37.

Naveh, J., and Y. Magen, 'Aramaic and Hebrew Inscriptions of the Second Century B.C.E. at Mount Gerizim', *'Atiquot* 32 (1997), pp. 9*-17*.

Negev, A., 'Seal-Impressions from Tomb 107 at Kurnub (Mampsis)', *IEJ* 19 (1969), pp. 89-106.

Newsom, C., *Songs of the Sabbath Sacrifice: A Critical Edition* (Harvard Semitic Studies, 27; Missoula, MT: Scholars Press, 1985).

Nikolaus, K., 'Oriental Divinities Represented on the Clay Sealings of Paphos, Cyprus', in M.B. de Boer and T.A. Edridge (eds.), *Hommages à Maarten J. Vermaseren* (Etudes preliminaires aux religions orientales dans l'Empire romain, 68.2; Leiden: E.J. Brill, 1978), pp. 849-53.

Nir-El, Y., and M. Broshi, 'The Black Ink of the Qumran Scrolls', *Dead Sea Discoveries* 3 (1996), pp. 157-67.

Nylander, C., *Ionians in Pasargadae* (Uppsala: Almqvist and Wiksell, 1970).

O'Callaghan, J., 'Papiros neotestamentarios en a cueva 7 de Qumran', *Biblica* 53 (1972), pp. 91-100; trans. W.L. Holladay, *JBL* 91.2 (1972) Supplement, pp. 1-14.

Oelsner, J., *Materialien zur babylonischen Gesellschaft und Kultur in hellenistischer Zeit* (Budapest: Eötvös University, 1986).

Oppenheim, A.L., 'Nebuchadnezzar II(c) Varia', in *ANET*, p. 308.

Oren, E.D., and U. Rappaport, 'The Necropolis of Maresha-Beth Govrin', *IEJ* 34 (1984), pp. 114-53

Orrieux, C., *Les papyrus de Zenon: L'horizon d'un grec en Egypte au IIIe siècle avant J.C.* (Paris: Editions MACULA, 1983).

Overbeck, B., *Das Heilige Land: Antike Münzen und Siegel aus einem Jahrtausend jüdischer Geschichte* (Munich: Staatliche Münzsammlung, 1993).

Pack, R.A., *The Greek and Latin Texts from Graeco-Roman Egypt* (Ann Arbor, MI: University of Michigan Press, 2nd rev. and enlarged edn, 1965).

Paper, H.H. (ed.), *Jewish Languages, Theme and Variations* (New York: Ktav, 1978).

Pardee, D., *Handbook of Ancient Hebrew Letters* (Chico, CA: Scholars Press, 1982).

Parker, D.C., 'Was Matthew Written before 50 CE? The Magdalen Papyrus of Matthew', *ExpTim* 107 (1995), pp. 40-43.

Parpola, S., and R.M. Whiting (eds.), *Assyria 1995* (Helsinki: Neo-Assyrian Text Corpus Project, 1997).

Parry, D.W., and S.D. Ricks (eds.), *Current Research and Technological Developments on the Dead Sea Scrolls* (Leiden: E.J. Brill, 1996).

Parsons, E.A., *The Alexandrian Library: Glory of the Hellenic World* (London: Cleaver-Hume, 1952).

Parsons, P.J., *The Oxyrhynchus Papyri*, XLII (London: Egypt Exploration Society, 1974).

Parsons, P.J. (ed.), *The Oxyrhynchus Papyri*, L (London: Egypt Exploration Society, 1983).

Parsons, P.J., and D. Lührmann, *The Oxyrhynchus Papyri*, LX (London: Egypt Exploration Society, 1994).

Patrich, J., 'Inscriptions araméennes juives dans les grottes d'el-Aleiliyât', *RB* 92 (1985), pp. 265-67.

Patterson, S.J., 'Reply to letters', *Bible Review* 10.1 (1994), p. 10.

Payton, R., 'The Ulu-Bürün Writing-Board Set', *Anatolian Studies* 41 (1991), pp. 99-110.

Pearson, B.A., 'Earliest Christianity in Egypt: Some Observations', in Pearson and Goehring (eds.), *The Roots of Egyptian Christianity*, pp. 132- 59 .

—'Nag Hammadi Codices', *ABD*, IV, pp. 984-93.

Pearson, B.A. (ed.), *The Future of Early Christianity: Essays in Honor of Helmut Koester* (Minneapolis: Fortress Press, 1991).

Pearson, B.A., and J.E. Goehring (eds.), *The Roots of Egyptian Christianity* (Philadelphia: Fortress Press, 1986).

Pestman, P.W., *A Guide to the Zenon Archive* (Leiden: E.J. Brill, 1981).

Peterman, G.L., 'Discovery of Papyri in Petra', *BA* 57 (1994), pp. 55-57.

Peters, J.P., and H. Thiersch, *Painted Tombs in the Necropolis of Marissa* (London: Palestine Exploration Fund, 1905).

Petersen, W.L., J.S. Vos and H.J. de Jonge (eds.), *The Sayings of Jesus: Canonical and Non-Canonical. Essays in Honour of Tjitze Baarda* (NovTSup, 89; Leiden: E.J. Brill, 1997).

Petitmengin, P. and B. Flusin, 'Le livre antique et la dictée', in Lucchesi and Saffrey (eds.), *Mémorial André-Jean Festugière*, pp. 247-62.

Pickering, S.R., 'Looking for Mark's Gospel among the Dead Sea Scrolls: The Continuing Problem of Qumran Fragment 7Q5', *New Testament Textual Research Update* 2 (1994), pp. 94-98.

—*Recently Published New Testament Papyri: P89-P95* (Sydney: Ancient History Documentary Resource Centre, Macquarie University, 1991).

Pleket, H.W., and R.S. Stroud (eds.), *Supplementum Epigraphicum Graecum* 41 (Amsterdam: J.C. Giëben, 1994).

Ploeg, J.P.M. van der, and A.S. van der Woude, *Le Targum de Job de la grotte XI de Qumran* (Leiden: E.J. Brill, 1971).

Politis, L., 'Nouveaux manuscrits grecs découverts au Mont Sinaï, rapport préliminaire', *Scriptorium* 34 (1980) pp. 5-17.

Porten, B., and A. Yardeni, *Textbook of Aramaic Documents from Ancient Egypt* (4 vols.; Winona Lake, IN: Eisenbrauns, 1986–99).

Porten, B., A. Yardeni *et al.*, *The Elephantine Papyri in English: Three Millennia of Cross-Cultural Continuity and Change* (Documenta et monumenta Orientis antiqui, 22; Leiden: E.J. Brill, 1996).

Porter, S.E., 'Did Jesus ever Teach in Greek?', *TynBul* 44 (1993), pp. 199-235.

Posener-Krieger, P., and J.L. de Cenival, *Hieratic Papyri in the British Museum, Fifth Series* (London: British Museum, 1968).

Posner, E., *Archives in the Ancient World* (Cambridge, MA: Harvard University Press, 1972).

Postgate, J.N., 'Middle Assyrian Tablets: The Instruments of Bureaucracy', *Altorientalische Forschungen* 13 (1986), pp. 10-39.

Puech, E., 'Abécédaire et liste alphabétique de noms hébreux du début du IIe s. A.D.', *RB* 87 (1980), pp. 118-26.

—'Des fragments grecs de la grotte 7 et le Nouveau Testament? 7Q4 et 7Q5, et le papyrus Magdalen grec 17 = $\mathfrak{P}^{64}$', *RB* 102 (1995), pp. 570-84.

—'Inscriptions funéraires palestiniennes: tombeau de Jason et ossuaires', *RB* 90 (1993), pp. 482-533.

—'Ossuaires inscrits d'une tombe du Mont des Oliviers', *Liber Annuus* 32 (1982), pp. 355-72.

—'Palestinian Funerary Customs', *ABD*, V, pp. 130, 131.

—'Sept fragments de la Lettre d'Hénoch (Hén 100, 103 et 105) dans la grotte 7 de Qumrân (=7QHén gr)', *Revue de Qumran* 18.2=70 (1997), pp. 313-23.

—'The Tell el-Fûl Jar Inscription and the Netînîm', *BASOR* 261 (1986), pp. 69-72.

—'Une inscription araméenne sur un couvercle de sarcophage', *Eretz Israel* 20 (1989), pp. 161*-65*.

Qedar, S., 'Two Lead Weights of Herod Antipas and Agrippa II and the Early History of Tiberias', *Israel Numismatic Journal* 9 (1986–87), pp. 29, 30.

Qimron, E., *The Hebrew of the Dead Sea Scrolls* (Harvard Semitic Studies, 29; Atlanta: Scholars Press, 1986).

Qimron, E., and J. Strugnell, *Qumran Cave 4.V. Miqsat Ma'ase Ha-Torah* (DJD, 10; Oxford: Clarendon Press, 1994).

Rahmani, L.Y., *A Catalogue of Jewish Ossuaries in the Collections of the State of Israel* (Jerusalem: Israel Academy, 1994).

Rajak, T., 'The Native Language of Josephus', in T. Rajak, *Josephus the Historian and his Society* (London: Gerald Duckworth, 1983).

Rapin, C., 'Les textes littéraires grecs de la trésorie d'Aï Khanoum', *Bulletin de Correspondance hellénique* 111 (1986), pp. 225-66.

Ratner, R., and B. Zuckerman, 'A Kid in Milk?: New Photographs of KTU 1.23, Line 14', *HUCA* 57 (1986), pp. 15-60.

Rea, J.R., R.C. Senior and A.S. Hollis, 'A Tax Receipt from Hellenistic Bactria', *ZPE* 104 (1994), pp. 261-80.

Reed, R., *Ancient Skins, Parchments and Leathers* (London: Seminar Press, 1972).

—-*The Nature and Making of Parchment* (Leeds: Elmete Press, 1975).

Reich, R., 'Ossuary Inscriptions from the "Caiaphas" Tomb', *'Atiqot* 21 (1992), pp. 72-77.

Reif, S.C., 'Codicological Aspects of Jewish Liturgical History', *BJRL* 75 (1993), pp. 117-31.

—*A Guide to the Taylor-Schechter Genizah Collection* (Cambridge: Cambridge University Library, 1973).

—*Judaism and Hebrew Prayer* (Cambridge: Cambridge University Press, 1993).

Reinhardt, W., 'The Population Size of Jerusalem and the Numerical Growth of the Jerusalem Church', in Bauckham (ed.), *Palestinian Setting*, IV, pp. 237-65.

Renan, E., *La vie de Jésus* (Paris: Calmann Lévy, 19th edn, 1888).

Rey-Coquais, J.-P., 'Decapolis', *ABD*, II, pp. 116-21.

Reynolds, J.M., *Aphrodisias and Rome* (London: Society for the Promotion of Roman Studies, 1982).

Reynolds, L.D. (ed.), *Texts and Transmission: A Survey of the Latin Classics* (Oxford: Clarendon Press, 1983).

Richard, M.D., *L'enseignement orale de Platon* (Paris: Cerf, 1986).

Richards, E.R., 'The Codex and the Early Collection of Paul's Letters', *Bulletin for Biblical Research* 8 (1998), pp. 151-66.

—*The Secretary in the Letters of Paul* (WUNT, 2. Reihe, 42; Tübingen: J.C.B. Mohr, 1991).

Ricks, S.D. (ed.), *Current Research and Technological Developments in the Dead Sea Scrolls* (Leiden: E.J. Brill, 1996).

Riesenfeld, H., *The Gospel Tradition and its Beginnings* (London: Mowbray, 1957).

Riesner, R., 'Synagogues in Jerusalem', in Bauckham (ed.), *Palestinian Setting*, IV, pp. 179-211.

Robert, J., and L. Robert, 'Bulletin Epigraphique', *Revue des Etudes Grecques* 72 (1959), pp. 149-283.

Roberts, C.H., *An Unpublished Fragment of the Fourth Gospel, in the John Rylands Library* (Manchester: University Press, 1935).

—*The Antinoopolis Papyri* (London: Egypt Exploration Society, 1950).

—'Books in the Graeco-Roman World and in the New Testament', in Ackroyd and Evans (eds.), *Cambridge History of the Bible*, I, pp. 48-66.

—*Buried Books in Antiquity* (London: The Library Association, 1963).

—'The Codex', *Proceedings of the British Academy* 40 (1954), pp. 169-204.

—*Manuscript, Society and Belief in Early Christian Egypt* (The Schweich Lectures 1977; London: Oxford University Press for the British Academy, 1979).

—'P Yale 1 and the Early Christian Book', in A.E. Samuel (ed.), *American Studies in Papyrology*. I. *Essays in Honor of C. Bradford Welles* (New Haven: American Papyrological Society, 1956), pp. 25-28.

—*Two Biblical Papyri in the John Rylands Library, Manchester* (Manchester: John Rylands Library, 1936).

Roberts, C.H., and T.C. Skeat, *The Birth of the Codex* (London: Oxford University Press for the British Academy, 1983).

Robertson, A.T., *A Grammar of the Greek New Testament in the Light of Historical Research* (London: Hodder & Stoughton, 3rd edn, 1919).

Robinson, J.M., *The Pachomian Monastic Library at the Chester Beatty Library and the Bibliothèque Bodmer* (Occasional Paper, 19; Claremont, CA: Institute for Antiquity and Christianity, Claremont Graduate School, 1990).

Robinson, J.M. (ed.), *The Nag Hammadi Library* (Leiden: E.J. Brill, 1977).

Rosenbaum, J., and J.D. Seger, 'Three Unpublished Ostraca from Gezer', *BASOR* 264 (1986), pp. 51-60.

Rosenthal, E.S., 'The Giv'at ha-Mivtar Inscription', *IEJ* 23 (1973), pp. 72-81.

Rössler, O., 'Die Numider: Herkunft—Schrift—Sprache', in Horn and Rüger (eds.), *Die Numider*, pp. 79-89.

Rostovtzeff, M.I., A.R. Bellinger, F.E. Brown and C.B. Welles, *The Excavations at Dura-Europos: Preliminary Report on the Ninth Season of Work, 1935–1936, Part* 1 (New Haven: Yale University Press, 1944).

Roxan, M.M., *Roman Military Diplomas 1954–1977* and *1978–1984* (Occasional Papers, 2, 9; London: Institute of Archaeology, 1978, 1985).

Rudolph, K., 'Gnosticism', *ABD*, II, pp. 1033-40.

Ruudiger, U., 'Die Anaglypha Hadriani', *Antike Plastik* 12 (1973), pp. 161-74.

Safrai, S., 'Oral Tora', in Safrai (ed.), *The Literature of the Sages*, pp. 35-119.

Safrai, S. (ed.), *The Jewish People in the First Century* (CRINT I, II; Assen: Van Gorcum, 1974–76).

—*The Literature of the Sages* (CRINT, II. 3a; Assen: Van Gorcum, 1987).

Sagnard, F., *Irénee de Lyon: Contre les hérésies* (Paris: Cerf, 1952).

Samuel, A.E. (ed.), *American Studies in Papyrology*. I. *Essays in Honor of C. Bradford Welles* (New Haven: American Papyrological Society, 1956).

Schams, C., *Jewish Scribes in the Second Temple Period* (JSOTSup, 291;Sheffield: Sheffield Academic Press, 1998).

Schechter, S., *Documents of Jewish Sectaries*. I. *Fragments of a Zadokite Work* (Cambridge: Cambridge University Press, 1910).

Schlatter, A., *Der Evangelist Johannes* (Stuttgart: Calwer Verlag, 1930).

—*Der Evangelist Matthaus* (Stuttgart: Calwer Verlag, 1929).

—*Das Evangelium des Lukas* (Stuttgart: Calwer Verlag, 1931).

Schmeling, G.L., *Chariton* (New York: Twayre Publishers, 1974).

Schmidt, C., and V. MacDermott, *Pistis Sophia [Askew Codex]* (Leiden: E.J. Brill, 1978).

—*The Books of Jeu and the Untitled Text in the Bruce Codex* (Leiden: E.J. Brill, 1978).

Schmidt, K.L., *Der Rahmen der Geschichte Jesu* (Berlin: Trowitzsch, 1919).

Schøyen, M., and E.G. Sørenssen, *The Schøyen Collection: Checklist of Manuscripts 1–2393* (Oslo: In Principio Press, 1997).

Schürer, E., *A History of the Jewish People in the Time of Jesus Christ* (trans. J. Mac-pherson, S. Taylor, P. Christie; 5 vols.; T. & T. Clark, Edinburgh, 1885–91).

Schürer, E., G. Vermes, F. Millar and M. Black (eds.), *The History of the Jewish People in the Age of Jesus Christ* (rev. edn; 3 vols.; Edinburgh: T. & T. Clark, 1973–87).

Seboek, T.A. (ed.), *Linguistics in South-West Asia and North Africa* (Current Trends in Linguistics, 6; The Hague: Mouton, 1970).

Segal, M.H., *A Grammar of Mishnaic Hebrew* (Oxford: Clarendon Press, 1927).

Segré, A., 'PYale Inv.1528 and PFuad 21', *JRS* 30 (1940), pp. 153-54.

Sevenster, J.N., *Do You Know Greek ? How Much Greek could the First Jewish Christians Have Known ?* (NovTSup, 19; Leiden: E.J. Brill, 1968).

Seyrig, H., 'Cachets d'archives publiques du quelques villes de la Syrie romaine', *MUSJ* 23 (1940), pp. 85-107.

Sharpe, J.L., III, 'The Dakleh Tablets and Some Codicological Considerations', in Lalon (ed.), *Les tablettes à écrire de l'antiquité à l'époque moderne*, pp. 127-48.

Sherk, R.K., *Roman Documents from the Greek East: senatus consulta and epistulae to the Age of Augustus* (Baltimore, MD: The Johns Hopkins University Press, 1969).

Siegel, J.P., 'The Alexandrians in Jerusalem and their Torah Scroll with Gold Tetragrammata', *IEJ* 22 (1972), pp. 139-43.

—*The Severus Scroll and 1QIs^a* (Missoula, MT: Scholars Press, 1975).

Simonides, C., *Fac-similes of Certain Portions of the Gospel of St. Matthew, and of the Epistles of St. James and St. Jude, Written on Papyrus in the First Century* (London: Trübner, 1861).

Sims-Williams, N., 'Nouveaux documents sur l'histoire et la langue de la Bactriane', *CRAIBL* (1996), pp. 633-54.

Sirat, C., 'Le livre hébreu dans les premiers siècles de notre ère: le témoignage des textes', in Lemaire and van Balberghe (eds.), *Calames et cahiers*, pp. 169-76; reprinted in Blanchard (ed.), *Les débuts du codex*, pp. 115-24.

Skeat, T.C., 'A Codicological Analysis of the Chester Beatty Papyrus Codex of Gospels and Acts (P45)', *Hermathena* 155 (1993), pp. 27-43.

—'The Length of the Standard Papyrus Roll and the Cost-advantage of the Codex', *ZPE* 45 (1982), pp. 169-75.

—'The Oldest Manuscript of the Four Gospels', *NTS* 43 (1997), pp. 1-34.

—'The Origin of the Christian Codex', *ZPE* 102 (1994), pp. 263-68.

—'Roll *versus* Codex: A New Approach?', *ZPE* 84 (1990), pp. 297-98.

—'Theological Texts. Job 42:11-12', in Parsons (ed.), *The Oxyrhynchus Papyri*, L, pp. 1-3.

Skehan, P.W., and A.A. Di Lella, *The Wisdom of Ben Sira* (AB, 39; New York: Doubleday, 1987).

Skehan, P.W., E. Ulrich and J.E. Sanderson, *Qumran Cave IV.4: Palaeo-Hebrew and Greek Biblical Manuscripts* (DJD, 9; Oxford: Clarendon Press, 1992).

Smallwood, E.M., *Documents Illustrating the Principates of Gaius, Claudius and Nero* (Cambridge: Cambridge University Press, 1967).

Smith, M., 'A Comparison of Early Christian and Early Rabbinic Tradition', *JBL* 82 (1963), pp. 169-176.

Smith, M.F., *Diogenes of Oinoanda: The Epicurean Inscription* (Naples: Bibliopolis, 1993).

—*The Philosophical Inscription of Diogenes of Oinoanda* (Vienna: Austrian Academy, 1996).

Sokoloff, M., *The Targum of Job from Qumran Cave XI* (Ramat-Gan: Bar-Ilan University, 1974).

Solin, H., O. Salomies and U.-M. Liertz (eds.), *Acta Colloquii Epigraphici Latini* (Helsinki: Societas Scientiarum Fennica, 1995).

Sotheby & Co., *Western Manuscripts and Miniatures* (Auction sale catalogue; London; 17 June, 1997).

—*Western Manuscripts* (Auction sale catalogue; London; 21 June, 1988).

Sperling, S.D., 'Fragments of Tannaitic Letters Preserved in Rabbinic Literature', in Pardee (ed.), *Handbook of Ancient Hebrew Letters*, pp. 183-96.

Stanton, G.N., 'The Early Reception of Matthew's Gospel: New Evidence from Papyri?', in Aune (ed.), *The Gospel of Matthew in Current Study* (forthcoming).

—'The Fourfold Gospel', *NTS* 43 (1997), pp. 317-46.

—*A Gospel for a New People* (Edinburgh: T. & T. Clark, 1992).

—*Gospel Truth? New Light on Jesus and the Gospels* (London: Harper-Collins, 1995).

Starcky, J., 'Un contrat nabatéen sur papyrus', *RB* 61 (1954), pp. 161-81.

Starr, R.J., 'The Circulation of Literary Texts in the Roman World', *The Classical Quarterly* 37 (1987), pp. 213-23.

Stern, E. (ed.), *The New Encyclopedia of Archaeological Excavations in the Holy Land* (4 vols.; New York: Simon & Schuster, 1993).

Stern, M., 'Aspects of Jewish Society: The Priesthood and Other Classes', in Safrai (ed.), *The Jewish People in the First Century* I.2, pp. 561-630.

Strange, J.F., 'First Century Galilee from Archaeology', in Edwards and McCollough (eds.), *Archaeology and the Galilee*, pp. 39-41.

Stuiber, A., and A. Hermann (eds.), *Mullus: Festschrift T. Klauser* (JAC Ergänzungsband, 1; Münster: Aschendorffsche Verlagsbuchhandlung, 1964).

Supplementum Epigraphicum Graecum I- (Alphen an den Rijn: Sijthoff & Noordhoff; Amsterdam: J.C. Gieben, 1923–).

Symington, D., 'Late Bronze Age Writing-Boards and their Uses: Textual Evidence from Anatolia and Syria', *Anatolian Studies* 41 (1991), pp. 111-23.

Syon, D., 'The Coins from Gamala—Interim Report', *Israel Numismatic Journal* 12 (1992–93), pp. 34-55.

Syon, H., 'Gamla—Portrait of a Rebellion', *BAR* 18.1 (1992), pp. 20-37.

Ta-Shma, I.M., 'Responsa', *EncJud*, XIV, cols. 83-88.

Talmon, S., 'Fragments of Scrolls from Masada', *Eretz Israel* 20 (1989), pp. 278-86 (Hebrew).

—'Hebrew Written Fragments from Masada', *Dead Sea Discoveries* 3 (1996), pp. 168-77.

—'Oral Tradition and Written Transmission, or the Heard and the Seen Word in Judaism of the Second Temple Period', in Wansborough (ed.), *Jesus and the Oral Gospel Tradition*, pp. 121-58.

—'The Three Scrolls of the Law that Were Found in the Temple Court', *Textus* 2 (1962), pp. 14-27.

Tcherikover, V.A., A. Fuks and M. Stern (eds.), *Corpus Papyrorum Judaicarum* (3 vols.; Cambridge, MA: Harvard University Press, 1957–64).

Teixidor, J., 'Deux documents syriaques du IIIe siècle provenant du moyen Euphrate', *CRAIBL* (1990), pp. 144-66.

—*Un port romain du désert: Palmyre et son commerce d'Auguste à Caracalla* (=*Semitica* 34, Paris, 1984).

Testa, E., *Herodion*, IV. I, *Graffiti e gli ostraca* (Jerusalem: Franciscan Printing Press, 1972).

Thayer, J.H., 'Language of the New Testament', *HDB*, III, pp. 36-43.

Thiede, C.P., *The Earliest Gospel Manuscript* (Exeter: Paternoster Press, 1992).

—'Notes on $\mathfrak{P}^4$ = Bibliothèque Nationale Paris, Supplementum Graece 1120/5', *TynBul* 46 (1995), pp. 55-58.

—'Papyrus Magdalen Greek 17 (Gregory-Aland $\mathfrak{P}^{64}$): A Reappraisal', *ZPE* 105 (1995), pp. 13-20.

—'Das unbeachtete Qumran-Fragment 7Q19 und die Herkunft der Höhle 7', *Aegyptus* 74 (1994), pp. 123-28.

Thiede, C.P., and M. d'Ancona, *The Jesus Papyrus* (London: Weidenfeld & Nicholson, 1996).

Thompson, Sir Herbert, *The Gospel of St John According to the Earliest Coptic Manuscript* (London: British School of Archaeology in Egypt, 1924).

Thompson, M.B., 'The Holy Internet: Communication between Churches in the First Christian Generation', in Bauckham (ed.), *The Gospels for All Christians*, pp. 49-70.

Torrey, C.C., *The Four Gospels: A New Translation* (London: Hodder & Stoughton, 1934).

Tov, E., *The Greek Minor Prophets Scroll from Nahal Hever (8HevXIIgr)* (DJD, 8; Oxford: Clarendon Press, 1990.

—'Scribal Markings in Texts from the Judaean Desert', in Parry and Ricks (eds.), *Current Research and Technological Developments on the Dead Sea Scrolls*, pp. 41-77.

Towers, S.K., *Letter Writing in Greco-Roman Antiquity* (Philadelphia: Fortress Press, 1986).

Tsafrir, Y., and I. Magen, 'Sartaba-Alexandrium', in E. Stern (ed.), *New Encyclopedia*, pp. 1318-20.

Tubb, J.N., 'Preliminary Report on the Fourth Season of Excavations at Tell es-Sa'idiyeh in the Jordan Valley', *Levant* 22 (1990), pp. 21-42.

Tuckett, C.M. (ed.), *Luke's Literary Achievement* (JSNTSup, 116; Sheffield: Sheffield Academic Press, 1995).

Turner, E.G., *Athenian Books in the Fifth and Fourth Centuries B.C.* (London: H.K. Lewis, 1951).

—*Greek Manuscripts of the Ancient World* (Institute for Classical Studies Bulletin Supplement, 46; London: Institute for Classical Studies, 2nd edn, rev. P.J. Parsons, 1987).

—*Greek Papyri* (Oxford: Clarendon Press, 1968).

—'Roman Oxyrhynchus', *JEA* 38 (1952), pp. 78-93.

—*The Typology of the Early Codex* (Philadelphia: University of Pennsylvania Press, 1977).

Ulrich, E., and F.M. Cross, *Qumran Cave 4: VII* (DJD, 12; Oxford: Clarendon Press, 1994).

VanderKam, J., 'The Calendar, 4Q327 and 4Q394', in Bernstein, García Martínez and Kampen (eds.), *Legal Texts and Issues*, pp. 179-94.

VanderKam, J. (ed.), *Qumran Cave 4: VIII Parabiblical Texts, Part 2* (DJD, 13; Oxford: Clarendon Press, 1995).

Van Groningen, B.A., 'EKDOSIS', *Mnemosyne* 16 (1963), pp. 1-17.

Vaux, R. de, *Archaeology and the Dead Sea Scrolls* (London: Oxford University Press, 1973).

Vaux, R. de, and J.T. Milik, *Qumrân Grotte 4 II (Archéologie et 4Q128-4Q157)* (DJD, 6; Oxford: Clarendon Press, 1977).

Vermes, G., *The Dead Sea Scrolls in English* (Harmondsworth: Penguin Books, 1995).

Vernus, P., 'Schreibtafel', in Helck, Otto and Westendorff (eds.), *Lexikon der Ägyptologie* 5 (1984), pp. 703-708

Vitto, F., 'Rehob' in Stern (ed.), *New Encyclopedia*, pp. 1272-74 .

Wacholder, B.Z., *Eupolemus: A Study of Judaeo-Greek Literature* (Cincinnati: Hebrew Union College, 1974).

—'Greek Authors in Herod's Library', *Studies in Bibliography and Booklore* 5 (1960), pp. 104-109.

Wachtel, K., '$\mathfrak{P}^{64/67}$ Fragmente des Mattäusevangeliums aus dem 1. Jahrhundert?', *ZPE* 107 (1995), pp. 73-80

Waldbaum, J.C., 'Greeks *in* the East or Greeks *and* the East? Problems in the Definition and Recognition of Presence', *BASOR* 305 (1997), pp. 1-17.

Walker, W.O. (ed.), *The Relationship among the Gospels* (San Antonio, TX: Trinity University Press, 1978).

Walls, A.F., 'Papias and Oral Tradition', *VC* 21 (1967), pp. 137-40.

Walser, G., *Römische Inschrift-Kunst* (Stuttgart: F. Steiner, 1988).

Wansborough, H. (ed.), *Jesus and the Oral Gospel Tradition* (JSNTSup, 64; Sheffield: Sheffield Academic Press, 1991).

Weidner, E.F., 'Jojachin, König von Juda, in babylonischen Keilschrifttexten', in *Mélanges syriens offerts à M. René Dussaud* (Paris: Geuthner, 1930), pp. 923-35.

Weill, R., *La cité de David* (Paris: Geuthner, 1920).

Welles, C.B., 'The Yale Genesis Fragment', *Yale University Gazette* 39 (1964), pp. 1-8.

Welles, C.B., R.O. Fink and J.F. Gilliam, *The Excavations at Dura-Europos, Final report V, Part I, The Parchments and Papyri* (New Haven: Yale University Press, 1959).

White, J.L., *Light from Ancient Letters* (Philadelphia: Fortress Press, 1986).

Whitley, J., 'Cretan Laws and Cretan Literacy', *AJA* 101 (1997), pp. 675-61.

Widengren, G., 'Tradition and Literature in Early Judaism and in the Early Church', *Numen* 10 (1963), pp. 42-83.

Wilcox, M., 'Semitisms in the New Testament', *ANRW*, II, 25.2 (Berlin: W. de Gruyter, 1984), pp. 978-1029.

Williamson, C., 'Monuments of Bronze: Roman Legal Documents on Bronze Tablets', *Classical Antiquity* 6 (1987), pp. 160-83.

—'The Display of Law and Archival Practice in Rome', in Solin, Salomies, Liertz (eds.), *Acta Colloquii Epigraphici Latini*, pp. 239-51.

Willis, W.H., 'A Census of the Literary Papyri from Egypt', *GRBS* 9 (1968), pp. 205-41.

Wilson, B.E., 'The Two Notebook Hypothesis: An Explanation of Seven Synoptic Problems', *ExpTim* 108 (1997), pp. 265-68.

Wilson, J.A., 'The Journey of Wenamun to Phoenicia', *ANET*, pp. 25-29.

Wise, M.O., 'Accidents and Accidence: A Scribal View of Linguistic Dating of the Aramaic Scrolls from Qumran', in Muraoka (ed.), *Studies in Qumran Aramaic*, pp. 124-67.

—'Languages of Palestine', in Green, McKnight and Marshall (eds.), *Dictionary of Jesus and the Gospels*, pp. 434-44.

Wiseman, D.J., 'Assyrian Writing Boards', *Iraq* 17 (1955), pp. 3-13.

Wiseman, D.J. *et al.*, *Notes on Some Problems in the Book of Daniel* (London: Tyndale Press, 1965).

Wouters, A., 'From Papyrus Roll to Papyrus Codex: Some Technical Aspects of the Ancient Book Fabrication', *Manuscripts of the Middle East* 5 (1990–91 [1993]), pp. 9-19.

Wright, D.F., 'Papyrus Egerton 2 (the *Unknown Gospel*)—Part of the Gospel of Peter ?', *The Second Century* 5 (1985–86), pp. 129-50.

Yadin, Y., *Tefillin from Qumran* (Jerusalem: Israel Exploration Society, 1970).

—*Jerusalem Revealed: Archaeology in the Holy City 1968–1974* (trans. R. Grafman; Jerusalem: Israel Exploration Society, 1976).

Yadin, Y., J. Naveh and Y. Meshorer, *Masada*. I. *The Aramaic and Hebrew Ostraca and Jar Inscriptions. The Coins of Masada* (Jerusalem: Israel Exploration Society, 1989).

Yamauchi, E., *Persia and the Bible* (Grand Rapids, MI: Baker Book House, 1990).

Yardeni, A., 'A Draft of a Deed on an Ostracon from Khirbet Qumran', *IEJ* 47 (1997), pp. 233-37.

—'Documentary Texts Alleged to be from Qumran Cave 4', in Cotton and Yardeni, *Aramaic, Hebrew and Greek Documentary Texts from Nahal Hever and Other Sites*, pp. 283-317 .

Yarshater, E., (ed.), *Encyclopaedia Iranica* (London: Routledge & Kegan Paul, 1982–).

Yon, M., M. Sznycer and P. Bordreuil (eds), *Le pays d'Ougarit autour de 1200 av. J.-C.* (Ras Shamra-Ougarit, 11; Paris: Editions Recherche sur les Civilisations, 1995).

Youtie, H.C., 'ΑΓΡΑΜΜΑΤΟΣ: An Aspect of Greek Society in Egypt', *Harvard Studies in Classical Philology* 75 (1971), pp. 161-76.

—'Βραδέως γράφων: Between Literacy and Illiteracy', *GRBS* 12 (1971), pp. 239-61.

—'P.Mich.Inv. 855: Letter from Herakleides to Nemesion', *ZPE* 27 (1977), pp. 147-50.

—*Scriptiunculae* (2 vols.; Amsterdam: Hakkert, 1973).

Zevit, Z., S. Gitin and M. Sokoloff (eds.), *Solving Riddles and Untying Knots: Biblical, Epigraphic and Semitic Studies in Honor of Jonas C. Greenfield* (Winona Lake, IN: Eisenbrauns, 1995).

INDEXES

INDEX OF REFERENCES

OLD TESTAMENT

NEW TESTAMENT

RABBINIC SOURCES

SUBJECT INDEX

INDEX OF FOREIGN WORDS